PROCESS CONSULTATION

MAOM CAPSTONE COURSE
FOR THE UNIVERSITY OF PHOENIX

EDGAR H. SCHEIN

Pearson
Custom
Publishing

PEARSON CUSTOM PUBLISHING
75 Arlington Street, Boston, MA 02116
A Pearson Education Company

University of Phoenix Introduction

Question: What does todays manager need to prepare for the next century?
Answer: A way to self-renew.

The safest one can be in this continuous white water world is to be prepared for nano-second reinvention. How else will one be able to stay ahead of (or keep up with) the proverbial power curve? It is knowing what, how, and where to learn. It is knowing how to apply that learning for the continuous improvement of our careers, organizations, and lives. This is the popular concept of the learning organization translated and reduced to the individual level. But, it is not so much *what* we learn as it is *how* we learn and *apply* our learning.

The curriculum of the MAOM program has a set of common threads that run through it. These common threads for learning are reinforced and applied anew in each course in ways that sew the MAOM together when the student has completed the entire course of study. To facilitate that goal, we have included an *Applied Learning Journal* for students to address the most important concepts and their application in and from each individual course.

The Capstone Course requires the student to synthesize and integrate the theory and practice learned from all of the courses in the MAOM curriculum and apply them toward the development of recommended solutions for specific managerial situations found within an organizations environment. This synthesis is based upon the concepts of *Process Consultation*. We believe the student who is capable of acting as an internal consultant and change agent for his or her organization will have the ability to facilitate organizational success in the next century.

Congratulations on reaching this milestone in the MAOM curriculum. We hope you will use this Capstone Course as a final opportunity to reflect on your past learning and to apply that learning to both an individual and study group consult of organizations in the private, public, or non-profit sectors. We also hope that this course and the MAOM program will be stepping stones to your future success as managers in the new century.

Jack Abbott, M.B.A., Faculty Member
Robert V. Conter, Ph.D., Faculty Member
Thomas H. Kemp, Ph.D., Faculty Member
Lee M. Finkel, J.D., Associate Dean
Robert W. Key, M.Ed., Project Manager
The MAOM Curriculum Management Team
University of Phoenix School of Graduate Business and Management

Overview
<u>Table of Contents</u>

Volume 1

Volume 2

Process Consultation
Volume I

Foreword

The Addison-Wesley Series on Organization Development originated in the late 1960s when a number of us recognized that the rapidly growing field of "OD" was not well understood or well defined. We also recognized that there was no one OD philosophy, and hence one could not at that time write a textbook on the theory and practice of OD, but one could make clear what various practitioners were doing under that label. So the original six books by Beckhard, Bennis, Blake and Mouton, Lawrence and Lorsch, Schein, and Walton launched what has since become a continuing enterprise. The essence of this enterprise was to let different authors speak for themselves instead of trying to summarize under one umbrella what was obviously a rapidly growing and highly diverse field.

By 1981 the series included nineteen titles, having added books by Beckhard and Harris, Cohen and Gadon, Davis, Dyer, Galbraith, Hackman and Oldham, Heenan and Perlmutter, Kotter, Lawler, Nadler, Roeber, Schein, and Steele. This proliferation reflected what had happened to the field of OD. It was growing by leaps and bounds, and it was expanding into all kinds of organizational areas and technologies of intervention. By this time many textbooks existed as well that tried to capture the core concepts of the field, but we felt that diversity and innovation were still the more salient aspects of OD today.

The present series is an attempt both to recapture some basics and to honor the growing diversity. So we have begun a series of revisions of some of the original books and have added a set of new authors or old authors with new content. Our hope is to capture the spirit of inquiry and innovation that has always been the hallmark of organization development and to launch with these books a new wave of insights into the forever tricky problem of how to change and improve organizations.

We are grateful that Addison-Wesley has chosen to continue the series and are also grateful to the many reviewers who have helped us and the authors in the preparation of the current series of books.

Cambridge, Massachusetts   Edgar H. Schein
New York, New York   Richard Beckhard

Preface

This book was originally written to communicate to my academic colleagues what I did when I went off to work with a company and to describe for consultants and managers my view of important events that occurred in organizations. It is only in retrospect, after some two decades of working as a process consultant, that I can see more clearly the philosophical and attitudinal assumptions that underlie this approach.

When I started out I was learning what seemed to work best. As I look back, I realize that there are some very important reasons why process consultation works, and these reasons — the assumptions underlying process consultation — have stood the test of time.

In revising this book, therefore, I have tried to stay close to the original formulations. I have added material only where it seemed to enhance the original theme. My thinking has, of course, evolved somewhat as a result of continued experience both with the consultation model and with the original version of this book. For example, I have found that this approach to working with people is highly relevant not only to consultants but to managers themselves. Many of the most enthusiastic readers of this book have been managers. I therefore also wrote a second volume that articulates the same basic philosophy and attitude but directs them more pointedly at the managerial audience and refines the concepts presented here further (Schein, 1987a).

I had originally planned to incorporate all of these ideas into the revision of this book, but that would have made it double in length and destroyed the integrity that this book has had. The reader who wants to get a quick overview of the assumptions, foci, and methods of PC can get all of that in this revised volume 1. The reader who is interested enough to consider how this really works out in practice, what its pitfalls and problems are, and what additional theories and models are needed to fully understand the vicissitudes of PC should go on to volume II.

The decision to revise this book and the planning of how to do it were greatly facilitated by my colleague Marc Gerstein, who offered many helpful ideas on what to preserve and what to change. I am grateful to Addison-Wesley for having revived the entire OD series, and am, as usual, greatly indebted to my colleague and co-editor, Richard Beckhard. My students and clients have been most helpful in sharpening the ideas presented here.

Sherie Potts was most helpful in the difficult chore of getting a text that had been prepared in the technological dark ages of typewriting onto a word processor so that editing would be easier. Also, in the frantic effort to get this book to press on time, not only did I have the emotional support of my wife, Mary, but she even pitched in on the typing and editing.

Cambridge, Massachusetts   E.H.S.

Contents

Part I

Process Consultation Defined

In this part the basic concept of process consultation is defined and compared to other major consultation concepts. It is emphasized that process consultation is a kind of philosophy about and attitude toward the process of helping individuals, groups, and organizations. It is not merely a set of techniques to be compared to and contrasted with other techniques.

Process consultation underlies the broader concept of organization development and is the key philosophical underpinning to organization development in that most of what the consultant does in helping organizations is based on the assumptions of process consultation. Understanding such assumptions is therefore critical to understanding the broader concept of organization development.

1

What Is Process Consultation?

This book is about a special kind of consultation that I am calling *process consultation* (PC). I will describe what it is and what role it plays in organization development (OD).

In focusing on process consultation I will be looking at one of the key activities that go on at the beginning of (and throughout) any OD effort. OD is typically defined as a planned organizationwide kind of program, but its component parts are usually activities that the consultant carries out with individuals or groups, and the attitudes with which these activities are carried out reflect the assumptions that underlie PC.

This volume will focus on these kinds of activities and, therefore, will deal primarily with interpersonal and group events. More important than the focus of such activities, however, are the attitude and philosophy that underlie the consultant's behavior vis-à-vis the client and pervade all aspects of any OD program.

I will not try to give an overview of OD programs as a whole, but will focus on the process by which the consultant builds readiness for change, actually conducts training as part of the OD effort, and works with the key individuals of an organization as part of an OD program, always attempting to illustrate the importance of the attitude that the consultant takes toward the helping process.

The field of consultation has grown remarkably in recent years, yet there is still conceptual confusion about what a consultant actually does for an organization, how he[1] goes about doing it, and what his assumptions are about giving help. For example, does the consultant provide information, analyze information using special diagnostic tools, help clients to diagnose complex problems, give managers support and comfort, recommend solutions to organizational problems, help managers to implement difficult or unpopular decisions, or some or all of these in various combinations?

Many analyses of the consultation process argue that unless the client manager knows exactly what he is looking for from the consultant, he is likely to be sorely disappointed. In reality, however, the manager often does not know what he is looking for and indeed should not really be expected to know. All he knows is that something is not working right and he needs some kind of help. An important part of any consultation process, then, must be to help the manager or the organization to figure out what the problem is, and only then decide what further kind of help is needed.

Managers often sense that all is not well or that things could be better, but they do not have the tools with which to translate their vague feelings into concrete action steps. The kind of consultation I will attempt to describe in this book deals with problems of this sort. Process consultation does not assume that the manager knows what is wrong, or what is needed, or what the consultant should do. The only thing required for the process to begin constructively is some *intent* on the part of someone in the organization to improve the way it is operating. The consultation process itself then helps the manager to define diagnostic steps that lead ultimately to action programs and concrete changes that improve the situation.

Process consultation is a difficult concept to describe sim-

---

[1]To simplify the writing I will use "he" whenever I refer to consultants or clients in general with the understanding that this is not intended as a sexist reference.

ply and clearly. It does not lend itself to a simple definition or to the giving of a few illustrative examples, because it is more of a philosophy or a set of underlying assumptions about the helping process that lead the consultant to take a certain kind of attitude toward his relationship with the client.

I will try to give some perspective to these assumptions by contrasting PC with some other consultation models. Then I will provide some historical perspective to indicate why PC is an increasingly relevant activity in today's organizational world, and why it is particularly relevant to OD efforts. Finally, I will devote the bulk of this volume to the actual procedure of PC: what the consultant looks for, how the process starts, how a relationship with the client is developed, what kinds of interventions are made at various stages, how the process is evaluated, and how it is terminated.[2]

Models of Consultation

Consultation processes can be distinguished best by looking at the assumptions they make about the client, the nature of help, and the role of the consultant. Three basic models can be identified.

1. The Purchase of Expertise Model

The most prevalent model of consultation is certainly the purchase of expert information or an expert service. The buyer, usually an individual manager or some group in the organization, defines a need and concludes that the organization has neither the resources nor the time to fulfill that need. He will then look to a consultant to provide the information or the service.

For example: (1) A manager may wish to know how a particular group of consumers feels, or how a group of employees will react to a new personnel policy, or what the state of morale

---

[2]In volume 2 of *Process Consultation* (1987) more detail is given on how the consultant makes his moment-to-moment decisions as he works with the client and what underlying concepts are relevant to an understanding of the consulting process.

is in a given department. (2) The manager may wish to know how to organize a particular group and may need the consultant to find out how other companies organize such groups, for example, how to organize the accounting and control system given the capabilities of current information technology. (3) The manager may wish to know particular things about competitor companies, such as their marketing strategy, how much of the price of their product is determined by production costs, how they organize their research and development function, how many employees they have in a typical plant, and so on.

In each of these cases there is an assumption that the manager knows what kind of information or service he is looking for. The likelihood that this model will work then depends on

1. whether or not the manager has correctly diagnosed his own needs;
2. whether or not he has correctly communicated those needs to the consultant;
3. whether or not he has accurately assessed the capabilities of the consultant to provide the information or the service;
4. whether or not he has thought through the consequences of having the consultant gather such information, and/or the consequences of implementing changes that may be recommended by the consultant.

The frequent dissatisfaction with consultants and the low rate of implementation of their recommendations can easily be explained when one considers how many assumptions have to be met for the purchase model to work effectively.

Process consultation, in contrast, involves the manager and the consultant in a period of *joint diagnosis*. The consultant is willing to come into the organization without a clear mission or goal because of an underlying assumption that any organization can improve its processes and become more effective if it can accurately locate those processes that make a difference to its overall performance. No organizational structure or process is perfect. Every organization has strengths and weaknesses. Therefore, the manager who senses that "something" is wrong because performance or morale is not what it should be *should not* leap into action until he has a clear idea of the strengths and weaknesses of the present structures and processes. The main goal of the process consultant is to help the manager to make such a diagnosis and to develop a valid action plan for himself.

The importance of joint diagnosis derives from the fact that the consultant can seldom learn enough about any given organization to really know what a better course of action would be or even what information would really help them most, because the members of the organization perceive, think about, and react to information in terms of their traditions, values, and assumptions, that is, their organizational culture (Schein, 1985) and the particular styles and personalities of their key members.

However, the consultant can help the manager (1) to become a sufficiently good diagnostician himself, and (2) to learn how to manage organizational processes better so that he can solve problems for himself. It is a crucial assumption of the PC philosophy that problems will stay solved longer and be solved more effectively if the organization solves those problems itself. The consultant has a role in teaching diagnostic and problem-solving skills, but he should not attempt actually to solve the problems himself.

2. The Doctor–Patient Model

Another common consultation model is that of "doctor–patient." One or more managers in the organization decide to bring in a consultant to "check them over," to discover if there are any organizational areas that are not functioning properly and might need attention. Or the manager may detect symptoms of ill health, such as dropping sales, high numbers of customer complaints, or quality problems, but not know how to make a diagnosis of what is causing the problems.

The consultant is brought into the organization to find out what is wrong with which part of the organization and then, like the physician, recommend a program of therapy or prescribe a remedial measure. This model puts a great deal of power into the hands of the consultant in that he both diagnoses and prescribes, and is therefore a model that appeals to consultants.

As most readers will recognize from their own experience, this model is fraught with difficulties in spite of its popularity.

One of the most obvious difficulties is the assumption that the consultant can get accurate diagnostic information on his own. But the organizational unit that is defined as "sick" may be reluctant to reveal the kind of information that the consultant would need to make an accurate diagnosis.

In fact, it is quite predictable that on questionnaires or in interviews systematic distortions will occur. The direction of these distortions will depend on the climate of the organization. If the climate is one of distrust and insecurity, the respondents will most likely hide any damaging information from the consultant because of fear of retaliation, something that we have seen repeatedly in the misadventures of whistle-blowers.

On the other hand, if the climate is one of high trust, respondents are likely to view contact with the consultant as an opportunity to get all their gripes off their chests, leading to an exaggeration of the problem. In either case, unless the consultant spends a lot of time observing the department, he is not likely to get an accurate picture of what may be going on.

An equally great difficulty with this model is that the client/patient is likely to be unwilling to believe the diagnosis or to accept the prescription offered by the consultant. I suspect that most organizations have drawers full of reports by consultants that are either not understood or not accepted by the "patient." What is wrong, of course, is that the "doctor" has not built up a common diagnostic frame of reference with his client. If the consultant does all the diagnosing while the client/manager waits passively for a prescription, it is predictable that a communication gulf will arise that will make the prescription seem either irrelevant or unpalatable.

Even in medicine, doctors have increasingly realized that patients do not automatically accept diagnoses and do what the doctor recommends. One sees this most clearly in the cross-cultural context, where assumptions about illness or what one does about it may differ from our own, but one also sees it, for example, in the treatment of breast cancer where the oncologist has to involve the patient in the crucial choice as to whether to have a radical mastectomy or a program of chemotherapy and radiation. Similarly, in plastic surgery or in the decision of whether or not to have back surgery, the patient's goals and self-image become crucial variables in determining the ultimate success of the surgery.

In other words, the success of the doctor–patient model will depend on

1. whether or not the initial client has accurately identified which person, group, or department is, in fact, "sick";
2. whether or not the "patient" will reveal accurate information;
3. whether or not the "patient" will accept and believe the diagnosis that the "doctor" arrives at;
4. whether or not the "patient" will accept the prescription, that is, do what the "doctor" recommends.

Process consultation, in contrast, focuses on joint diagnosis and the passing on to the client of the consultant's diagnostic skills. The consultant may recognize early in his work what some of the problems are in the organization and how they might be solved. But he does not share his insights prematurely, for two reasons. One, he may be wrong. If he prematurely makes a diagnosis that is incorrect, he may damage his credibility with the client and undermine the relationship. Two, he recognizes that even if he is right, the client may well be defensive, may not listen or may wish to deny what he hears, or may misunderstand what the consultant is saying and thus subvert remedial efforts.

It is a key assumption underlying PC that the client must learn to see the problem for himself by sharing in the diagnostic process and be actively involved in generating a remedy. The consultant may play a key role in helping to sharpen the diagnosis and may provide suggestions for alternate remedies that may not have occurred to the client. But he encourages the client to make the ultimate decision on what remedy to apply.

Again, the consultant does this on the assumption that if he teaches the client to diagnose and remedy situations himself, problems will be solved more permanently and the client will have learned the skills necessary to solve new problems as they arise.

It should also be emphasized that the process consultant may or may not be an expert at solving the particular problems that may be uncovered. The important point in PC is that such expertise is less relevant than are the skills of involving the client in self-diagnosis and helping him to find a remedy that fits his particular situation and his unique set of needs. The process consultant must be an expert at giving help and at establishing a relationship with clients that makes it possible to be helpful. He does not need to be an expert in marketing, finance, or strategy. If problems are uncovered in such areas, the consultant can help the client to find an expert resource and, more important, help the client to think through how best to ensure that he will get the help he needs from those experts.

3. The Process Consultation Model and Its Underlying Assumptions

The main assumptions of what I am calling the process consultation philosophy or model can now be summarized:

1. Clients/managers often do not know what is wrong and need special help in diagnosing what their problems actually are.
2. Clients/managers often do not know what kinds of help consultants can give to them; they need to be helped to know what kinds of help to seek.
3. Most clients/managers have a constructive intent to improve things, but they need help in identifying what to improve and how to improve it.
4. Most organizations can be more effective than they are if they learn to diagnose and manage their own strengths and weaknesses. No organizational form is perfect; hence every form of organization will have some weaknesses for which compensatory mechanisms must be found.
5. A consultant probably cannot, without exhaustive and time-consuming study or actual participation in the client organization, learn enough about the culture of the organization to suggest reliable new courses of action. Therefore, unless remedies are worked out jointly with members of the organization who do know what will and will not work in their culture, such remedies are

likely either to be wrong or to be resisted because they come from an outsider.

6. Unless the client/manager learns to see the problem for himself and thinks through the remedy, he will not be willing or able to implement the solution and, more important, will not learn how to fix such problems should they recur. The process consultant can provide alternatives, but decision making about such alternatives must remain in the hands of the client.

7. The essential function of PC is to pass on the skills of how to diagnose and fix organizational problems so that the client is more able to continue on his own to improve the organization.

Process Consultation Defined

With these assumptions in mind, we can define PC:

PC is a set of activities on the part of the consultant that help the client to perceive, understand, and act upon the process events that occur in the client's environment in order to improve the situation as defined by the client.

The process consultant seeks to give the client insight into what is going on around him, within him, and between him and other people. Based on such insight, the consultant then helps the client to figure out what he should do about the situation. But the core of this model is that the client must be helped to remain "pro-active," in the sense of retaining both the diagnostic and remedial initiative. Allowing the client to become dependent on the consultant, as comfortable as that may be for both parties, is a prescription for failure in the helping process if complex human systems processes are involved.

The events to be observed and learned from are the human actions that occur in the normal flow of work, in the conduct of meetings, in the formal or informal encounters between members of the organization, and in the more formal organizational structures. Of particular relevance are the client's own actions and their impact on other people in the organization.

Implicit in this model is the further assumption that all organizational problems are fundamentally problems involving human interactions and processes. No matter what technical, financial, or other matters may be involved, there will always be humans involved in the design and implementation of such other processes. A thorough understanding of human processes and the ability to improve such processes are therefore fundamental to any organizational improvement.

As long as organizations are networks of people engaged in achieving some common goals, there will be various kinds of processes occurring between them. Therefore, the more we understand about how to diagnose and improve such processes, the greater will be our chances of finding solutions to the more technical problems and of ensuring that such solutions will be accepted and used by members of the organization.

Part II

Human Processes and How to Intervene in Them

In this part of the book I will review the major human processes that I have observed to be relevant to helping organizations improve their effectiveness. In the first chapter I will provide some historical perspective, and in each subsequent chapter I will analyze a major human process, such as communication or leadership, and highlight what the process consultant would observe and what he then might do about what he observes, that is, how he might intervene.

Not all possible human processes are analyzed, and in each case only the most relevant aspects of each process are described. The descriptions are often deliberate simplifications designed to make clear the underlying significance of what is going on.

Knowledge of how human processes work is essential for the consultant in order to diagnose the problems and select wisely the manner in which he intervenes. But even the process of observing and asking questions to find out what is going on constitutes interventions. So the consultant can never separate diagnostic and intervention activities in his behavior, even though these are conceptually distinct when we analyze the consultation process.

2

Human Processes
in Organizations:
An Overview

The study of human processes in organizations has been the direct result of improved techniques of observation and improved conceptual models of how processes in organizations affect ultimate outcomes. The key to understanding what makes an organization more or less effective is *how* it does things.

Organizations can be designed and structured in many different ways, each of which can be successful. If one is to understand why the same structures are successful at one time and unsuccessful at another, one must understand various processes — how goals are set, how the means to be used are determined, the forms of communication used among members, their processes of problem solving and decision making, how they run meetings and groups, how superiors and subordinates relate to each other, and ultimately how leaders lead.

The process consultant must be conversant in each of these areas, to be able both to observe such processes and to intervene effectively in them. In this chapter I will provide an overview and a road map. In subsequent chapters I will discuss each of the major processes in detail and provide some intervention tools to aid in improving those processes.

Structure versus Process: A Historical Note

Early studies of organizations were dominated by the "scientific management" school of thought leading to an almost exclusive preoccupation with the structural or static elements of the organization. What should be the correct division of labor? What is the right span of control? Should the organization be structured by functions, such as sales and manufacturing; by product lines, such as trucks, large autos, and small autos; or by geography? How many levels should there be in the hierarchy? Should each department have its staff people, such as personnel, or should there be a single centralized staff?

This concern for organizational "statics" is understandable and partially appropriate, because organizations are open systems that exist in uncertain and dynamic environments. In order to survive they must stabilize some elements in the face of recurring disintegrative pressures from the environment. Just as total societies develop a culture, social structure, laws, and traditions as a way of stabilizing themselves, so organizations must find ways to conserve and stabilize their culture and structure (Schein, 1985).

The appeal of the structural approach is strong in the field of consultation. Management consulting firms are often brought in to examine the existing structure and to recommend alternative forms that are presumed to be more effective for achieving organizational goals. If the recommendations are acted on, reporting relationships are likely to be changed, departments are likely to be phased out or moved, jobs are redesigned or eliminated, and so on. To the extent that individual personalities are taken into account, they are also treated as static and structural factors to be worked around rather than changed.

The problem with this approach is twofold. Most serious is the possibility that the diagnosis will be incorrect or that the prescription for a new structure will ignore some major cultural or personality constraints, thus making the recommendations unimplementable. The report simply gets filed.

Less serious is the possibility that the diagnosis is correct but that the recommendations are incomplete because they ignore the human processes at work. The network of positions and roles that define the formal organizational structure is occupied by people, and those people in varying degrees put their own personalities into getting the job done. Not only does each role occupant have a certain style of doing his own work, but he has his own unique way of relating to other people in the organization. These processes of relating to others have a decisive influence on outcomes and must themselves become objects of diagnosis and intervention if any organization improvement is to occur.

Paradoxically, some processes recur with such regularity that they become virtually part of the structure. An authoritarian entrepreneur who always barks orders and expects instant obedience creates a militaristic form of organization that expresses, both in its formal structure and in the daily behavior of its managers, recurring patterns of top-down influence, unwillingness to accept suggestions from subordinates, ruthless disciplinary processes, and so on. But the consultant should make a clear distinction in his own head between structure in terms of formally defined positions and roles, and structure in terms of observed regularities of behavior. Structured *processes* are very much the domain of the process consultant.

Some Historical Roots

The study of organizational processes has several roots. One of these roots is the field of group dynamics as developed originally under the leadership of Kurt Lewin (1947). A second root was the development of systematic techniques for studying small-group processes such as those developed by Chapple (1940) in applied anthropology, Bales (1950, 1979) in sociology, and Carter et al. (1951) in psychology.

The classical experiments by White and Lippitt (1953) on the effects of different kinds of leadership showed that group productivity and morale were very much affected by the leadership style of the formal leader. Bales, in his extensive and detailed analyses of small-group problem solving, showed that groups developed certain patterns of behavior that were quite predictable. For example, two kinds of leader tended to emerge: a task leader who helps the group to do its job, and a "socioemotional" leader who helps to build and maintain good relations among group members. Only rarely were these two kinds of leader the same person in the groups studied. Such experiments showed that it was possible to study group processes and that such research would pay off in finding nonobvious regularities in such human processes.

A third, and closely related, historical root was the development of group dynamics and leadership training associated with the National Training Laboratories (Bradford et al., 1964; Schein and Bennis, 1965). Deriving from Lewinian concepts of action research, a technology of group observation and intervention in group processes has been developed over the last thirty-five years. This approach represents the most important precursor to PC in that most of the assumptions PC makes in relation to working with an organization are derived from assumptions that group "trainers" make in working with laboratory-training groups. For example, the trainer sees himself not as a teacher or an expert but as someone who helps group members to discover the kinds of events that are occurring in the group and the effects such events are having on themselves and other members.

A fourth root is the study of group relations and interpersonal processes in industrial organizations. These studies — originating in the early works of Mayo, Roethlisberger, and Dickson; carried forward by Arensberg, Whyte, Homans, and others who studied the "informal" organization in industry; and taken to the management ranks in works such as Melville Dalton's (1959) — showed that *how people actually relate to each other* bears only a limited similarity to *how the formal organization structure says they should behave* (Schein, 1965, 1980). These studies more than any others illustrate the need to study human processes in organizations by actual observation rather than to accept at face value what people say in interviews or on survey questionnaires.

Finally, an important root has been the work of Muzapher Sherif et al. (1961), who showed that regularities could be demonstrated not only within small groups but also between groups, and thus opened up the whole area of intergroup relations. For example, the perceptions, feelings, and behavior of people when they are in an intergroup competition are sufficiently predictable that one can readily create a demonstration exercise that reproduces those phenomena within a period of a couple of hours (Blake and Mouton, 1961).

As can be seen, PC is anchored deeply in social psychology, sociology, and anthropology. The understanding of and intervention into human processes in organizations require not merely an attitude or a decision to pay attention to such processes but also a good deal of knowledge of what to look for, how to look for it, how to interpret it, and what to do about it. Helping an organization to do its own diagnosis and to solve its own problems requires, in addition, helping skills that can be acquired only with experience in a training, clinical, or consulting role.

What Human Processes in Organizations Are More Relevant?

In the next several chapters I will describe what are in my view the most important processes that the process consultant must know something about. Some of these deal with face-to-face relationships between two or more people, some deal with groups and intergroup situations, and some are more broad organizational issues, such as norms, culture, and leadership.

This is not intended to be an exhaustive treatment of interpersonal, group, and organizational processes. Instead I have tried to select those processes that most often catch my attention when I am trying to be helpful. I will describe each area in simple, straightforward language that not only makes sense to me but communicates well to the layman. These can be thought of as "simplifying models" that capture the essence of the phenomena.

In the consultant role I have often found it necessary to translate difficult psychological ideas into simple formulations. In that process one sometimes has to sacrifice rigor, but as long as one knows what the underlying theory and research findings are, it is worthwhile to translate concepts into something the client can understand and deal with. By the same token, the layman not familiar with the underlying theory or the research on which some of the points rest should be cautious in using these concepts in his efforts to be helpful.

The concepts to be reviewed will be illustrated whenever

possible from my own consulting experience and will generally mirror the most critical events as they occur chronologically in the consulting process. Many of the illustrations come from group events because most often the process consultant finds himself in one or another group situation, but this in no way implies that PC is primarily a group-oriented process. Rather, PC is characterized more by the attitude toward the helping process that one takes, as I will try to show.

To recap, PC is characterized by the desire and skill on the part of the consultant to create a relationship with the client (1) that the client will regard as helpful, (2) that will enable the client to focus on the critical process events in his own environment, and (3) will enable the client to diagnose and intervene in those processes to make his organization more effective.

3

Communication Processes

One of the most important basic processes in organizations, and one of the easiest to observe, is how people communicate with each other, particularly in face-to-face and small-group situations. The process consultant must be aware of such processes because they are central to the establishment of his relationship with the client in the one-on-one situation, and they are likely to be the most salient aspect of the kinds of settings in which he will find himself early in the relationship.

For example, if I decide to get involved with a client, I am likely, following the initial contact, to find myself with several members of the client organization at a group meeting with the opportunity to observe what goes on between them. Not only have I observed my own communication with the client so far, but I can now observe how different members in the client organization communicate with each other.

Many formulations of communication depict it as a simple problem of transfer of information from one person to another. But, as we all know, the process is anything but simple, and the information transferred is often highly variable and highly complex. We communicate facts, feelings, perceptions, innuendos, and various other things all in the same "simple" message. We communicate not only through the spoken and written word but through facial expressions, gestures, physical posture, tone of voice, timing of when we speak, what we do not say, and so on. The present chapter will start with simple observables about communication and then will move into deeper, less observable communication processes.

Who Communicates? How Often? For How Long?

The easiest analysis of communication is to focus only on the *relative frequency* and *duration* of communication acts. Thus, if the process consultant wishes to observe the communication behavior of a group or committee, he can list the names of all the members and put a check mark next to a name each time that person says something. He can measure duration by putting down a check mark every few seconds as long as the speaker continues.

After some period of time the chart can be summarized to show who has talked, how often, and how much of the total available time he has used. One can also determine who used short communications and who spoke for long periods. If one wanted to analyze written communications, an analogous chart could be set up to determine who sends, how often he sends, and how long the message is.

I have deliberately ignored such factors as the content of the message in order to illustrate that even very simple things can be observed and learned from. For example, in my experience both in training groups and in meetings, a frequent occurrence is that one or more "quiet" members are accused by the more vocal ones of not contributing their thoughts to the discussion. In many instances I have heard the "quiet" members deny this accusation, saying that they had been talking but that apparently no one had been listening to them.

To help the group to focus on this kind of issue, having a record of how many times each person actually spoke relative to other persons can be extremely valuable. In most instances I have found that the "silent" member is quite right; he had spoken several times but others had stereotyped him as silent and hence not heard what he had to say. Once the facts are recognized, it is possible to move on to the more important issue of *why* some members are listened to more than others.

It should be noted that the process consultant helps the group by gathering data, but when and how he uses these data will depend very much on his judgment of how ready the group is to look at its own process. The key assumption *always* is that the group or the individual manager who is the client must collaborate in formulating the diagnosis; nothing is gained by a premature feedback of data that will be either ignored or resisted. The most common intervention the process consultant therefore makes early in the consultation process is to remain silent, to ask questions if he is not clear about something that is going on, or simply to make generally encouraging remarks.

Even though the consultant may have made an extensive analysis of the group's communication patterns, he may withhold all of the data until he senses that the group is ready. Furthermore, sensing when the group is ready calls for a complex judgment based on other observations that I will describe below. The consultant cannot treat a simple request from the client as equivalent to being ready. All too often I have had a group ask for my observations of the group's process only to find, once I began to share them, that the group had trapped me in a position where I could be neutralized by being shown by some members how "wrong" my observations were.

Who Communicates to Whom?

The next level of complexity of observation would be to determine who talks or writes to whom. Such observation is not difficult with written communications, if they are addressed; it can be very tricky in a group situation, however, since people often are not explicit about to whom they are directing themselves. The observer may have to watch the speaker's eyes to see whom he is looking at when he is talking, or he may observe body posture for similar cues.

These observations, like the previous set, could be recorded in a matrix where all the members are listed on both the horizontal and vertical axes and a check mark is made in the appropriate cell of the matrix. Alternatively, the method could extend the previous one by simply listing for each communication who the speaker and who the recipients were.

This level of communication analysis can reveal a number of processes. For example, if one tracks who speaks to whom fairly carefully, one quickly discovers that some members talk to the whole group, some talk to the ceiling or floor, and some members have favorite audiences. Having identified, for example, the fact that Joe tends mostly to direct his comments at Jane, the question arises as to why this occurs, leading to a next level of observation of their behavior. At this next level it may turn out that Joe talks mostly to Jane because the latter tends to agree with everything the former says. A kind of subgroup or coalition exists within the larger group, which may have a variety of implications for the functioning of the total group.

Alternatively, I have found that sometimes people talk to those others from whom they expect the most opposition or resistance. Thus Joe may have learned that Jane is the member most likely to "shoot him down." He talks first to Jane to see whether he can expect to get his point past what he sees to be his toughest hurdle.

The above illustration highlights the fact that any given observation that the consultant makes does not mean anything very significant in and of itself. Rather, the observations of regularities and key events in group communication serve as a guide or a set of cues for progressively more meaningful questions that then determine new areas of observation. For example, if the manager of the group exhibits a bias in terms of whom he tends to talk to in his meetings, this fact by itself means relatively little. But if the consultant observes how the members who are and the members who are not talked to by the boss react to this behavior, he can formulate some important hypotheses about the functioning of the group.

Who Talks After Whom? Who Interrupts Whom?

Closely related to the issue of who talks to whom is the matter of who triggers whom and in what ways. I have noted in observing groups that there are clear patterns of triggering. Whenever John speaks the odds are pretty good that Sue will be the next to speak even if the remarks were not initially directed to her. Again, this may reflect either support or a desire to undo the point John has made. As every observant group member has noted many times, such undoing can take the most elaborately polite forms, yet it remains a "Yes, *but* . . . " reaction nevertheless. As one group member once put it, in his company examples of such encouragement or undoing are labeled "Attaboys" and "Yeabuts," and the norm is that it takes at least three attaboys to undo the damaging effect of one yeabut in the group discussion.

Sometimes this level of analysis seems trivial, superficial, and contrived. If the observer's analysis stopped at this level, it would indeed be insufficient. What we need to underline again is that the overt surface behavior provides the clues as to what is going on between the people beneath the surface. Such clues not only help the process consultant understand what is going on but are a visible manifestation to the members themselves. If the consultant's role is to set up a situation of shared diagnosis, he must concentrate on observables that are seen as readily by the clients as by him. One of the great problems of psychologically sophisticated consultants who forget their mission as defined here is that they correctly interpret to the group what is happening, but the interpretation is so far detached from observable behavior that the group members reject both it and the consultant.

Let us now turn to the other behavior mentioned in the heading above: who interrupts whom. Observing this type of communication behavior is important because it gives us clues as to how members perceive their own status or power in the group relative to the status or power of other members. It is a matter of common observation, and has been documented in careful studies of deference, that the person of higher rank, status, or power feels free to interrupt someone of lower rank. We generally let the boss finish his sentences more often than he lets us finish ours. In those instances where this trend seems not to hold, one often finds that the members feel themselves to be of equal status even though objectively their rank may be different. Even then they might be more careful in public than in private situations.

Assuming a working team of equals, what does it mean if the marketing manager often interrupts the production manager, but the reverse seldom occurs? The process consultant would ask himself whether there was in fact a status difference, or, if not, whether the marketing manager simply felt himself to be more important than the production manager. In the latter case, a fairly common kind of problem arises from the fact that the production manager begins to feel a loss of influence, to which he may react by starting to fight rather than continuing to work cooperatively.

Without insight on the part of either as to how they are signaling their feeling in overt communication acts, it is difficult for them to improve their working relationship. They can improve the relationship only if the consultant can create a situation where they discover for themselves how their self-perceptions, perceptions of each other, and subjective judgments about their own influence relative to others come out in overt behavior.

In general, I have observed that interrupting others is one of the more common and more destructive kinds of communication behavior. Most people have relatively little awareness of how often and how crudely they cut in on others, convinced that what they have to say is more important than what they believe the previous speaker would have continued to say. When this process is itself interrupted by a consultant intervention, it often turns out that the person who first interrupted did not in fact really understand what the previous speaker was trying to say. In his eagerness he was formulating his own thoughts rather than listening to what was said before him.

One of the unfortunate consequences of frequent interruption is that the group is likely to interpret this as a sign of lack of organization. The suggestion is usually made that the way to control interruptions and avoid having too many people talking at once is to give the chairman more power to cut people off, call on people, and generally establish order. This solution substitutes external discipline for internal control. It misdiagnoses the problem as one of organization rather than recognizing it as a lack of concern of the members for each other, resulting in insufficient listening. If the problem is one of listening, then the formal-chairmanship solution will not deal with the problem. Members will still not listen but will instead be busy formulating what they will say when called on to speak.

Communication Style

Communication style is intended to refer to a whole range of factors, such as whether the person is assertive, questioning, pedantic, or humorous; whether his tone of voice is loud, soft, grating, or melodious; whether he accompanies his words with gestures; and so on. Insofar as the process consultant is interested in member relations, he is less concerned about style as an indicator of underlying personality and more concerned about the possible effects of a given communication style on the people with whom the person communicates.

For example, I may notice that a person talks very loudly and assertively, causing others gradually to tune him out, yet he seems to be quite unaware that this is happening. He may even become aware of his declining influence in the group and yet remain unaware of what has caused this decline. He does not hear himself as loud and assertive. The other members of the group who are no longer paying attention to him are also in a trap. They may not be paying attention because of the communication *style* used by the speaker and yet erroneously feel it is the *content* of what he is saying that is failing to hold their interest. Communication in this situation cannot improve until both parties to the problem gain some insight into what they are doing and why they are doing it (for example, what cues they are sending and are reacting to).

Gestural Communication (Kinesics)

As anthropologists and linguists have known for some time, body posture, gestures, facial expressions, and other nonverbal behavior can and do become patterned according to the culture in which the person grew up. To the extent that they are patterned and have symbolic meanings, they can be understood just as clearly as verbal or written communication. Certain gestures, for example, reflect ethnic background. Careful analysis of films of people in spontaneous interaction has revealed that some groups (for example, first-generation Jewish immigrants) tend to accompany assertive words with forward-reaching, one-handed gestures, often described as "buttonholing." First-generation Italians, in contrast, tend to use both hands in gesturing and to rotate them outward rather than pointing toward the listener.

Hall, in his excellent book *The Silent Language* (1959), describes a whole range of culturally determined nonverbal cues that must be understood if the listener is to make correct interpretations of the speaker. For example, in every culture there is a kind of "ideal sphere" around a person. This "sphere" is the territory or space around a person that may not be violated unless you are on intimate terms with him, have some legitimate reason, or are deliberately and aggressively violating it. Two examples of violation are standing too close and touching. In countries where this normal distance is less than in America, the American is likely to feel uncomfortable because people are always crowding him in conversation or getting him into corners.

Systematic observations of postural and gestural behavior have been made by Birdwhistell (1961) using methods of analysis first developed in the field of linguistics. This field of analysis he calls *kinesics*. He has identified, for example, some of the nonverbal behavior associated with courtship patterns which is properly labeled as "preening." It can be observed that a young man, when he suddenly finds himself in the company of an attractive girl, will straighten his tie, pull up his socks, run his fingers through his hair, adopt a slightly more erect posture, and have a higher muscle tonus. If the girl similarly notices the young man and responds to him, she will also show higher muscle tonus, may flush slightly, stroke her hair, check her makeup, straighten her stockings, and sketchily rearrange her clothing (Scheflen, 1965).

Further postural and nonverbal cues are also associated with what Scheflen identified as stages of "positioning for courtship" and "actions of invitation." Since such cues are culturally learned, their meaning is clear to members of the same culture. Such cues are often called "body language" and can be meaningfully interpreted providing the sender and observer are using a common cultural frame of reference. But there is little evidence that body language has universal meaning.

Although methods of analysis of such complex gestures are still in their infancy, it is not too difficult to imagine that they could be used successfully in identifying cues that accompany aggressiveness, excessive deference, boredom, and various other feelings that are of great importance in group situations. In fact, I suspect that most experienced managers already rely on many such clues but do so unsystematically and without complete awareness of what it is on which they are relying.

Levels of Communication

So far I have discussed more or less manifest and easily observable communication events. In order to make some sense of these events and to understand more fully how members of any encounter react to each other, it is important to analyze less easily observable events. As background for this discussion, some psychological theory about the nature of communication is also relevant.

As most of us know from observation of our own behavior, not only do we tend to react to the manifest content of what another person says to us, but we interpret what he says and use various subtle clues to get at the real meaning of the message. Often the same message carries more than one meaning, both a manifest and a latent meaning. Occasionally these meanings tend to contradict each other. One simple example is the person who issues an invitation with the statement "Come over to our house anytime," but leaves it sufficiently ambiguous through his tone of voice that you realize he does not really want you to come and is merely being polite. Another example is in work teams, where it is not unusual for a person to argue against a proposal because he feels he has to be consistent with a previous position or defend a group he represents, but to argue in a way that lets others know he is privately prepared to be convinced and will go along eventually. Often we say one thing in order to save face but manage to communicate something else.

Double messages of this kind do not pose unusual difficulties because the sender is aware of them and can clarify misunderstandings. Greater difficulty arises from double messages that reflect parts of the person of which he is unaware. To illustrate, it is useful to think of the person as having several parts, as depicted in Figure 3–1. Quadrant 1 in the figure represents those areas of the person of which he himself is aware and which he is willing to share with others: the "open self." Quadrant 2 represents those parts of himself of which he is aware, but which he is consciously and deliberately trying to conceal from others. Typical examples that come up if one asks a group to reveal anonymously some of the things they conceal from others are areas of insecurity that the person is ashamed to admit, feelings and impulses that he considers to be antisocial or inconsistent with his self-image, memories of events where he failed or showed up particularly badly against his own standards, and most important, feelings and reactions to other people that he feels would be impolite or hurtful to reveal.

For example, Jill might think that the boss made a terrible presentation at the key meeting, leading to loss of the sale, but equally might feel she must withhold this reaction and compliment the boss "in order not to hurt his feelings or make him mad." As we will see later, one of the key insights resulting from

2 Concealed self	1 Open self
4 Unknown self	3 Blind self

Figure 3–1
The Parts of a Person *

*J. Luft, "The Johari Window," *Hum. Rel. Tr. News* 5, 1961, pp. 6–7.

PC is understanding of how much valuable loss of communication results from conscious concealment of reactions to interpersonal events.

Quadrant 3 in the figure is the key one for this discussion. The "blind area" of the self refers to those things that we unconsciously conceal from ourselves yet which are part of us and are communicated to others. "I am *not* angry," says the boss in loud tones, purple-faced, as he slams his fist on the table. "These meetings are quite relaxing for me," says the executive as his hand trembles, his voice cracks, and he either has a third martini or tries unobtrusively to slip a tranquilizer into his mouth. "I do not care about the opinions of others," says the manager, but then he gets upset if others do not notice him or his work.

All of us have, in the process of growing up, been rewarded for being certain kinds of people and punished for being other kinds. The young boy learns that it is all right to have aggressive feelings but that it is not all right to feel fear or tenderness when with other boys. So he begins to reject feelings of tenderness as being not part of himself. He suppresses them or refuses to recognize them as his own when they occur. Yet they may be quite visible to other people. How often have we said of a gruff, tough man that he is really very tender? What we are saying is that we see tender behavior but that the person himself cannot see his own tender side and must continue to deny it by maintaining a gruff exterior. I have seen executives who became aggressive in direct proportion to the amount of tenderness they felt for the people around them; and I have seen women who became studiously considerate and tender in direct proportion to the amount of aggression they were feeling but unwilling to admit to themselves.

Each of us thus has feelings and traits that we feel are not part of us, and we are blind to the fact that we do communicate many such feelings to others. We may also be blind to the fact that some of the feelings we try to conceal do leak out.

Quadrant 4 consists of those parts of the person of which neither he nor others are aware. Examples would be truly unconscious and deeply repressed feelings and impulses, hidden talents or skills, potentialities, and so on. For our purposes this area is irrelevant.

Let us now consider two people in interaction with each other (Fig. 3–2) and analyze the implications of the different kinds of messages and different levels of communication that occur. Most communication occurs between the two open selves of the persons (Arrow A), and most popularized analyses of the communication process confine themselves to this level.

A second level of communication is the signals or meanings that we pick up from a person's blind self and which he is unaware of sending (Arrow B).

A third level of communication occurs when we deliberately reveal something that we ordinarily tend to conceal (Arrow C). Usually we think of this as "confiding" in someone or "leveling" if we are sharing reactions or feelings generated by immediate events.

Finally, there is a less common but no less important level

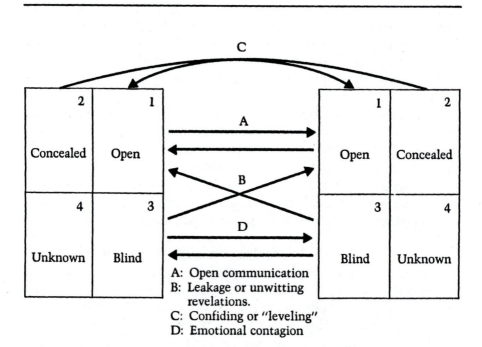

Figure 3–2
Types of Messages in a Two-Person Communication Situation

of communication, represented by Arrow D, which might best be labeled "emotional contagion." One person influences the feelings of another without either one's being consciously aware of the origin of the feeling. Sometimes the feeling that is aroused in the recipient mirrors that of the sender, as when tension that may be denied by the sender nevertheless makes the receiver tense as well. In other cases the feeling is different, as when a denied but displayed feeling in one person causes tension in the other because he does not know whether he should respond to the manifest level of communication (the denial of feeling) or to the latent level (the actually displayed feeling).

The process consultant must be aware of these subtleties and complications in levels of communication in order to understand fully the flow of interpersonal events. I have observed a group situation where the senior executive and chairman of the group became very angry at several members and punished them openly for failing to follow through on a project. Yet, surprisingly, he did not arouse any defensiveness or tensions on their part. The explanation was that they had learned over a long period of time that he was really frustrated over not being more involved in the project himself and was really communicating, without being aware of it, that he was feeling sorry for himself. His group reacted more to this second message and worked hard to involve him in the project. When they succeeded, his anger subsided. What this executive was unconsciously denying was his need to be involved and needed (a very tender feeling), yet these feelings were clearly perceived by his subordinates and they had no difficulty responding to them.

Once one recognizes several levels of communication, one can open up communication channels that ordinarily are not used. Once the participants in an interpersonal situation obtain some insight into their own communication behavior, they can examine rationally the pros and cons of opening more of the Arrow C, or "confiding," kind of channel. Specifically, they can examine whether or not the effectiveness of the group would be increased if more members shared withheld information or their private feelings relevant to the task at hand, particularly feelings pertaining to other members and to the work situation.

For example, the consultant may face a situation in which

the members of a work group or team will reveal feelings, such as frustration, anger, futility, tenderness, or concern, privately to him, but it never occurs to them to share these feelings with the people who elicit them. The reasons for such withholding are multiple: our culture says it is not polite; it may be hurtful to the other person; there is the danger of angering the other person, leading to retaliation on his part; it may make the relationship too intimate; or it is something that simply does not occur to the person to do.

The consultant can stimulate more open communications by interventions that show the group the price of *not* communicating at this level. The approach would be to start with rather safe topics and areas. A member is against a proposal, but instead of sharing his feeling he starts various political maneuvers to ensure that the proposal will not go through, or, worse, lets it go through and then resists implementing it. If the consultant can get the group to spend some time analyzing its own process, he can raise the question of how members originally felt about the proposal and thus stimulate in a safer environment some opening up of earlier feelings. If this exercise proves illuminating and productive to the group, they are likely to be a bit more open in the next work session, although the consultant has to expect this kind of learning to be very slow and erratic.

Exploration of the B-type communication is most relevant if the group is having serious communication problems. The consultant can then raise the question of whether members are confusing each other by sending more than one message at once, creating for the recipient the problem of which one to react to. It should be noted that if the group agrees to discuss this issue at all, the members must reveal some of their own reactions. In other words, if I tell someone that he is sending a B-type message, thus reducing one of his blind spots, I am at the same time revealing something of my reactions that I ordinarily hide, thus reducing the size of my own concealed areas. Discussions of either B- or C-type messages tend thus to stimulate each other. The desired result would be a situation in which all members could enlarge their own open areas in their dealings with each other, thereby reducing distortions, miscommunications, and ambiguities.

On the other hand, nothing in the PC philosophy argues

for openness as being in and of itself a good thing. It all depends on whether or not relevant information that would make accomplishment of the group's task easier is being withheld. Being more open then would increase group effectiveness, provided being open was culturally permissible. In many cultures there are areas that are interpersonally taboo and cannot be opened up no matter what the cost of withholding. In such instances the consultant would not be helpful if he simply encouraged more openness.

Filtering

The final, and perhaps most difficult, complexity to consider in the communication process is that both the sender and the receiver use a number of filters in selecting what they will send and what they will receive. I am not implying conscious censorship, although this occurs also. Rather, I am implying that all of us select what we say, how we say it, and when we say it in terms of a complex set of decision rules that we have learned over a lifetime and that reflect a number of specific factors:

1. Self-image. Both sender and the receiver have an image or concept of themselves and feelings of self-worth or self-esteem. What their self-concept is at any given time and what value they attach to themselves in a given situation will, in part, determine their communication. For example, if I think of myself as an expert in an area and have great confidence in myself (attach great worth to myself) in a given situation, I am more likely to communicate in the first place, more likely to choose an assertive, telling style of communication rather than a diffident one, and less likely to listen to others on that same topic. After all, I am the expert.

2. Image of the Other Person or Persons. Both the sender and the receiver have an image or concept of the others in the situation and attach certain values to these others as people. These images of the others will also, in part, determine communication. For example, if I see the others in the situation as being less expert and of lower status in the situation than I am, I am likely to talk down to them, to interrupt them when I think they are off target, to listen less for their original points of view and more for whether they are understanding me and/or agreeing with me. If I feel less expert or of lower status I will say less, listen harder, and try to figure out how to gain status in the situation (this, incidentally, may inhibit good listening also, diverting attention from the task to the relationship issue).

3. *Definition of the Situation.* Both the sender and the receiver have a certain picture of the situation in which they are jointly operating. Is it a meeting to solve a specific problem? Is it an informal bull session? Are we here to give the boss a chance to tell us his ideas? Often this process of "defining the situation" is not verbalized until someone raises the question "What are we here for?" or "What is our task?"

The definition of the situation goes beyond specifying the goals or task to be achieved; it is the complete set of perceptions pertaining to one's own and others' roles in the situation, its duration, its boundaries, and the norms that will govern it (for example, is it a formal or informal situation?). Obviously, what we say and how we say it will be largely governed by how we define the situation.

4. *Motives, Feelings, Intentions, Attitudes.* Another set of filters on the communication process both for sender and listener are the various needs and motives they bring to the situation, their intentions, and their attitudes toward others. If my needs are to sell a proposal or to influence others, I will communicate differently from how I will if I am curious about something and need to get information. If I am trying to influence, I will listen differently to what others say from how I will if I am gathering information, and I will listen for different things. For example, if I am trying to influence, I will listen harder for agreement or disagreement than for new ideas.

5. *Expectations.* The final category of psychological factors that create filters is our expectations of ourselves and of others in the situation, based either on actual experience or on preconceptions and stereotypes. If I expect my audience to be slow to understand, I will use simpler words; if I expect them to be receptive, I will talk in a more relaxed way; if I expect them to be critical, I will frame my points carefully and precisely.

From the point of view of the listener, if he expects the speaker to be very smart, he may read in more meaning than there is in the message; if he expects him to be inarticulate or unintelligent, he may fail to hear the good points. If he expects disagreement, he may read hostility into what the speaker says; and if he expects support, he may fail to hear disagreement.

Given all the various filters described, it is not surprising that the communication process between people is fraught with so much difficulty. The process consultant is not immune to the psychological factors described. He will have his own set of filters based upon his needs, expectations, images, intentions, and so on. Because he is a trained observer he may spot the effects of filters sooner than other members, but he certainly cannot see the truth in any absolute sense any better than other members can. It is partly for this reason that he must help the group to make a diagnosis rather than simply providing his own diagnosis as if it were the absolute truth. Only out of the joint efforts of all the members can a diagnosis of communications difficulties be made that is likely to be near enough to the truth to warrant remedial action.

The Circular Process and Self-fulfilling Prophecies

The various factors described above under the category of filtering make it possible for communications to break down in a particularly dangerous manner. If expectations are strong on the part of both the sender and the receiver, it is possible for each to interpret the cues from the other in such a way that both confirm their stereotypes and thus lock each other into roles from which it is difficult to escape. Let us take two examples.

Person A, on the basis of previous experience, has a positive self-image, is confident, needs to influence others, and expects to be able to do so. His communications are assertive, confident, and clear. His listeners respond to this clarity and assertiveness by paying attention to what he has to say, thus confirming A's image of himself as an influential person. He gains confidence from being listened to and assumes an increasingly strong role in the group.

Person B, on the basis of his previous experience, is not sure of himself, feels a lack of confidence in the presence of several others, is not sure he can influence people even though he would like to, and expects that he will have difficulty establishing himself in the group. His communications will, as a result, be hesitant, low key, and diffident, although they may be just as clear as A's.

His listeners may well respond to the diffidence and hesitancy by assuming that B does not have much to offer and may cease to pay attention to him, thus confirming his own initial impression of himself as having little to contribute. B loses confidence, communicates less and less, further confirming for the others his lack of potential contribution, and gradually assumes the role of a noncontributor.

In both cases the final outcome is the result of initial expectations that produce a certain communication style, which in turn leads to confirmation of the initial expectations. The danger is that the initial expectations may have little to do with the actual potential contribution of A and B to the group product; yet A will be a high contributor and B will be a low contributor. Only by becoming sensitive to this kind of self-fulfilling prophecy can the group protect itself from getting a mix of contributions that are unrelated to actual ability.

A key role for the process consultant is to ask himself, when he observes different rates of participation and contribution to the group, whether this accurately reflects ability to contribute or is the result of circular processes of the sort described. If the consultant finds evidence for the latter, he must help the group reassess its own operations, reexamine its stereotypes of who can contribute what, and build norms that permit the low-confidence contributor to gain confidence by being listened to by others.

Summary

In the previous sections I have examined various facets of the communication process. Starting with relatively overt processes, such as who talks, who talks to whom, who interrupts whom, and what style of communication is used, I then reviewed more subtle communication issues, such as the meaning implicit in nonverbal communication, the role of different levels of communication stemming from our blind spots and tendencies to conceal certain things about ourselves, and the problems stemming from our tendencies to filter in the role of both sender and receiver.

This set of issues by no means exhausts all aspects of communication that could be reviewed. For example, we did not cover problems of semantics, nor did we examine issues involving how to communicate in a more persuasive way — subjects one might find in courses on "good" communications. Topics covered reflect those aspects of communication that tend to be especially important in work teams, staff meetings, bull sessions, committees, and other settings where member relations have to be "good" in order for work output to be high. The process consultant must help the group to perceive the connection between the subtle communication processes described and the kind of factual exchange that leads to effective working relations and high output.

4

The Process of Building and Maintaining a Group

One of the most salient phenomena I encounter in the early contacts with a client organization is groups at all stages of development. The clients who come to visit me to explore a possible consultation may not have worked with each other before and thus may be a brand new small group. The committee meeting that I am asked to attend may be a special meeting of a group that has regular meetings every week or, on the other hand, may be a group that has met for the very first time to consider the consulting project. The people that the client may have invited to meet with me may include some who have worked extensively with each other and a few others who are, in effect, strangers to each other at the initial meeting. Given this variety of circumstances, it is essential for the consultant to have a simplifying model of how a group gets started and develops.

The underlying theoretical premise is that when two or more people come together to form a work- or task-oriented group, there will first be a period of essentially self-oriented behavior reflecting various concerns that any new member of a group could be expected to experience. As the self-oriented behavior declines, members begin to pay more attention to each other and to the task at hand. The kinds of behavior that help the group to build and maintain itself then occur concurrently with behaviors designed to accomplish the work of the group. I would like to describe the steps in a chronological sequence because they occur more or less in sequence, although each phase may overlap the others.

Phase 1: Problems in Entering a New Group; Self-oriented Behavior

The problems that a person faces when he enters a new group stem from certain underlying emotional issues that must be resolved before he can feel comfortable in the new situation. Four such issues can be readily identified (see Fig. 4–1).

Problems	*Resulting feelings*	*Coping responses (self-oriented)*
1. *IDENTITY* Who am I to be?	Frustration	1. *"TOUGH" RESPONSES* Fighting, controlling resisting authority.
2. *CONTROL & INFLUENCE* Will I be able to control and influence others?	Tension	2. *"TENDER" RESPONSES* Supporting, helping forming alliances, dependency.
3. *NEEDS & GOALS* Will the group goals include my own needs?	Anxiety	3. *WITHDRAWAL OR DENIAL RESPONSES* Passivity, indifference, overuse of "logic and reason"
4. *ACCEPTANCE & INTIMACY* Will I be liked and accepted by the group? How close a group will we be?		

Figure 4–1
Problems in Entering a New Group Which Cause Self-oriented Behavior

1. Identity First and foremost is the problem of choosing a role or identity that will be acceptable to the person himself and viable in the group. In other words, each new member, whether he is aware of it or not, must find an answer to the question "Who and what am I to be in this group?"

This issue exists in the first place because all of us have a large repertory of possible roles and behavioral styles to bring into play in any given situation. Should I be the dominant aggressive leader, a behavior pattern that may have worked for me in some situations; or should I be the humorous tension reliever, which may have worked for me in other situations; or should I be the quiet listener, which has worked in still other situations? In varying degrees we are different people in different life situations. Therefore we always have some degree of choice in new situations.

In formal committees or work groups, this kind of issue is often partially resolved through the initial mandate. A person is told to join a task force to represent the "personnel point of view," or a strong chairman tells members what kinds of roles he wants them to play. Such resolutions are at best only partial, however, in that there is still great latitude for the person to develop a style that will satisfy him and be acceptable to the others in the group. As Figure 4–1 indicates, as long as the emotional issue is there, whether the person recognizes it consciously or not, it operates as a source of tension, leads the person to be primarily preoccupied with himself, and consequently leads to less listening and concern for others or the group task.

2. Control, Power, Influence A second issue that any new member faces and which must be resolved in any new group is the distribution of power and influence. It can be safely assumed that every member will have some need to control and influence others, but the amount of this need and its form of expression will vary from person to person. One member may wish to influence the actual task solution, another may wish to influence the methods or procedures used by the group, a third may wish to achieve an overall position of prominence in the group, and so on.

The dilemma for all members early in the group's history

is that they do not know each other's needs or styles, and hence cannot easily determine who will be able to influence whom and what. Consequently, the consultant will frequently observe a great deal of fencing, testing each other out, and experimenting with different forms of influence in early meetings. The consultant must be careful not to misunderstand this behavior. On the surface it seems like a definite flight from whatever task the group is facing. Underneath it represents an important sorting out, getting acquainted, and coming to terms with each other which the members need to do in order to relax their self-concerns and focus on the task.

If a chairman insists on a tight formal schedule that prevents some of this getting acquainted and testing out, he runs the risk of either producing superficial solutions because members are not ready to really work on the task, or of forcing them to do their fencing in the context of the task work, thereby slowing down the progress and undermining the potential quality of the solution. In this kind of situation, the consultant must help the chairman to understand the functions the initial sorting-out behavior performs for the members, to understand the need for group building time, and to understand that good communications cannot develop until members' self-preoccupations have been reduced.

3. Individual Needs and Group Goals A third issue that faces every group member is his concern that the group goals that are initially set or will emerge from discussion may not include his personal goals and needs. Preoccupation with this issue typically leads the person to wait and see how the group develops, not to invest himself too heavily in it until he sees whether things will go his way. The problem for the group as a whole is that if a substantial number of people take the wait-and-see attitude, it is difficult to get any group action started. In this situation the group typically turns to any available authority to set the agenda, formulate goals, or suggest a task. If the chairman responds to the pressure and sets the goals, he is partially solving the problem, but he still cannot ensure that the goals he sets will involve all the members sufficiently to get them committed to the task.

A sounder procedure would be to face the paradox directly: *Until member needs are to some degree exposed and shared, it is not possible to set up valid group goals.* Consequently, enough meeting time should be allocated to permit members to explore what they really want to get out of the group. The role of the process consultant in this situation is usually to slow down the group and to reassure members that the early struggles to communicate with each other are a necessary and important part of group growth.

4. *Acceptance and Intimacy* These two issues are lumped together because they deal with the same underlying problem: Will I be liked and accepted by the others in the group, and how close or intimate will we have to be to achieve a comfortable level of mutual respect and acceptance? For every set of people and every situation, norms must be developed by the group that help to resolve these issues. There is no optimal or absolute level of acceptance and intimacy for all groups at all times. It depends on the members, on the group task, on the length of time available to the group, and a host of other factors. But the issue is always there as a source of tension until working norms have been established.

Initially the issue will appear in terms of forms of address and patterns of politeness. As the group develops, the issue will center on formality or informality of group procedures. At a still later stage the issue will center on whether group discussion must stick to the formal task or whether more personal exchanges are permissible and desirable.

The group can attempt to legislate solutions by the adoption of Roberts's Rules of Order or similar devices, but such procedures are more likely to sweep the issue under the rug than really to resolve it. The role of the consultant can be to help the group to recognize that the issue is a legitimate one to be worked on.

Types of Coping Responses to Emotional Issues

As indicated above, each of the underlying problems in gaining membership leads to tension, frustration, and self-preoccupation. What does the person typically do in coping with the underlying problems and the resulting tensions? Three basic kinds of coping patterns can be observed (see Fig. 4–1):

1. Basically tough, aggressive coping
2. Basically tender, support-seeking coping
3. Coping by withdrawal behavior based on denial of any feelings

The *tough, aggressive response* shows up in various kinds of fighting, such as arguing, cutting down other members' points, ridiculing, deliberate ignoring of others, cutting and hostile humor, and the like. Although the behavior may be legitimate within the rules of group discussion under the guise of "debating the point" or "exploring our differences," the observer should be careful to note whether the underlying feelings expressed are concern for a better task solution or are, in fact, ways of challenging and testing other members in the process of solving emotional issues.

The aggressive response also is reflected in attempts to control other members through setting up procedures, calling on people, telling other members what they should be talking about, and the like. With respect to any authority figures in the group, such as the chairman, this type of emotional behavior shows up as counterdependency. Counterdependency refers to feelings of wanting to resist authority: "Let's find out what the chairman wants us to do and then *not* do it," or "Let's do it our own way, not the way he wants us to do it."

In most formal groups such behavior is likely to be quite subtle because standards of politeness and formal power differences militate against open expressions of counterdependency. Yet it is not difficult for the process consultant to observe such behavior, to help the group to recognize the legitimacy of it, and to help differentiate emotional coping from genuine expression of differences on the task level.

The *tender, support-seeking response* is reflected in a variety of ways. Members look for someone with whom they seem to agree and try to form a supportive alliance or subgroup within the larger group. Members attempt to avoid conflict, give support, help each other, and generally try to suppress aggressive, divisive feelings. With respect to authority, such behavior shows up as dependency — looking for someone to lean on, to give guidance, and to solve the problems that the members feel they have.

How does the process consultant differentiate this kind of behavior from constructive problem-solving behavior? First, he notes at what point in the group's or member's history the behavior is occurring. As I have indicated, the emotionally based self-oriented behavior occurs early in the history when members are trying to establish themselves in the group. The same kind of behavior later could simply mean genuine support in reference to the task.

A second criterion is whether the consultant feels that the support is based on genuine mutual understanding or is a kind of blind response. The emotionally based behavior I am describing here is often indicated by members forming alliances without really showing evidence of understanding each other's points of view at all. The consultant must help the group to distinguish hasty support seeking, indiscriminate helping, and inappropriate dependency from similar behaviors that may occur later in the process of problem solving.

The *withdrawal or denial response* is characterized by a suppression of tension and feeling, often resulting in a rather passive, indifferent, bland kind of response. It is as if the person were saying, "You people go ahead and fight it out and get this group rolling while I watch; I don't really have any feelings about it, so I'll get on board when things get properly organized."

Another version of this emotional behavior is for the person to argue that feelings have no place in group discussion and should be legislated out of existence and suppressed at all costs. When a fight breaks out, the person says, "Fellow members, we are all civilized, mature individuals; we can settle this logically and calmly. Let us not let our feelings get the better of us; let's stick to the facts."

If the person were being truly rational and logical, he would realize that the feelings in the situation are some of the facts that must be taken into account. They can be suppressed and legislated off the agenda, but they cannot be made to disappear and they cannot be prevented from affecting each member's problem-solving behavior. If a group member has tensions and self-preoccupations, he will in fact not be listening to or concerned about other members and hence will not contribute to effective problem solving.

Each of us, as a human being, is capable of each of these basic types of response in our efforts to cope with the emotional issues of the group. Which style of response we tend to use will depend on our personalities, on our past histories in interpersonal situations, on the behavior of other members in the group, and on the formality and structure of the situation. For example, a formal, tightly controlled group is much more likely to produce withdrawal and denial responses, which in the long run will produce a poorly motivated, alienated group. When such a group tries to solve a difficult problem, there is no guarantee that members will either be motivated enough to direct their energies to the problem or be able to communicate with each other well enough to build a genuine group solution. Permitting and exploring emotional expressions, on the other hand, will lead to initial discomfort but will, in the long run, produce a higher level of communication and a stronger, more effective group.

Resolution of Emotional Issues

I have described four kinds of emotional issues that every person faces when he enters a new group situation — the problem of identity, the problem of influence and power, the problem of needs and goals, and the problem of acceptance and intimacy. Until the person finds a role for himself in the group and until the group develops norms pertaining to goals, influence, and intimacy, he will be tense and will respond in various emotional ways.

The price of such behavior for the group is that the members are preoccupied with their own feelings and hence less able to listen to each other and solve problems. Yet every group must go through some growing pains while members work on these issues and find their place. If the formal structure does not permit such growth, the group never becomes a real group capable of group effort. It remains a collection of individuals held together by a formal structure.

The process consultant can help the group to resolve emotional issues in a number of ways. First of all, he must be aware of what is going on and not become anxious over the initial communication problems that members have. Second, he must help the group to realize that the early fighting, alliances, and withdrawal responses are efforts on the part of members to get to know each other, to test each other out, and to find their own place in the group. He can do this by giving the group perspective on itself through capsules of group theory of the sort I have given here. He can indicate his belief that members are working on a legitimate group-building task, not just wasting time.

In order to be helpful, the consultant must fully understand how groups form and which issues are involved in the evolution of group norms and eventually a group culture (Schein, 1985). In particular he must be aware that, as individual self-oriented behavior declines and the group begins to take shape, it must manage both its external relations and its internal functioning in order to survive and function well.

Process management takes insight, time, and energy. I find myself, as a process consultant, having to help managers accept the reality of the investments they must make in group functioning. Managers typically expect groups to be able to get right to work and do not allow for a period of group building. If the group does not solve problems quickly, members get angry and disillusioned with group effort. The consultant must then encourage managers to be patient, to allocate enough time to group meetings to permit the group to grow, and to realize that their own anger and impatience are a reflection of the same emotional issues that the other members are facing.

Finally, the consultant must be expert in giving helpful and useful feedback to members concerning their own behavior. Much of the coping is likely to be occurring without awareness on the part of the group members as to what is happening and why. If they are to gain some insight into this behavior and become more expert in diagnosing it themselves, the consultant must try to help each member to understand his own coping behavior.

As members acquire this insight, as they begin to know how others are feeling and responding, and as they begin to realize that the group can include them and their potential contribution, they gradually relax and their ability to pay attention to others increases. When this happens one can sense a change in the climate and mood of the group. There is less urgency, more listening, less running away from tasks to be performed, more willingness to cooperate as a total group, less formality and falling back on arbitrary rules, but more self-discipline and willingness to suppress personal agendas for the sake of the total group performance. The important thing to realize is that such a state can be achieved only if the group is permitted to work out its internal and external problems. It cannot be imposed or legislated.

Phase 2: Task and Group-Maintenance Functions

So far I have discussed what happens in the early life of a group before it is ready to solve problems effectively. In the following sections I will deal with various aspects of group problem solving and the contributions that members make to it. Figure 4–2 shows a list of what have been called *task* functions and *maintenance* functions. These are behaviors that must occur to some degree inside the group in order for the group to progress effectively. The group must also maintain itself in its environment and fulfill *boundary maintenance* functions.

From the point of view of the process consultant, the lists are important as a checking device to determine which kinds of functions are being performed adequately and which are either missing altogether or not adequately performed. The observer of process can also study the distribution of the functions to determine whether they are evenly distributed, whether some members consistently do one kind of thing, which functions the leader performs, and so on.

A. Task Functions

Let us look at some task functions first. In order for the group to make progress on a task, there must be some *initiating*. Someone must state the goal or problem, make proposals as to how to work on it, set some time limits or targets, and the like. Often this function falls to the leader or to whoever called the

Task Functions	***Building and Maintenance Functions***
Initiating	Harmonizing
Information seeking	Compromising
Information giving	Gatekeeping
Opinion seeking	Encouraging
Opinion giving	Diagnosing
Clarifying	Standard setting
Elaborating	Standard testing
Summarizing	
Consensus testing	

Boundary Management Functions

Boundary defining
Scouting
Negotiating
Translating
Guarding
Managing entry and exit

Figure 4–2
Task, Building, and Maintenance Functions in Groups

group together in the first place, but as a group grows and gains confidence, initiating functions will increasingly come from a broader range of members.

In order for progress to be made there must be some *opinion seeking and giving* and *information seeking and giving* on various issues related to the task. The kinds of information and opinions a group seeks in pursuing its tasks are often crucial for the quality of the solution. The observer should note carefully and help the group to observe for itself whether sufficient time was given to the information- and opinion-seeking functions. It is also important to distinguish seeking from giving and information from opinion. Groups often have difficulty because too many members give opinions before sufficient information seeking and giving has occurred, leading then to fruitless debate. The consultant can help by asking what kinds of information might be needed to resolve the issue among different opinions that are on the floor.

Clarifying and *elaborating* are critical functions in a group in order to test the adequacy of communication and in order to build on the ideas of others toward more creative and complex ideas. If such activities do not occur, the group is not really using its unique strength. One of the most common and powerful interventions that the process consultant can make is to ask clarifying questions or test his own listening by elaborating some of the ideas of members.

Summarizing is an important function to ensure that ideas are not lost because of either the size of the group or the length of time of discussion. Effective summarizing will include a review of which points the group has already covered and the different ideas that have been stated, so that as decision points are reached, the group is operating with full information. One common problem I have observed in committees, task forces, and executive teams is that they tend to work sequentially and process one idea at a time, never gaining any perspective on the totality of their discussion. What is missing is the summarizing function. It can be fulfilled by having a recorder note ideas on a blackboard as the group proceeds so that it has its own visible summary before it at all times; or a person can, from time to time, simply review what he has heard and draw out tentative generalizations from it for the group to consider. This, along with clarifying, is a most useful function for the consultant.

Finally, the group needs someone periodically to test whether it is nearing a decision or should continue to discuss. *Consensus testing* could involve simply asking the question "Are we ready to decide?" or could involve some summarizing: "It seems to me we have expressed these three alternatives and are leaning toward number two; am I right?" The success of this function in moving the group forward will depend largely on the sensitivity of the person in choosing the right time to test, although ill-timed tests are still useful in reminding the group that it has some more discussing to do.

Task functions such as these are so obviously relevant to

effective group problem solving that it is easy for the process consultant to get the group thinking of process in terms of them. One of the consultant's greatest problems is choosing which behavior to bring to the group's attention. The task functions provide one simple alternative that is not too likely to be resisted as irrelevant.

B. Building and Internal Maintenance Functions

In order for the group to survive and grow as an effective instrument of problem solving, members must concern themselves with the building and maintenance of good relationships. Ideally such concerns would be expressed throughout the life cycle of the group, but, as we have already seen when examining the early phases of group life, members do become preoccupied with their own needs and thus may damage their relationships to others.

The problem for the group is how to rebuild damaged relationships and/or minimize initial tendencies for them to become damaged. By a damaged relationship I mean, for example, two members who are angry at each other because they have opposing views on a task issue, members who were outvoted or ignored and thus feel left out, members who feel misunderstood or sidetracked, and so on. In each case, the person is temporarily preoccupied with personal needs and feelings, and is therefore relatively less able to contribute to group effort. If no group maintenance occurs, the member is not brought back into harmony with the group and is consequently lost as a resource to the group or, worse, becomes an active saboteur of group effort.

Some member activities can best be thought of as preventive maintenance. For example, the function of *gatekeeping* ensures that members who have a contribution to make to problem solution have an opportunity to make it. Gatekeeping thus involves both reducing the activity of overactive members and increasing the activity of overly passive members. I have often sat in a group and observed one person repeatedly open his mouth and actually get one or two words out when a more aggressive person interrupts him, takes the floor away, and make his own point. After two or three attempts, the person gives up, unless someone notices the problem and provides an opportunity for the person to get his point in.

Encouraging may serve a similar function in helping a person to make his point, partly to give the group the benefit of the content, but also to ensure that he and others will feel that the group climate is one of acceptance.

Harmonizing and *compromising* are deliberately placed on the maintenance function list rather than the task function list because they are useful in reducing destructive types of disagreement between individuals, but are definitely of limited usefulness in solving task problems. This is a crucial point because process consultants, in being concerned about group effectiveness, are likely to be seen as favoring harmony and smooth group functioning at all times. In fact, it may be quite necessary for the group to confront and work through tough disagreements to some genuine integrative solution that does not involve any compromising or harmonizing. The consultant may often have to help the group to confront and work through a problem when it would rather back off and compromise. However, if communication has broken down and several members are arguing or taking positions for such self-oriented reasons as maintaining their own status in the group, it may be necessary as a maintenance step to harmonize the conflict and help each member to take stock of his own behavior as a way of reestablishing good communication.

Diagnosing, standard setting, and standard testing are most relevant as remedial measures when relationships have to some degree broken down. What the group then needs is some period of suspending task operations while it (1) looks at its process, checks out how people are feeling about the group, its norms, and its method of operating; and (2) airs the problems and conflicts that may have arisen. Most groups do not engage in this kind of behavior unless a consultant is present or one of the members takes a real process orientation. Yet such periods of reassessment and catharsis are absolutely necessary for most task groups if they are to remain effective.

C. Boundary Management Functions

Every group exists in some kind of organizational or social environment; one of its primary tasks, therefore, is to manage its relationship to that environment (Ancona, 1988).[1]

Boundary defining by specifying who is in and who is not in the group is one of the most fundamental of these functions, and the consultant will observe a variety of behaviors that serve to communicate both to insiders and to outsiders who the group is — special uniforms, styles of communication, names that groups give themselves, minutes of meetings that communicate who is in and who is out through the distribution of who gets them, and so on.

Scouting refers to activities that provide the group the information it needs about its environment. Such information may refer to what is going on so that the group can forecast its own future, which resources are available, what key people in the environment think of the group, which sources of support and sources of danger exist, and so on. The process consultant, himself in a boundary-spanning role, can be especially helpful in identifying when some of the critical scouting functions are not being performed, thus putting the group into jeopardy from unanticipated environmental events.

Negotiating with the environment involves a whole host of activities designed to ensure that the group gets what it needs, manages sources of opportunity or threat, and generally maintains good relations with those people in the environment who can affect the fate of the group. Thus the group will from time to time send out information and appoint ambassadors to negotiate with key outsiders if conflicts of interest are involved or to open up communication channels to other groups as these become necessary.

Translating refers to all those functions involved in figuring out what others' messages mean to the group and in formulating its own messages to the outside in terms that others will understand. In this process of information exchange with the

---

[1]Much less work has been done on defining boundary maintenance functions than on defining internal maintenance functions. The particular ones identified here are based on extensive work by Ancona (1988).

environment, the group will need to filter, classify, and elaborate information to ensure internal comprehension and external acceptance. Here the consultant again has a special opportunity to raise questions about what different words will mean to others as he listens to the group.

An especially important activity in this arena is *technological gatekeeping*, the activity of bringing to the group whatever special information it needs to perform its task (Allen, 1977). In technically oriented groups, such as product development teams in engineering, some members scan the external technical environment to bring to the group those critical information items that bear on their particular task.

Guarding or *patrolling the border* refers to the activities that ensure that the group's sense of integrity will not be violated. Who is invited to meetings, what information is shared with which outsiders, what agreements are made among members about keeping information confidential, how unwelcome visitors are managed, how members are dealt with who leak information or embarrass the group, and so on are among the activities here.

Entry and exit management refers to the processes the group uses to bring in new members (immigrants) and to release present members who leave (emigrants or outcasts). Thus socialization activities, indoctrination, training, and rites of entry would occur around new members, and various kinds of exit rites would be involved for departing members depending on the conditions under which they are leaving. Do members leave because they have been promoted out of the group, because they have been sent on a mission by the group, because they do not like the group, because they do not fit into the group, or because they have violated group norms and are being excommunicated?

Other functions can be identified, and the particular lists I have provided are not necessarily the best ways to classify the various activities and roles that members of a group fulfill. The important point for the process consultant is to recognize that every group must manage its own creation and its own maintenance both internally and externally. By observing how the group manages these various activities and which ones get over- or undermanaged, the consultant can formulate in his mind where interventions are most necessary.

The two phases I have focused on do not describe the entire life cycle of a group (Schein, 1985). As the group matures and develops a culture, it also develops new issues and problems, but these are typically beyond the scope of the consultant's involvement unless he is called to help a group that is stagnating and needs revitalization.

Helping the Group to Learn

How can the process consultant encourage the performance of these kinds of functions on a regular basis? One of the simplest techniques is to suggest that at the end of every meeting (or on some periodic basis) the group allocate some small period of time, such as fifteen to thirty minutes, to review its own meeting and to collect member feelings about how the meeting has gone. Such feelings can be collected in an open-ended way or with the help of such diagnostic instruments as that shown in Figure 4–3. This particular set of questions focuses on internal relationships, but it would be equally appropriate to create a set of questions around external boundary management if the consultant felt that the group needed help in that area.

If a diagnostic questionnaire is used, somewhat more time must be allocated to analysis. If the group is skeptical of the value of any diagnosis, it is better to start with short periods of open-ended discussion, keeping the questionnaire in reserve until the group learns the value of such discussions and is willing to allocate more time to them. The consultant can always start the discussion by focusing on only one or two of the questions where he feels particular issues may have arisen.

The role of the consultant during diagnostic periods must be carefully managed. The great temptation is to rush in, once the group has opened the door, and report all the meaty observations that the consultant has made over the past several hours. This temptation is often heightened by the group's actually inviting the consultant to tell the group all of his observations. "How do you feel we did during the meeting?" "You've been sitting observing us for a couple of hours; what thoughts do you have?"

The consultant must at this time remind himself of his basic mission: to get the group to *share* in diagnosis and to help the group to *learn* to diagnose its own processes. If he succumbs

Rating Group Effectiveness

A: Goals

Poor	1	2	3	4	5	6	7	8	9	10	Good

Confused; diverse;
conflicting; indifferent;
little interest.

Clear to all; shared
by all; all care about
the goals, feel
involved.

B: Participation

Poor	1	2	3	4	5	6	7	8	9	10	Good

Few dominate; some
passive; some not
listened to; several
talk at once or
interrupt.

All get in; all are
really listened to.

C: Feelings

Poor	1	2	3	4	5	6	7	8	9	10	Good

Unexpected; ignored
or criticized.

Freely expressed;
empathic responses.

D: Diagnosis of group problems

Poor	1	2	3	4	5	6	7	8	9	10	Good

Jump directly to
remedial proposals;
treat symptoms
rather than basic
causes.

When problems arise
the situation is care-
fully diagnosed before
action is proposed;
remedies attack basic
causes.

(continued)

Figure 4–3
Sample Form for Analyzing Group Effectiveness

E: Leadership

Poor	1	2	3	4	5	6	7	8	9	10	Good

Group needs for leadership not met; group depends too much on single person or on a few persons.

As needs for leadership arise various members meet them ("distributed leadership"); anyone feels free to volunteer as he sees a group need.

F: Decisions

Poor	1	2	3	4	5	6	7	8	9	10	Good

Needed decisions don't get made; decision made by part of group; others uncommitted.

Consensus sought and tested; deviates appreciated and used to improve decision; decisions when made are fully supported.

G: Trust

Poor	1	2	3	4	5	6	7	8	9	10	Good

Members distrust one another; are polite, careful, closed, guarded; they listen superficially but inwardly reject what others say; are afraid to criticize or to be criticized.

Members trust one another; they reveal to group what they would be reluctant to expose to others; they respect and use the responses they get; they can freely express negative reactions without fearing reprisal.

H: Creativity and growth

Poor	1	2	3	4	5	6	7	8	9	10	Good

Members and group in a rut; operate routinely; persons stereotyped and rigid in their roles; no progress.

Group flexible, seeks new and better ways; individuals changing and growing; creative; individually supported.

Figure 4–3 *(Continued)*

and takes the lead in making observations, there is great danger that the group will abdicate its own responsibility for diagnosis. Furthermore, if the consultant makes observations with which some members disagree, he quickly finds himself in a position of having been neutralized. Finally, if the consultant comes in with his own observations first, he is forgetting that his own filters are operating and that he may be reporting things that are relatively less important or which are a reflection of his own biases.

Given these pitfalls, it is important that the process consultant encourage the group not only to allocate time for diagnosis but to take the lead itself in trying to articulate and understand its own processes. Once the group has identified an area where members themselves have observations to make, it is entirely appropriate for the consultant to add his own observations and to use the opportunity to deepen members' understanding by offering not only observations but some group theory. But the group must take the lead, and the consultant must work within the areas defined by the group as relevant. If the group urges the consultant to do this job *for them*, he must politely decline and urge the group in turn to try its own hand at diagnosis.

Summary

Thus far we have been focusing on various aspects and functions of the individual's behavior in the group. We have examined the causes of self-oriented behavior and types of self-oriented behavior. We then examined various task functions relevant to getting a job done, and various maintenance functions relevant to keeping the group in good working order and managing the group's relationship with its external environment. Having dealt with these basics, let us proceed to an analysis of the processes involved in the actual work of the group: problem solving and decision making.

5

Group Problem Solving and Decision Making

Groups in organizations generally exist for a purpose. They have a function or are supposed to work on a task or to solve a problem. Whether we are focusing on a two-person group, such as a client and I trying to establish a relationship, or a task force meeting that I have been asked to attend as part of getting acquainted with the client organization, there is always a task explicitly or implicitly defined, there are always problems to be solved, decisions to be made, and time and effort to be managed. How does a group tackle and solve problems?

Problem Solving

Problem solving as a process is much discussed and little understood. I propose to give the reader not an ultimately valid model of this process but a practical model that is amenable to observation and analysis. The steps or stages I will describe and analyze are applicable to any kind of problem-solving process, whether it occurs in an individual manager's head, in a two-person group, in a large committee, or in the total organization. My focus will remain, as in past chapters, on the small group because it is in this size unit that the process consultant is often most likely to be able to make his contribution.

The basic model as presented in Figure 5–1 is an elaboration of a model originally developed by Richard Wallen for use in sensitivity training programs. It distinguishes two basic cycles of activity — one that occurs prior to any decision or action, and one that occurs after a decision to act has been taken. The first cycle consists of three stages:

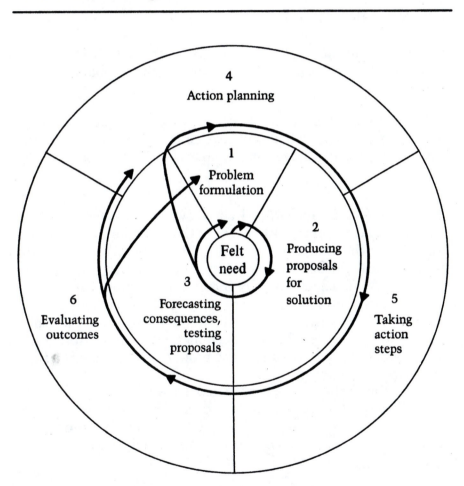

Figure 5–1
A Model of the Stages of Problem Solving

1. Problem formulation
2. Generating proposals for action
3. Forecasting consequences of proposed solutions or testing proposed solutions and evaluating them conceptually before committing to final action.

This cycle ends when the group has made a formal decision on what to do. The second cycle then involves the following:

4. Action planning
5. Action steps
6. Evaluation of the outcomes of the action steps, often leading back to the first cycle with problem redefinition.

The basic reason for breaking the total process into stages such as these is that when problem solving goes awry, it is generally because a given stage is mismanaged or is missing altogether.

Cycle 1

Problem Formulation In my own experience in solving problems and watching others solve them, by far the most difficult step is the first one — defining the problem. The difficulty arises in part because of a confusion between *symptoms* and the *problem*. A manager typically starts a problem-solving process when someone brings some difficulty to his attention or he discovers something that is not as it should be. Sales have fallen off, a schedule for delivery has not been met, an angry customer is on the phone, the production line has broken down, there is a fire in the shop, or whatever.

None of the things mentioned are really "the problem" to be worked on, however. Rather, they are the symptoms to be removed. Before the manager can begin to solve the problem he must identify or find it, and this is the crucial and often most difficult stage of the whole cycle.

Let us take the example of sales falling off, to illustrate the complexity. Manager X has called together his key subordinates and they sit down to discuss "the problem" of declining sales. If the manager is not sensitive to the issue raised above, he may soon be in the midst of a discussion of whether the advertising budget should be raised or ten more men should be sent into the field. But has he as yet defined his problem? Has he even identified what the various alternative problems might be that could cause a reduction in sales?

Falling sales could have any number of causes — erroneous sales forecast (which implies doing nothing out in the field but something in the marketing department), a competitor entering the market suddenly, a drop in product quality, loss of two key salesmen to a competitor, a change in consumer taste, and so on. Without some preliminary diagnosis — which, incidentally, may take time and effort — the manager won't know what is really causing the discrepancy between forecast and actual sales. He won't know what he should really be working on.

The process consultant can often play a key role at this stage because he is less likely to react to the time pressure the manager is under, and therefore is more likely to notice premature shortcuts in reasoning and misdiagnoses. His role is often to help the group to slow down and recognize that it may be acting hastily on an ill-defined problem, and that some initial time invested in identifying what is really the problem will pay off in less wasted time and effort later.

A special category of problems deserves particular mention in this regard — those involving interpersonal relations. A manager says he has a "problem" in motivating a subordinate, or coordinating with another department, or influencing his boss, or integrating the efforts of several people. Often these "problems" are felt as frustrations and tensions, with a minimum of clear understanding on the part of the manager of what is actually frustrating him or making him tense. In a sense he knows something is not right, but he does not know what the problem really is.

In instances such as these, the process consultant can help the manager or the group to identify its problem by asking them to identify concrete incidents or examples of events that led to their feelings of frustration. By carefully going over these incidents in detail and trying to identify which event actually triggered the frustration, one can often define the real problem. The essential step is to examine the concrete incidents and to generalize the problem from these.

This process, as shown in Figure 5–2, is a necessary step in any problem formulation and is the one most often skipped, leading to premature closure on what may be an incorrect diagnosis of the problem. In the falling sales example, the group should carefully reconstruct when and where exactly all the instances of falling sales have occurred, and then determine what those instances have in common.

Producing Proposals for Solution Once the problem has been adequately formulated, the group can move on to producing ideas or courses of action that might resolve the problem. At this stage the most likely pitfall is that proposals are evaluated one at a time. Thus the group is never permitted to gain perspective on the problem by looking at a whole array of possible ideas for solution.

The process consultant can help here by pointing out the consequences of premature evaluations: (1) there is insufficient opportunity for ideas to be judged in perspective because they cannot be compared to other ideas, and (2) the evaluation tends to threaten not only a given idea but the person who proposed it. Members whose ideas have been rejected early may feel less inclined to offer ideas at a later stage.

The group should be encouraged to start this stage with some version of brainstorming — producing a number of ideas and keeping them all in front of the group before any of them are evaluated as such. Brainstorming is built on the rule that no evaluation of ideas should be permitted during the idea-production phase to stimulate the creativity that is needed at this point.

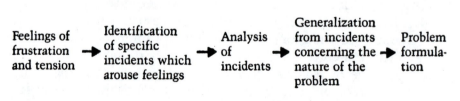

Figure 5–2
Necessary Steps in Initially Formulating the Problem

Once a number of ideas have been laid out, the group can weed out the obviously unworkable ones and go to the next stage with the two or three ideas for problem solution that look like they might work.

Forecasting Consequences and Testing Solutions The next stage of testing ideas by forecasting the consequences of any given solution and evaluating those consequences is often a difficult one because the criteria the group should be using to do its evaluating are not clear. Testing criteria include (1) personal experience, (2) expert opinion, (3) surveying of existing data or information, and/or (4) planned scientific tests or research.

Personal experience and expert opinion are the easiest to obtain but the least valid. Surveys and research are more valid but also more time consuming and expensive. One of the key functions of the process consultant at this stage is to provide to the group this range of alternatives, to enable it to correctly match its validation method to the kind of idea it is trying to test. For example, if the group is trying to decide between two products to develop, it should probably do some market research and test marketing; if the group is trying to decide whether to put surplus funds into capital expansion or investment programs, it should obtain advice from financial experts; and so on. All too often a group uses just one validation method, no matter what ideas are being evaluated.

At each stage of problem solving the discussion may reveal new features that lead to a reformulation of the problem. For example, in testing the idea that a new advertising campaign is needed, examining existing information may reveal that the advertising campaign was perfectly sound. This discovery then raises the question whether the initial formulation of the problem as "consumer sales resistance" was correct. The consultant should help the group to recognize that this kind of recycling, from initial formulation through idea production and idea testing to reformulation of the problem, is a very sound way to solve the problem. Reassurance from the consultant is usually necessary until a group becomes experienced in sensing its own problem-solving cycle because of the tendency to believe that constant reformulation of the problem is merely wasting time.

Cycle 2

All of cycle 1 involves steps that occur in discussion and that do not involve commitment to action unless the group chooses to gather some additional data for idea evaluation. As the group reaches some consensus on a proposed solution and makes a decision to act, we go into cycle 2, or the action cycle. The making of the decision is not shown in the diagram but is represented by the act of crossing the boundary between cycle 1 and cycle 2.

Although a decision has been made on a given proposal or idea for solution, the problem-solving process is far from finished. The group must then still plan a detailed course of action, take action steps, and provide for some method to determine whether or not the action steps are solving the problem. This last step should be thought out in advance: "What information should we be looking at to determine whether or not our action steps are achieving the desired results?"

At any of these stages, it is again possible for the group to discover that it had not formulated the problem correctly; hence it may revert back to cycle 1 for some new reformulation and idea proposing and testing. Again I want to emphasize that such recycling is entirely desirable and should not be considered a waste of time. It is far more costly to be working on the wrong problem, and discover this only after expensive action steps have been taken, than to make an initially greater effort to define the problem correctly. Yet, as a process consultant I have found it difficult to get groups to go back to step 1 and ask themselves the questions: "Have we formulated the problem correctly? Are we working on the right thing?"

Action Planning and Implementation The stage of action planning can be treated as a new problem requiring its own problem formulation stage (What is the problem in implementing the proposal we have decided on?), idea production (What are some alternative ways of implementing this proposal?), and idea testing (Which of our alternatives is the best way to implement this proposal?).

If these substages are short-circuited or avoided, a good proposal may be carried out inadequately and the group will erro-neously conclude that the proposal was deficient instead of recognizing insufficient action planning as the culprit. Here again, the key role for the consultant may be to slow the group down and encourage it to plan carefully before leaping into action.

One of the major pitfalls of this stage is to make general plans without assigning clear responsibilities for who is to implement what. I have sat in many a group meeting where a decision was reached, the meeting was adjourned, and nothing happened because everyone thought that someone else would now do something. The clear allocation of responsibility for action not only ensures that action will be taken but provides a test of the decision in that the responsible implementer may raise questions about the decision that had not been considered before.

In some cases the whole second cycle is delegated to some other person or group. For example, the original problem-solving group decides "Let's beef up our advertising campaign." Once it has reached this decision, the group orders the advertising department to increase advertising on certain products. The group then relaxes and reverts to watching sales figures. Is this a sound approach? The answer in many cases is "No."

The major problem, when different people or groups perform cycle 1 and cycle 2, is that the second person (or group) may neither understand clearly nor be particularly committed to the proposal or solution that the cycle 1 person (or group) has offered. He has not struggled with the problem definition; he has not had a chance to see the reasons why other alternatives that may now occur to him have been rejected; and he may not feel that the general proposal given to him is clear enough to permit implementation.

Equally problematic is the case where a group delegates cycle 1 to a task force or a consulting organization and then waits for a proposal in writing. In nine cases out of ten, if the originating group has not involved itself in cycle 1 and if the task force has not thought through cycle 2, the group will not like the proposal and will find an excuse to shelve it.

Given these kinds of problems, it is desirable to ensure a high degree of communication between cycle 1 and cycle 2 persons or groups. The ideal situation would, of course, be that they are the same problem-solving unit. If that is not possible, the cycle 1 unit should provide for an interim phase that permits the cycle 2 unit to get completely on board before the two units sever their communication link.

One way to do this is to bring the implementer into the problem-solving process at the earliest possible stage, or, at least, review completely with the implementer all the steps the cycle 1 unit has gone through in its efforts to arrive at a proposal for solution. In such a review, the key process would be to permit the implementer to satisfy himself completely by asking as many questions as he would like concerning the reasons that certain other alternatives, which might strike him as better ones, were not selected. Either he should get satisfactory answers, or the cycle 1 group should go back and review the additional alternatives brought up by the implementer.

A good problem-solving group will protect itself against communication breakdown at the implementation stage by consulting the implementers at the earliest stages of idea production. If all their ideas are inserted early, there is less likelihood of missing important alternatives, and less likelihood of choosing something that will not make any sense to, or may be misunderstood by, the implementer. The role of the process consultant here is to help the group understand how difficult it is to communicate a complex solution to an implementer, and to ensure this understanding early enough in the problem-solving process to institute protective measures against communication breakdown. And there is no better protective method than to involve the ultimate implementer in the problem solving at the earliest possible stage.

Evaluating Outcomes To ensure adequate evaluation, the group should reach consensus on (1) the criteria that will be used for evaluation, (2) the timetable — when results should first be expected, and (3) who will be responsible for reporting back information to be evaluated.

The other critical point about this stage is that one should be psychologically prepared to go back into cycle 1 with an effort to reformulate the problem, not merely to rush in with more effort or a new solution. A good problem formulation is three-quarters of the solution, so the group should always be prepared to reconsider what it sees the problem to be, and the consultant should constantly raise the question "What problem are we working on?"

The purpose of presenting the problem-solving process as a series of cycles rather than a linear progression is to highlight the importance of going back to earlier stages as new information is revealed.

Group Decision Making

One of the key steps in the problem-solving process is the making of decisions. Decisions are involved at every stage of the process but are only highly visible in the transition from cycle 1 to cycle 2, where the problem-solving unit commits itself to trying out a proposal for action. Prior to this step the group has had to decide when and where to meet, how to organize itself, how to allocate time, by what procedures or rules to run its discussion (for example, with or without a formal chairman, with or without Roberts's Rules of Order), how to tell when the problem has been sufficiently well formulated to move on to idea production, and so on. Often group members do not recognize that they have made so many process decisions and that these have real consequences for the climate of the group and the quality of problem solutions. The consultant must be prepared, therefore, to draw attention to the many mechanisms by which groups make decisions.

In reviewing the different decision-making methods listed below, it is important that we do not quickly judge any one method as better than another. Each has its use at the appropriate time, and each method has certain consequences for future group operations. The important point is for the group to understand these consequences well enough to be able to choose a decision-making method that will be appropriate to the amount of time available, the past history of the group, the kind of task being worked on, and the kind of climate the group wants to establish.

1. Decision by Lack of Response ("Plop") The most common and perhaps least visible group decision-making method occurs when someone suggests an idea, and, before anyone else has said anything about it, someone else suggests another idea, until the group finds one it will act on. All the ideas that have been bypassed have, in a real sense, been decided on by the group. But the decision has been simply a common decision *not* to support them, making the proposers feel that their suggestions have "plopped." The floors of most group meeting rooms are completely covered with plops.

2. Decision by Formal Authority or Self-authorization Many groups set up a power structure or start with a power structure that makes clear the fact that the chairman or someone in authority will make the decisions. The group can generate ideas and hold free discussion, but at any time the chairman can say that, having heard the discussion, he has decided to do thus and so. This method is highly efficient. Whether it is effective depends a great deal on whether the chairman is a sufficiently good listener to have culled the right information on the basis of which to make his decision. Furthermore, if the group must move on to the next stage or implement the decision, the authority-rule method produces a minimum amount of involvement of the group. Hence it undermines the potential quality of the implementation of the decision.

I have often sat in meetings where the chairman has decided something after listening to the group for a few minutes, but the action taken proved to be somehow out of line with what the chairman wanted. Upon later reconstruction it turned out that the group either misunderstood the decision or did not agree with it in the first place, and hence was neither able nor motivated to carry it out effectively.

3. Decision by Minority One of the most common complaints of group members is that they feel railroaded in reference to some decision. Usually this feeling results from one, two, or three people employing tactics that produce action and therefore must be considered decisions, but which are taken without the consent of the majority.

A single person can railroad a decision, particularly if he is in some kind of chairmanship role, by not giving opposition an opportunity to build up. Let us take an example pertaining to a decision as to how the group should work. The chairman says: "I think the way to go at this is to each state our opinion on the topic to see where we all stand. Now my own opinion is . . . " Once he has given his own opinion, he turns to the person on his right and says, "What do you think, Harry?" When Harry has spoken, the chairman points to the next person and the group is off, having made in effect a decision about how it is going to go about its work. Yet no one agreed to this method of work, except the initiator.

Another similar tactic is to say, "Well, we all seem to be agreed, so let's go ahead with John's idea," even though the careful observer may have detected that only John, the chairman, and maybe one other person has spoken favorably about the idea. The others have remained silent. If the initiator is asked how he concluded there was agreement, chances are that he will say, "Silence means consent, doesn't it? Everyone had a chance to voice opposition." If one interviews the group members later, one sometimes discovers that an actual majority was against John's idea but each one hesitated to speak up because he thought that all the other silent ones were for it. They too were trapped by "silence means consent."

Finally, a common form of minority rule is for two or more members to come to quick and powerful agreement on a course of action, to challenge the group with a quick "Does anyone object?", and, if no one raises his voice in two seconds, to proceed with "Let's go ahead, then." Again the trap is the assumption that silence means consent.

The process consultant plays an important role with respect to these first three decision-making methods, primarily because they are rarely labeled as decision-making methods in the first place. Yet a great many group decisions, particularly pertaining to the important issue of group procedures, rules of order, and the like, are made in these rather rapid ways. For a group member to challenge such proceedings, to say, "We don't really agree," is often seen as blocking; hence there are strong pressures on group members to stay silent and let things take their course, even though they are not in agreement.

The consultant must first make the group aware of decisions it has made and the methods by which it has made them;

then he must try to get the group to assess whether they feel that these methods were appropriate to the situation. For example, the members may agree that the chairman did railroad the decision, but they may feel that this was appropriate because time was short and someone needed to make that decision quickly so the group could get on with more important things.

On the other hand, the group might decide that a decision such as having each person in turn state his point of view introduces an element of formality and ritual into the group which undermines its ability to build creatively on ideas already advanced. The group might then wish to choose a different method of idea production. The important thing is to legitimize such process discussion and to have some observations available in case the group is finding it difficult to discern what the consultant is talking about.

4. Decision by Majority Rule: Voting and/or Polling We come next to more familiar decision-making procedures, those which are often taken for granted as applying to any group situation because they reflect our political system. One simple version is to poll everyone's opinion following some period of discussion, and, if a majority feels the same way, to assume that that is the decision. The other method is the more formal one of stating a clear alternative and asking for votes in favor of it, votes against it, and abstentions.

On the surface this method seems completely sound, but surprisingly often decisions made by this method are not well implemented even by the group that made the decision. What is wrong? If one can get the group to discuss its process, or if one interviews members of the minority, it turns out that two kinds of psychological barriers exist: (1) the minority member often feels that there was an insufficient period of discussion for him to really get his point of view across; hence he feels misunderstood and sometimes resentful; (2) the minority member often feels that the voting has created two camps within the group, that these camps are now in win–lose competition, that his camp lost the first round but it is just a matter of time until it can regroup, pick up some support, and win the next time a vote comes up.

In other words, voting creates coalitions, and the preoccupation of the losing coalition is not how to implement what the majority wants but how to win the next battle. If voting is to be used, the group must be sure that it has created a climate in which members feel they have had their day in court and where members feel obligated to go along with the majority decision. A key role for the process consultant is to highlight for the group the pitfalls of each method and to get enough discussion of group climate to ensure that the group will choose an appropriate decision-making process.

5. Decision by Consensus One of the most effective but also most time-consuming methods of group decision making is to seek consensus. Consensus, as I will define it, is not the same thing as unanimity. Rather, it is a state of affairs where communications have been sufficiently open, and the group climate has been sufficiently supportive, to make everyone in the group feel that he has had his fair chance to influence the decision. Someone then tests for the "sense of the meeting," carefully avoiding formal procedures, such as voting.

If there is a clear alternative that most members subscribe to, and if those who oppose it feel they have had their chance to influence the decision, then a consensus exists. Operationally it would be defined by the fact that those members who would not take the majority alternative nevertheless understand it clearly and are prepared to support it. It is a psychological state that might be described as follows:

> I understand what most of you would like to do. I personally would not do that, but I feel that you understand what my alternative would be. I have had sufficient opportunity to sway you to my point of view but clearly have not been able to do so. Therefore, I will gladly go along with what most of you wish to do.

In order to achieve such a condition, time must be allowed by the group for all members to state their opposition and to state it fully enough to get the feeling that others really do understand them. This condition is essential if they are later to free themselves of preoccupation with the idea that they could have gotten their point of view across if others had only understood what they really had in mind. Only by careful listening to the opposition can such feelings be forestalled and effective group decisions reached.

The process consultant can help the group to determine what kinds of decisions should be made by consensus. Which decisions are important enough to warrant the effort? One guideline he might suggest is that procedural decisions, those which pertain to how the group works, are the ones where it is most important that everyone be on board; hence these should probably be made by consensus. The group might decide to give complete authority to the chairman, or it might decide to try for very informal discussion procedures, or it might wish to brainstorm some ideas. But whatever is decided, it should be completely clear to everyone and there should not be residual feelings of being misunderstood or desires to sabotage the group procedure. Unfortunately, this is the kind of decision that most often is made by minorities, costing the group untold hours of wasted effort because of low morale, lack of involvement, and lack of clarity in communication.

6. *Decision by Unanimous Consent* The logically perfect but least attainable kind of decision is where everyone truly agrees on the course of action to be taken. For certain key kinds of decisions it may be necessary to seek unanimity, but for most important ones consensus is enough, if it is real consensus. The process consultant can help the group here by pointing out that the group may be setting too high a standard for itself in some cases. Unanimity is not always necessary and may be a highly inefficient way to make decisions. The important thing is to take some time to agree on which method to use for what kinds of tasks and in what kinds of situations.

A Final Thought

Often the method of decision making is simply announced to the group by the convener or chairman. If this is the case, the process consultant must try to determine whether the group is comfortable with the method being used, and, if not, find an opportunity to raise with the chairman the issue of whether he should permit some discussion by the group of how to handle the decision-making area. In my experience, chairmen often tend to feel threatened by such discussion because they fear that they will lose control of the group and that disorder and chaos will result. One way to reassure them is by pointing out that different ways of making decisions do not necessarily imply a disorderly communication process. If the consultant can provide some viable alternatives, he can often get the chairman to experiment with different methods and draw his own conclusions.

Summary

Problem solving can be thought of as consisting of two cycles, one of which involves primarily discussion and the other primarily action-taking. The first cycle consists of the phases of problem identification and formulation, idea or proposal generation, and idea or proposal testing through attempting to forecast consequences. The most difficult stage is that of identifying and formulating what is really the problem; often this stage requires additional diagnostic effort.

The second cycle involves action planning, action steps, and evaluation of outcomes. The action planning is itself a problem-solving process and should be treated as such. The major difficulty in the total cycle is making the transition from cycle 1 to cycle 2 if different parties are involved. Those who have to implement the decisions should be involved in making them at the earliest possible stage.

The decision process itself can be handled by

1. lack of group response;
2. authority rule;
3. minority rule;
4. majority rule;
5. consensus; and/or
6. unanimity.

It is important for a group to become aware of these different decision-making methods and to learn to choose an appropriate method for the kind of task or decision it is working on.

6

Group Growth and Development: Norms and Culture

As a group works together and faces common problems, it gradually builds common assumptions about itself and norms of conduct. In other words, the group as a group learns how to cope with its problems of external survival in its environment and to manage and integrate its internal processes. The sum total of this learning, embodied as a set of implicit assumptions that come to be taken for granted, can be thought of as the "culture" of that group. One of the main aspects of this culture will be the norms that guide group members' behavior.

The process by which norms and, eventually, cultural assumptions develop can be observed if one watches for critical incidents in the group's life and how the group deals with them (Schein, 1985). For example, as a process consultant I often observe that there are moments in the problem-solving process where the manager or someone influential attempts to get his way and one or more other members argue or refuse to go along. Some form of "insubordination" occurs. If the manager reacts punitively and makes it clear that he expects his suggestions to be taken as orders, and if the other group members now cease to argue and accept the punishment, a norm of how to deal with authority has been established.

Or, to give another example, in my observer role I note varying degrees of openness of communication. One group member suddenly says to another, "I think you did a lousy job of handling that customer." How the other group members, especially people in positions of authority, deal with this comment will begin to build a norm around openness and confrontation. If there is a shocked silence and the chairman acts as if nothing had happened and changes the subject, he is sending a clear signal that such openness is not welcome. On the other hand, if he says, "John, I understand how you feel and would like to hear a bit more about what you observed that made you reach this judgment," he is not only accepting such remarks as legitimate, but is furthering the dialogue by asking for additional information. He may also be starting to try to build a norm that judgments are legitimate only if they are backed up by facts and figures.

Norms are not easy to define or to identify in group process, yet they are very influential in determining member behavior, perceptions, and feelings. Part of their influence derives from the fact they operate invisibly, in that they are carried in each member's head as personal guidelines.

A norm can be defined as a set of assumptions or expectations held by the members of a group or organization concerning what kind of behavior is right or wrong, good or bad, appropriate or inappropriate, allowed or not allowed. Norms are usually not articulated spontaneously, but members can state them if asked to do so. For example, some typical norms in a group might be:

"We should not swear or use foul language in this group."

"We should get to meetings on time."

"We should not challenge or question the statements of the chairman of the group."

"We should be informal with each other, use first names."

"Everyone in the group should participate."

"We should reach consensus and not fall back on voting."

"We should not start the meeting until all the members are present."

Those norms which are open, verbalized, or even written down function as the rules and regulations of the group and can for this purpose be called explicit norms. Those which are unspoken can be thought of as implicit norms. We know they are there from observing member reactions when they are violated: shocked silences, rebukes, "Dutch Uncle" talks, and the like. If norms are violated repeatedly, members are punished in various ways and ultimately expelled from the group if their behavior does not conform in critical areas.

One important function of the process consultant is to attempt to decipher norms and to check how much consensus there is in the group on certain issues. In the previous chapter this was identified as the setting and testing of standards. One of the most destructive aspects of group behavior comes about from lack of consensus — when members assume that a norm is operating, but, in fact, none is. Valuable ideas and suggestions are suppressed because members assume that they would not be accepted, leading sometimes to the group doing something that no one really wanted to do. Jerry Harvey (1974) has identified this condition as the Abilene Paradox; he argued persuasively that to avoid going to Abilene when, in fact, no one really wants to go, it is necesary to state and check one's assumptions.

The process consultant can also help the group by observing closely how critical incidents are handled and trying to infer the kinds of norms the group is building for itself. If the group later engages in some process analysis of its own, the consultant can help the group to identify and reconstruct some of its norms and to test for itself whether the norms are helpful or constitute a barrier to effective action. For example, a group may discover that it has built a norm that people should speak up only when asked directly for an opinion or some information. The group may feel that such a formal mode of operating is getting in the way of good idea production. Having identified the norm, the group can then set about to change it explicitly to bring it into line with their feelings about how the group should operate.

The group may also discover that explicit and implicit norms tend to counteract each other. For example, there may be an explicit norm to say exactly what is on one's mind, but an implicit norm that one must not contradict the ideas of certain powerful people in the group. Or there may be an explicit norm that all members of the group are equal and have an equal voice in the discussion, but an implicit norm that higher-status people in the group should speak first and others in the group should try to go along with their views. Such norms can be very subtle in their operation, and the process consultant must be able to identify concrete examples if the group is to learn to observe the effects of the norms for itself.

As norms develop and become interlocked with each other, one can begin to think of the group's "culture." One of the reasons culture is so difficult to change is that when norms begin to support each other, one must change the whole set of norms instead of just the one or two that may be getting in the way. For example, assume that a group has developed the norm that one should always seek consensus on important decisions, and this norm is supported by other norms, such as "One must speak up if one disagrees with the decision that is being made," "One must always be truthful and open in task-oriented discussion," and "One must not try to take an action oneself unless the group has achieved consensus on that action." To change the decision norm toward "One must do what the chairman asks" (perhaps in order to get decisions made more quickly) is not likely to be possible unless people also change their attitudes toward participation and implementation. The process consultant must help the group to see these interconnections so that change processes are undertaken realistically.

Much more could be said about culture, but that would be beyond the scope of this discussion. Suffice it to say that the process consultant must be very mindful of cultural norms because they are so powerful in their operation.[1]

---

[1]The reader wishing more detail and discussion of culture as a topic and its effects on organizational life is referred to *Process Consultation: Volume 2* (1987a) and to my book *Organizational Culture and Leadership* (1985).

Group Growth

Relationships and groups do develop and grow from the early stages of getting acquainted described in Chapter 4 to the mature stages of effective, smooth functioning, and ultimately to stable states and stagnation. But it is often difficult for the members of the group to realize that the group has developed and grown, because the criteria of growth are usually not well defined. The process consultant can be most helpful in identifying for the group some of the ways it has developed and matured.

There is no single criterion that can be universally applied to test the degree of maturity of a group, but there are a number of dimensions along which a group can assess itself in order to identify where it has grown and where it may still need further development. These dimensions can be put into a simple self-rating questionnaire that the members can fill out periodically to determine how they feel about each dimension and how these feelings change over time. A sample of such a questionnaire is shown in Figure 6-1, but there is nothing absolute about the particular dimensions chosen.

The dimensions in Figure 6-1 reflect some of the basic criteria of maturity that have been developed for judging individual personality. Similar criteria can be applied to groups:

1. Does the group have the capacity to deal realistically with its environment, and is it independent of its environment to an optimal degree?
2. Is there basic agreement in the group about mission, goals, and ultimate values?
3. Does the group have a capacity for self-knowledge? Does the group understand why it does what it does?
4. Is there an optimum use of the resources available within the group?
5. Is there an optimum integration of the group's internal processes — communication, decision making, distribution of authority and influence, and norms?
6. Does the group have the capacity to learn from its expe-

A MATURE GROUP POSSESSES:

1. Adequate mechanisms for getting feedback:

   Poor   1   2   3   4   5   Excellent feedback
   feedback   Average   mechanisms
   mechanisms

2. Adequate decision-making procedure:

   Poor   1   2   3   4   5   Very adequate deci-
   decision-   Average   sion making
   making
   procedure

3. Optimal cohesion:

   Low   1   2   3   4   5   Optimal cohesion
   cohesion   Average

4. Flexible organization and procedures:

   Very   1   2   3   4   5   Very flexible
   inflexible   Average

5. Maximum use of member resources:

   Poor   1   2   3   4   5   Excellent use of
   use of   Average   resources
   resources

6. Clear communications:

   Poor   1   2   3   4   5   Excellent communi-
   communi-   Average   cation
   cation

   (continued)

Figure 6–1
Criteria of Group Maturity

7. Clear goals accepted by members:

| Unclear goals— not ac- cepted | 1 | 2 | 3 Average | 4 | 5 | Very clear goals— accepted |

8. Feelings of interdependence with authority persons:

| No inter- depen- dence | 1 | 2 | 3 Average | 4 | 5 | High interdepen- dence |

9. Shared participation in leadership functions:

| No shared participation | 1 | 2 | 3 Average | 4 | 5 | High shared participation |

10. Acceptance of minority views and persons:

| No accept- ance | 1 | 2 | 3 Average | 4 | 5 | High acceptance |

Figure 6–1 (*Continued*)

rience? Can it assimilate new information and respond flexibly to it?

No group is going to achieve some perfect level on all of these dimensions. Their major usefulness is that they permit the group to study its own progress over time and to identify weak spots in how it is operating. This implies capacity to learn and puts special emphasis on criterion number 6 in the above list. One can elaborate this criterion further by identifying what for groups and organizations can be thought of as a healthy learning or coping cycle — the steps that have to be successfully negotiated if the group is to learn from its own experience (Schein, 1980):

1. *Sensing* a change in some part of the environment, either internal or external;
2. *Importing* the relevant information into those parts of the group or organization than can act on it, and *digesting* the information (instead of denying or subverting it);
3. *Changing* internal processes according to the information obtained while, at the same time, reducing or managing the undesirable side effects of the changes made;
4. *Exporting* new behavior or "products" to respond to whatever environmental changes had been sensed;
5. *Obtaining feedback* on the degree to which the new responses successfully deal with the environmental change.

The process consultant can play a crucial role in helping the group to identify these stages of the coping process and to evaluate which steps are well handled and which are poorly handled by the group. It is especially important to identify those areas where the group is doing well and has shown real evidence of growth, because so often members see only the dysfunctional aspects of what they do and get discouraged prematurely about their work with each other.

Summary

The origin, function, and meaning of group norms and culture were discussed. I highlighted the importance that norms have in the life of the group, making norms and norm formation one of the key processes to focus on and track. Some dimensions along which a group can measure its growth and development were identified, and the underlying criteria for group growth and successful group learning were described.

7

Leading and Influencing

All interpersonal relationships involve efforts to lead and influence. We always have intentions and goals, whether they be external task related or simply the need to develop a friendship or have a good time or be liked. How we influence the situation to achieve our goals is, however, one of the most complex and multifaceted processes in the human situation.

This area has been analyzed from the perspective of "leadership," "management," "authority," and "power." It is a confusing area because the premises or assumptions on which influence attempts are usually built remain implicit and often deliberately concealed, leading us to negative influence concepts such as "manipulation" or "coercion."

In order to develop some simplifying models of this complex area, I need first to clarify what I will mean by the key terms:

1. *Leadership:* behavior on the part of some members of the group or organization that creates or changes basic assumptions and values in the group.
2. *Management:* behavior on the part of some members of the group or organization that helps the group to

achieve some goals, but within the assumptions or values previously agreed on by the group.

3. *Power:* the ability to control/influence the behavior of others because of (a) the possession of resources that those others need; (b) personal characteristics (charisma) that make one influential; and/or (c) the perception that one controls resources that others need.

4. *Authority:* the amount of influence that is legitimately granted to an organizational position or to a person; if others do not consent to the basis of legitimacy (promotion, election, and so on), the person may have formal authority but no influence.

5. *Coercion:* the ability to influence others whether or not they consent because of actual control of resources, such as freedom, food, or safety, that those others need.

6. *Manipulation:* influencing others without making visible the motivation behind the influence attempts; the legitimacy of the manipulation is a function of how one would evaluate the motivation.

Given these definitions, how does one now make sense of the multitude of influence attempts one can observe in any human situation? One approach to simplifying this area is to note that historically there have been several major models or sets of assumptions that have guided managerial thought based on our understanding of what went on in organizations. These can be thought of as four "models of human nature" (Schein, 1980).

1. Rational-economic Assumptions This set of assumptions, closely paralleling McGregor's Theory X, is built on the view that human beings work for money, that they must be motivated and controlled by economic incentives, and that, being lazy, without managerial effort they would basically do nothing. Therefore, the manager must motivate, organize, control, and, in effect, bear the responsibility and burden of his subordinates' performance.

2. Social Assumptions This set of assumptions is built on the view that human beings' basic needs are to have good relationships with both fellow workers and supervisors. The manager must therefore set up a congenial work situation, care about his subordinates, understand their needs and go to bat for them, and establish close and harmonious relations with them.

3. *Self-actualizing Assumptions* This set of assumptions is built on the view that human begins have a hierarchy of needs and, as lower-order needs are satisfied, higher-order needs come into play, culminating in the human need to use all of one's potential and thereby to actualize oneself. The manager must therefore provide adequate challenge, a work situation that permits subordinates to use their talents fully, and enough understanding of his subordinates to know when and how to challenge them. There is no need to control and motivate them because the motivation is already there waiting to be released. The capacity for self-control is also already present in humans. This set of assumptions is closely parallel to McGregor's Theory Y.

4. *Complex Assumptions* This set of assumptions is built on the view that human beings are different from each other and that they change and grow in their motives as well as in knowledge and skills. Therefore, a person can start out being rational-economic but learn to be self-actualizing. It will depend on the organization, his personality, and a whole host of other factors. The manager must therefore be a good diagnostician in order to know what the motivations and abilities of his subordinates actually are, and must be flexible enough to use different influence attempts with different people.

The process consultant often has the opportunity to observe a manager in action. He can see him handle people, run groups, issue written memoranda, and think out loud. One way the consultant can attempt to interpret what he hears and observes is to ask himself what underlying assumptions about people the manager holds, and how these assumptions are in turn influencing the manager's leadership style. As opportunities arise to discuss issues, the consultant can then direct the manager's thinking to his own assumptions. The consultant can provide observations and help the manager to interpret the implications of his own behavior.

For example, I have spent some time with a manager who

told me that he wants his immediate subordinates to take more initiative in running their own operations. A little while later he showed me a list of nineteen (!!) questions he had asked of one of these subordinates about a proposal this particular person had made. I asked the manager whether he thought there was any inconsistency between the messages he was sending to his subordinate: "Take more initiative" and, at the same time, "Here are nineteen things you had better think about before you act."

After further exploration, it turned out that the manager really didn't trust his subordinates to the extent he professed. His elaborate questioning attitude was a clear signal of this mistrust. Consequently, subordinates behaved very cautiously. Only after some real exploration of his own behavior did the manager realize that ideally he wanted initiative, but in practice he wanted pretty tight control. Once he recognized these feelings in himself he became less upset over the cautious behavior of his subordinates.

Another example illustrates a more far-reaching organizational phenomenon. A company president who prides himself on creating a climate in which engineers and other professionals really feel challenged by their work was told that the company's internal communications system was being overused and costing too much. He verified the fact of the high costs and then instructed his office manager to issue a memorandum that turned out to be punitive and rather supercilious in its tone. It was as if it had been written for either stupid or recalcitrant people. The president asked me what I thought of it, prior to his sending it out.

The ensuing discussion was aimed at helping this man see the inconsistency between a climate in which people were supposed to be treated as professionals and a memorandum that treated them as if they were recalcitrant children. I argued that if the memorandum went out in its original form, the communications systems might indeed be used less but the climate of professionalism might be irreparably damaged. The president would be sending a message that implied that he didn't really trust his people at all, which would have been quite inconsistent with his actual feelings. Being unused to thinking in terms of the total organizational effects of a managerial communication, he did not initially see the inconsistency. Once he saw it, he could choose the kind of message he was willing to have go out to his organization.

Many managers are, of course, truly ambivalent. They want to trust people and they send signals accordingly; at the same time they are afraid to trust them and unwittingly send out other signals that imply mistrust. The process consultant can help best by encouraging self-examination so that the ambivalence itself comes to be recognized as a real feeling. The manager can then choose whether to lean in one direction or the other, or to continue to be ambivalent. But whatever course he now chooses, he does so with some insight into the probable effects of his behavior on the people around him.

Sources of Power or Bases of Legitimacy

One of the most critical areas to observe is how successful influence attempts actually come about. When *A* influences *B*, what is the real reason that *B* was influenced? Power, influence, and leadership are such complex concepts in part because there is no simple answer to why *B* was influenced. The reason could be any of several possibilities:

1. *Coercion, nonlegitimate influence:* B went along with what A wanted because he felt he had no choice. A controlled some critical resource B needed, such as his job, or his next raise, or his future in the company.
2. *Tradition:* B went along because he had always gone along with what A wanted because A was by prior history in a position where it was "right" to go along. A might be B's father, or the king in the traditional monarchy, or the founder/owner of the business.
3. *Legitimate authority:* B went along because he accepted A as his legitimate boss. This implies that B accepts the system by which people get to positions of authority, whether that be a system of election or appointment. It is the acceptance of the system that creates legitimacy, so B will take orders even from a boss who may be per-

sonally not respected. But if he is the boss and got there by legitimate means, he is accepted in that role.

4. *Derivative authority:* B went along because A was a friend of someone that B respects or was appointed by B's legitimate boss, or in some other way derives his authority from someone else who granted him power.

5. *Expertise:* B went along because he respects A's ability to solve problems of the sort that are at issue. B has learned from past observation of A that A has the expertise and knowledge, and, therefore, can be trusted to give sensible orders.

6. *Personality or charisma:* B went along because A was such a powerful pesonality that B could not resist. In fact, he may develop a blind loyalty to A and do even things that do not make sense if A has the kind of personality that commands admiration and allegiance.

Which of these various sources of power or influence was involved makes a difference in how B feels, how stable the situation is in the long run, and how well implemented the decision will be. If B feels that the influence attempt was not legitimate, he may agree but sabotage the decision or implement it with so little effort and enthusiasm that it will not solve the problem. The process consultant must therefore help the manager/leader to understand on what basis his power or authority rests. If he miscalculates in this area, he risks becoming ineffective.

It is particularly risky if the manager attributes to himself more legitimacy, expertise, or charisma than he in fact has. If the subordinate goes along because of coercion or tradition, the boss may be fooled into thinking that the relationship is stable and that implementation will be effective when, in fact, neither of these conditions will hold. The consultant must help the manager to think realistically about the source of his influence.

Leadership and Decision-Making Style

We have previously referred to the different means by which groups make decisions. Looking at this process from the

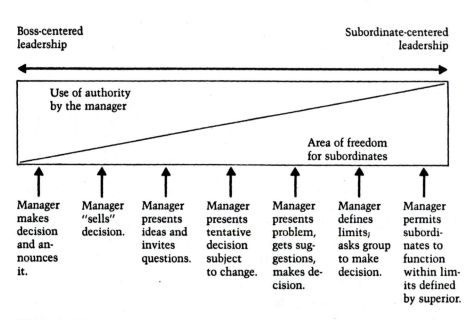

Boss-centered leadership

Subordinate-centered leadership

Use of authority by the manager

Area of freedom for subordinates

| Manager makes decision and announces it. | Manager "sells" decision. | Manager presents ideas and invites questions. | Manager presents tentative decision subject to change. | Manager presents problem, gets suggestions, makes decision. | Manager defines limits; asks group to make decision. | Manager permits subordinates to function within limits defined by superior. |

Figure 7–1
*A Continuum of Managerial Behavior**

*Tannenbaum, R., and Schmidt, W. H., "How to choose a leadership pattern." *Harv. Bus. Rev.*, March-April, 1958.

perspective of the manager, we can now analyze what options are open to him when he must initially structure an interpersonal situation. This issue applies to staff meetings, task forces, or any kind of situation where some people are brought together for the eventual solution of a problem. The most useful formulation of the action alternatives available to the manager has been provided by Tannenbaum and Schmidt (1958). They identify a basic dimension that runs from *total leader autocracy* on one end to *total group autonomy* on the other end (see Fig. 7–1). At one extreme the manager makes the decision and simply announces it to the others involved; at the other extreme the manager states the ultimate target to be achieved but gives the group complete freedom in how to achieve it.

Most managers recognize these extremes readily. What they are less likely to recognize is that there are a number of in-between positions and that one can choose different positions at different times. For example, the manager can make the decision himself but make a real effort to explain and sell it to others. He can retain the power to make the decision but tell the group what his ideas are and invite comment prior to making the decision. Still further along on the continuum, he can present the problem and invite ideas and alternatives from the group prior to making a decision, or he can let the group know of several alternatives among which they might choose. He can state some limits outside of which the group may not go but permit the group to decide within those limits. And he can vary his behavior from one decision to the next.

What factors will determine the appropriate position for any given managerial situation? Tannenbaum and Schmidt identify three sets of forces that should be considered:

1. Forces in the leader himself
2. Forces in the subordinates
3. Forces in the situation

Examples of forces in the leader are his value system, his confidence in the group, his own natural inclinations or style, and the security he feels in the situation. Examples of forces in the group are their prior experience in making decisions, their actual competence, their tolerance for ambiguity, their ability to become involved in the problem, and their expectations and need for growth. Examples of forces in the situation are the amount of time pressure, the type of problem to be solved, and the type of organization in which the process is occurring.

The process consultant can be most useful in helping the manager to see the alternatives available to him and to make a diagnosis of the various forces that have been outlined. There are no right or wrong assumptions about people in the abstract, and there is no right or wrong leadership style in the abstract. The problem for the manager is to make an accurate diagnosis and choose a course of action appropriate to that diagnosis.

It should be noted that this kind of leadership/managerial

model says relatively little about the traits or characteristics of the leader. I do not believe that there is some magic set of traits that can be identified in all leaders, nor do I believe that all leadership/managerial situations call for the same mix of traits. The unique requirements for being a good president may be quite different from the requirements for a good vice president. The production manager often has to be a different type of person from a sales manager or a research manager. (Each may wish to be a leader, but what he must do to lead effectively varies with the job and the situation.)

Given the above ideas, the process consultant cannot really help a company to identify who should be in what job or who should be promoted. Indeed, his initial psychological contract with the organization would probably preclude involvement in such activities. On the other hand, the consultant might be most useful by helping a manager to think through whether his own traits, values, motives, and temperament are suited for a particular kind of leadership position he is in or aspires to be in. If he has observed the manager in action, he can certainly provide observations that may help the manager to think more clearly about his own style and select a leadership pattern that fits him best. If he finds incompatibilities between job demands and his personal style, he can then, on his own, seek a niche where his style matches job requirements better.

Leading versus Managing

In the above discussion I have used leadership, management, and influence more or less interchangeably. If one wants to distinguish these concepts I would propose that leading and managing both involve influence, but that leadership implies influencing ultimate goals, mission, and culture, while management implies influencing how things are implemented and carried out. As Warren Bennis has put it very succinctly: Managers do things right; leaders to the right thing (Bennis and Nanus, 1985).

I have also argued that leadership involves the unique function of assesing and, if necessary, changing organizational culture. If the process consultant finds himself in a situation where leaders need help in this process, he can be most helpful by providing diagnostic tools to help assess what the culture is and help in the implementation of change processes. Most likely such help will involve getting the leader to see how difficult and traumatic culture change can be for the members of an organization (Schein, 1985).

Summary

Leading, managing, and influencing have been identified as highly variable kinds of behavior resting on many different kinds of implicit assumptions. Effective behavior depends on the person, his subordinates, the nature of the task to be accomplished, and the organizational setting within which the process takes place. Therefore, no easy generalizations can be made about influence processes, except that they are highly contingent on the particulars of the situation.

The kinds of assumptions that the leader/manager holds about people will determine to a large extent how he will attempt to influence them. Becoming aware of one's own assumptions is therefore crucial, and helping others to become aware of their assumptions is essential. The leader/manager has a choice within his assumption set of how tightly to centralize control and how flexible to be from one decision to the next. By diagnosing the forces in himself, his subordinates, and the situation, he can increase his flexibility and, thereby, his effectiveness.

8

Appraising Performance and Giving Feedback

The process consultant will observe in any human organization a constant stream of judgments that people make about each other. Sometimes these judgments will be articulated publicly, that is, will be "fed back" to the person about whom they are made. Often they are made privately. One of the most common dilemmas for the process consultant is what to say when after a meeting the manager asks him what he "thinks of so-and-so."

In order for the consultant to think clearly about this, he must have a model of how human behavior and performance can be measured and evaluated, and what the pitfalls are in this process.

Why Are People and Their Performance Appraised?

It is intrinsic to organizational life and to the process of management that evaluations are made of individual employees. But why? Who needs this information and why do we gather it?

Most managers would give one or more of the following reasons for appraising performance:

1. *As a basis for personnel actions.* Every organization needs to know whom to select for a given job, whom to promote, how to distribute limited rewards among several people doing similar jobs, whom to transfer out, and whom to terminate.

2. *As a basis for human resource planning.* Every organization needs some kind of process for ensuring that it will have the right number of people with the right mix of talents at some point in the future.

3. *As a basis for individual development planning.* Most organizations want to maximize their pool of human talent, so they need some system for identifying who needs what kind of development. Such information is also necessary to facilitate whatever career counseling is needed in connection with development.

4. *To improve performance.* The most fundamental reason for performance appraisal, of course, is to ensure that everyone's performance will improve so that the overall effectiveness of the total organization will improve.

Awareness of these multiple purposes should alert the process consultant to the fact that different kinds of information and appraisal processes may be relevant to these different purposes. No one system may meet all of the needs. So when a manager is seeking help in appraising someone, the consultant might well start with the question "For what purpose or purposes are you trying to make a judgment here?"

What Is Appraisal?

The next question to be addressed is "What do we mean by appraisal, anyway?" This process can be broken down into four logically distinguishable steps:

1. Some *observations* of the behavior of the person being judged, hopefully in situations that are performance related.

2. The *evolution of some standard or criterion* that defines very high levels, expected levels, and substandard levels of performance.
3. Some *comparison* of the observed behavior with the standard or the criterion, implying some ability to measure or rate the behavior and the criterion.
4. Some *judgment* or *assessment* of what the gap between the observed behavior and the criterion means evaluatively.

The process consultant should be aware that in practice these steps tend to be collapsed into instant judgments, such as "Joe is one of my best men," "Pete is messing up," or "Jane can't handle people." Instead of being seduced into agreeing or disagreeing, the consultant should help the manager to surface each of the above questions — what data is he basing his judgment on, what standard is he using and why, how does the person in fact compare to the standard, and so what? If the consultant can help the manager to think through each of the steps and check out the client's logic, he is helping him to make evaluations without having to make evaluations himself on minimal data.

What Is Appraised?

To complicate matters further, it is often not clear just what the manager is, in fact, looking at when he makes an appraisal. Several categories of information can be identified:

1. *Stable traits.* These are usually personality or skill characteristics that are presumed to be unchangeable, for example, "He is a very dynamic person," "He lacks aggressiveness," "She is one of our best computer people."
2. *Malleable traits.* These are personality or skill characteristics that are presumed to be changeable through experience or training, for example, "He comes on too strong with people, but may well mellow with experience," "She needs to become more assertive in meetings," "Right now all she lacks is self-confidence."
3. *Averaged performance.* This is a summary over a period

of time of some specific behavioral characteristic or result, for example, "He always does a good job with our customers," "She handles the pressure of the job very well," "She has done consistently high-quality work with our key accounts."

4. *Specific performance.* This is an appraisal of a specific situation, for example, "She handled the shop steward very well at that meeting," "His presentation to the group was weak and lacking in conviction," "She missed the deadline for the sales promotion."

5. *Future potential.* This is an assessment of strengths and weaknesses relative to future jobs. At one extreme, potential is simply an assessment of whether the person is promotable to the next higher level or to a different function (promotability). At the other extreme, potential refers to how many promotions the person might be able to handle and to what goal job he could aspire (ultimate potential).

The consultant should be alert to possible confusion that can arise when the evaluator is not clear about what kind of information he is using for what purpose. For example, if the goal is to improve performance, the most relevant information is specific performance feedback (category 4 above). If the goal is human resource planning, averaged performance and potential become more relevant. If salary action or promotion is the issue, malleable traits and averaged performance are the most relevant. And if personal development is the issue, a discussion of stable and malleable traits is most relevant. The consultant does not have to get into the evaluator role in order to be helpful to the manager in thinking through the evaluation process with the aid of categories such as those shown above.

Giving and Receiving Performance Feedback

One of the major issues surrounding the appraisal process is what happens to the evaluative information. Is it simply entered into personnel records and kept under lock and key, or is it revealed to the person? And if it is revealed, how much is revealed?

The norms in the organization around the issue of openness of appraisal information can become complicated because the feedback norms and the manner in which appraisal is done interact with each other. To be specific, if the organization has clear norms that "one should fully disclose to the employee everything that is said about that employee in the appraisal process," it is predictable that the appraisal process itself will gravitate toward less extreme judgments and evaluations. Supervisors will not make extreme judgments in the first place if they know that they will feel uncomfortable discussing them with the subordinate.

If, on the other hand, the organization has clear norms that one need not give employees anything more than very generalized feedback and can withhold whatever the organization considers to be privileged information, one will get a much more honest, true assessment, but employees will not benefit from it except as they do or do not get raises, promotions, and transfers.

The situation now becomes paradoxical as the different goals of the appraisal process as outlined earlier lead to conflicting procedures. If one wants the most accurate information for personnel actions and human resource planning, the system should be biased toward minimizing feedback to employees; but if one wants to improve performance and employee development, the system should be biased toward maximizing feedback to employees. No one set of procedures will fulfill both sets of goals effectively.

How can the process consultant help managers get out of this box? The most important point to recognize is that the conflict is intrinsic because of the inherent difficulty of giving feedback about performance. The consultant can be supportive to managers by helping them to recognize that reluctance to appraise and give feedback is a normal response in most cultures because of the wider social norms about protecting "face."

The manager must then be helped to figure out which of the goals of performance appraisal are, in fact, the most important, and then how to achieve those. Since performance improvement is likely to be high on the list, and since that always involves learning to give some kind of feedback to the employee, the manager can be helped to develop his skills in giving performance feedback.

The consultant can also raise the question of whether or not a single appraisal system can fulfill all of the needed functions, and, if necessary, help managers to develop several systems. In many organizations there is a performance appraisal system that maximizes feedback and a separate human resource planning system that emphasizes promotability and potential, the data from which are not shared with employees except in general form.

In any case, the skills of giving feedback are central to the appraisal process and, since they are also critical to the activities of the process consultant, he is in a good position to do some coaching on how best to give feedback. I have found it useful in this context to give a short lecture on giving and receiving feedback that emphasizes the following points.

Giving Feedback: Problems, Pitfalls, and Guidelines

Feedback can be defined as information that provides the recipient guidance concerning whether or not he is on target relative to some goal that he is trying to achieve. Feedback always implies some goals on the part of the recipient. Therefore, the first and most important pitfall is

1. *Failure to agree on goals to be achieved and/or performance standards to be met.*

If the boss and the subordinate disagree on goals and performance standards, what may be corrective information from the point of view of the boss may be irrelevant criticism from the point of view of the subordinate.

Feedback can emphasize positives (things the subordinate did well), be descriptive and neutral (things the subordinate did, without any judgment or evaluation), or emphasize negatives (things the subordinate did not do well). Most learning theory has shown that the consequences of the three types of information are different.

Positive feedback is easiest to learn from and most pleasant in that it guides future behavior directly into more of what is already effective. *Descriptive neutral feedback* can be effective if the subordinate has clear standards and only needs to know what he did. In areas where people are very sensitive and "ego-involved," this may be the only kind of information they can accept.

Negative feedback is often necessary in order to ensure that certain kinds of behavior will not be repeated, but it is also the most problematic because of the likelihood that it will arouse defensiveness, be denied or not heard, and in other ways rejected. Furthermore, negative feedback does not offer any guidance on what the person should do and hence does not provide a learning direction.

The second pitfall in the feedback process, then, is

2. *Overreliance on negative feedback and insufficient descriptive and positive feedback.*

Feedback is a communication process subject to all of the pitfalls of communication as outlined in Chapter 3. Basic lack of clarity in the feedback message or semantic confusion when personality traits are involved are therefore potential problems, as illustrated below.

The third pitfall in the feedback process, then, is

3. *Vagueness and generality in the message instead of specific examples and guidelines.*

Several examples will make clear what I mean by these two points. In each of the examples I am deliberately highlighting the pitfalls.

Unclear: "You are too aggressive" (negative, vague, general).

Clear: "I have observed you shouting other people down when they are trying to express their own views, and I think this may undermine communication" (descriptive, precise, specific).

Unclear: "You don't handle your people well" (negative, general).

Clear: "You should involve your subordinates more in making decisions and give them a chance to express their own views" (negative, specific).

Unclear: "You need to show more initiative" (negative, general).

Clear: "Instead of waiting for me to discover that your costs are overrunning, you should set up your own systems for finding this out and correct it before it goes too far" (positive, specific).

The key to semantic clarity is specificity. The more general the comment, whether positive or negative, the more likely it is to be misunderstood.

The next problem with feedback has to do with the perceived motivation of the giver of feedback. If the recipient believes that the giver is genuinely interested in helping the recipient, he is more likely to listen and pay attention than if he has doubts about or mistrusts those motives. We have all had the experience of feeling angry with someone and, as a way of expressing the anger, saying, "Let me give you some feedback." Needless to say, the receiver senses that the giver's needs are being served more than the receiver's. The fourth pitfall in giving feedback, then, is

4. *Lack of clarity about the giver's motives.*

Again, several examples will make clear what is involved

Confused: "You should motivate your subordinates to control their costs more because this quarter we have again gone beyond our budget" (the boss wants to improve performance, but the subordinate feels he has been criticized for continuing to be a poor manager and gets preoccupied with career issues).

Clear: "Basically the operation is going well, but I continue to worry about the fact that we are again overrunning our budget; what suggestions do you have for getting your subordinates to be more cost-conscious?" (the boss makes his own feelings clear and focuses on the specific issue with a specific question).

Confused: "I think you need to learn to handle customers

better" (the boss may perceive the subordinate to be a person of high potential who has to overcome only one area of weakness, but the subordinate may perceive himself to be generally failing and, therefore, become defensive).

Clear: "You are already very effective and could improve that effectiveness even more if you concentrated on learning how to handle customers better" (the boss makes clear his motive to make already good performance even better).

Confused: "I could get you only a 5 percent raise this year because things are generally lean in the company" (the boss is trying to be truthful, but the subordinate may conclude that he is being subtly told that he is only an average performer and become demoralized).

Clear: "Your performance overall was excellent this last year, and I wish I could reward it with money, but the company has had a generally lean year, so no one got more than a 5 percent raise" (the boss is being specific and puts the subordinate performance into the proper context).

A closely related problem in giving feedback is the natural tendency not to want to be critical because criticism so often produces defensiveness and unpleasant hassle. Or, even more serious, critical comments are denied or not heard at all, thus making all of the effort to give negative feedback seemingly a waste of time. The fifth pitfall, then, is

5. *Withholding of negative critical information in order to avoid hassle.*

What the consultant must learn and what he can teach to the manager is that the solution here, as in the above cases, is to substitute clear, specific examples for vague generalities. I can accept criticism of some specific behavior in a specific situation, but find it much harder to accept criticism of my traits and more general characteristics. In the former case I can attribute my behavior to situational circumstances and learn how to avoid such behavior; in the latter case my self-image and self-esteem become involved and I cannot readily change general parts of my personality. Hence I will resist or deny the criticism.

On the other hand, if the negative feedback deals with some concrete behavior that both the giver and receiver have witnessed, the giver can express his own feelings about the behavior and his evaluation of it, and the receiver can avoid ego-involvement. In other words, if I am angry at *you*, this may be a problem for you, but if I am angry at something specific that *you did*, you may get some new insights from that feedback. Some examples of how to give negative criticisms follow.

General trait oriented: "We need more team players at higher levels in this company, and your performance so far has made me doubt whether you want to be or can be enough of a team player."

Specific behavior oriented: "My problem in seeing you move ahead into higher levels of this company is that whenever you get into a group, you immediately want to take over, like in the XYZ committee. And when you were on the ABC task force, the group never made its best possible contribution because your loyalty to your department made the discussions into win–lose debates. When I see you putting down others that way, it makes me angry and I worry about whether or not you can learn enough new behaviors to move ahead in the company."

General trait oriented: "You really lack initiative; you are just not aggressive enough for this kind of work."

Specific trait oriented: "Several things have concerned me about your performance this past year. When we got stuck on the ABC project, you seemed willing to let matters drift instead of coming up with some proposals for how to move forward and confront the problems. When the other division challenged the direction you were going, you backed off instead of showing them why your solution was the right one. I have seen both of these patterns on other projects and am concerned about the lack of initiative and aggressiveness that is implied by such behavior."

In the above examples, the giver did make evaluative comments, but they were directed at specific behavior instead of at the total person. When goals and standards are clear and have been agreed to, such evaluations are sound. But if such agreement does not exist, feedback will work better if it stays descriptive. The giver and receiver can then jointly evaluate the behavior.

In either case, specificity is the key. The more general the evaluation, the more likely it is to be misunderstood, resisted, denied, and the trigger to defensive behavior.

The next pitfall, then, is

> 6. *Evaluations are applied to general traits or the total person, instead of specific situations and behaviors.*

Many of the examples given above make this point in arguing for specificity. What can be especially devastating is when a general target becomes the object of feelings and judgment as well.

Unsafe: "You really blew it at the last sales meeting; we almost had it sewed up until you stuck your oar in and made the client back off."

Safer: "When you brought up that XYZ issue at the last sales meeting, I thought you really blew it; we almost had it sewed up until your comments were made, and they seemed to make the client back off" (the emphasis is shifted to the person's behavior, and the giver softens his evaluation by making it his own opinion rather than an absolute judgment).

If the subordinate is to learn from the feedback, the message must somehow be related by the receiver to himself. If the feedback comes too long after the event, the receiver may not remember the incident and thus be able to deny it. Or if the feedback is too general, the receiver may not know to what it refers. Specificity has already been dealt with, but timeliness has not. The next pitfall, then, is

> 7. *The feedback is poorly timed.*

Proper timing has two components. As previously mentioned, feedback should come soon enough after a given event so that both receiver and giver can clearly remember what happened. Perhaps even more important, however, is that the receiver be ready to listen to feedback. If the *giver* decides when to give it, he may encounter a preoccupied, nervous, or defensive receiver. On the other hand, if the *receiver* decides when to receive feedback, he will make himself psychologically ready to listen. The giver who is concerned about this issue will, therefore, attempt to create a situation where the receiver can take the initiative on when to hold the feedback session. The boss can say that he wants to discuss performance sometime in the next few days and allow the subordinate to pick the time.

The final point about feedback is that it should deal primarily with malleable behavior so that the receiver can do something about what he has been told. On the other hand, if some stable characteristic of the person prevents him from attaining some goals that he desires, it may, on occasion, be necessary for someone to tell him this rather than allowing him to live with illusions and unrealistic expectations.

Process Consultation as Feedback Management

In concluding this chapter it can be noted that much of what the process consultant does when he intervenes with individuals or groups is manage the feedback process. He makes observations that provide feedback information, he asks questions that direct the client's perception to the consequences of his own behavior, he makes suggestions that have implicit evaluations built into them (any given suggestion implies that other things that have not been suggested are less appropriate than what has been suggested).

The process consultant must therefore be highly aware of the psychological dynamics of appraising human behavior and providing feedback about it. In fact his skill in this area is one of the most important things to pass on to his clients so that they can improve the management of their own organizations.

9

Intergroup Processes

One of the most important and least studied aspects of organizational process is intergroup relations within an organization. Whether or not groups form in organizations is no longer an issue. The evidence is overwhelming that they do — along formal departmental lines, along geographical lines, and in terms of who has to interact with whom in the course of getting the work done. It is also well known that groups develop norms, members feel loyal to their groups and adopt the norms, and the goals of different groups sometimes run at cross-purposes with each other.

Not only do groups develop cultures over a period of time, but the larger cultures of the society, the occupation, the community, and the organization all influence the formation of those cultures and define to some degree how groups should relate to each other. In a capitalist society in which free market competition is the norm for economic enterprises, it is not surprising that groups within organizations similarly tend to be competitive with each other.

Nor is it surprising that most managerial theories encourage such competition on the grounds that it increases motivation and, thereby, productivity. I have often found myself being asked to advise managers on how they could introduce more of a competitive element into their organization by having departments and groups be measured against the same standard and rewarding the winners. This has long been an individual motivational tool, especially in sales departments; that the same tool would seem to be attractive in the intergroup context is not surprising.

What is relatively less well known is that the long- and short-run consequences of intergroup competition may be *dysfunctional* to organizational performance. For one thing, not all managers agree that competition, even though it increases motivation, is good for improving the quality of solutions. In the rush to win, perhaps groups compromise on quality. Or some kinds of groups, such as sales departments in independent regions, can constructively compete, but if the groups are the manufacturing department and the sales department, having them compete would produce obvious problems since they are so interdependent.

Studying Intergroup Processes

Part of the problem of making sense of this area is that the key processes are relatively invisible. If the engineering department has poor relations with the production department, the production workers might be motivated *not* to correct errors that they find in the drawings given to them. Douglas McGregor told of standing at the end of a production line with the foreman watching finished trucks roll off the line. The foreman was comfortably puffing his pipe as he said with faint amusement in his voice, "Well, there she goes . . . but she'll be back."

The ultimately bad product is visible enough, but the lack of interest on the part of the production worker (who failed to correct what he knew was a fault) is hard to observe; it is a private decision on his part *not* to do something. Similarly, the giving of false information or the withholding of information, which typically results from groups competing with each other in a win–lose situation, is difficult to observe, even when one suspects strongly that it exists.

The process consultant can use a variety of techniques in an effort to learn about and intervene in such intergroup processes:

1. He can interview members of each group about their feelings toward the other group and inquire how they translate these feelings into overt behavior.

2. He can try to observe meetings or settings where members of both groups are present and assess the degree of openness of communication, spirit of cooperation, and so on.

3. He can try to theorize what should happen between the groups and check his theories by observing specific situations. For example, if relationships are good, he would theorize that errors by one group would be sympathetically and helpfully dealt with by the other group. He can then try to find an incident where an error occurred and either observe what happens, or, if the incident is past, ask what happened at the time.

4. A final and more complicated method for assessing and working on intergroup processes is to arrange an intergroup exercise of some sort. One model that was developed by Robert Blake and Jane Mouton (1961) involves the following steps:

    a. Each group separately describes its own image of itself and its image of the other group.

    b. Through representatives these images are then reported by each group to the other. Both groups now have some new data about how they are perceived by each other. During the reports each group must just listen, no matter how upset they might be about what they are hearing.

    c. The next stage is not to react, but to meet separately to consider what kind of behavior on the part of each group may have led to the image the other group holds. This forces each group to take the stance of the other group and consider sympathetically how the group might have arrived at its conclusions.

    d. These behavioral hypotheses are then shared and discussed openly by both groups. Only at this step is interaction between the groups allowed.

e. In the final stage the groups work together toward reducing the discrepancy between self-image and the image held by the other group, by planning how to relate differently to each other in future contacts.

This process brings both groups into the common task of exploring why discrepancies of perceptions exist, and thus reduces the competitive task each group faces in trying to outdo the other group and show up well with the rest of the organization or higher-level authorities.

It is particularly important for the higher-level manager to understand intergroup processes because he often has the choice of whether to reward competition, collaboration, or complete independence. Since the most common tendency appears to be to arrange competitive conditions, the process consultant must often attempt to get across some of the possible consequences of competition *before the win–lose situation arises*. These consequences have been derived from laboratory and field experiments and can be reliably reproduced in simulations that involve two groups in win–lose competition.

What happens as a result of competition can be studied in the simulation before a decision is reached, during open competition, and after one group has won out over the other. The kinds of results described below seem to occur no matter what kind of task is given to the groups.

What Happens Within Each Competing Group in the Early Phase?

1. Each group becomes more closely knit and elicits greater loyalty from its members; members close ranks and bury some of their internal differences.
2. The group climate changes from informal, casual, playful, to work and task oriented; concern for members'

psychological needs declines while concern for task accomplishment increases.

3. Leadership patterns tend to change from more democratic toward more autocratic; the group becomes more willing to tolerate autocratic leadership.
4. Each group becomes more highly structured and organized.
5. Each group demands more loyalty and conformity from its members in order to be able to present a solid front.

What Happens Between the Competing Groups?

1. Each group begins to see the other groups as the enemy rather than merely a neutral object.
2. Each group begins to experience distortions of perception: it tends to perceive only the best parts of itself, denying its weaknesses, and tends to perceive only the worst parts of the other group, denying its strengths. Each group is likely to develop a negative stereotype of the other ("they don't play fair the way we do").
3. Hostility toward the other group increases, while interaction and communication with the other group decreases; thus it becomes easier to maintain negative stereotypes and more difficult to correct perceptual distortions.
4. If the groups are forced into interaction — for example, if they are forced to listen to representatives plead their own and the others' cause in reference to some task — each group is likely to listen more closely to their own representative and not to listen to the representative of the other group, except to find fault with his presentation. In other words, group members tend to listen only for that which supports their own position and stereotype.

After a decision has been rendered what happens to the winner and loser?

What Happens to the Winner?

1. The winner retains its cohesions and may become even more cohesive.
2. The winner tends to release tension, lose its fighting spirit, become complacent, casual, and playful (the condition of being "fat and happy").
3. The winner tends toward high intragroup cooperation and concern for members' needs, and low concern for work and task accomplishment.
4. The winner tends to be complacent and to feel that winning has confirmed the positive stereotype of itself and the negative stereotype of the "enemy" group. There is little incentive or basis for reevaluating perceptions, or reexamining group operations in order to learn how to improve them, hence the winner does not learn very much about itself.

What Happens to the Loser?

1. If the outcome is not entirely clear-cut and permits a degree of interpretation (if, for example, the decision was rendered by judges who may be seen as biased, or if the outcome was very close), there is a strong tendency for the loser to *deny* or *distort the reality of losing.* Instead, the loser will find psychological escapes, such as "the judges were biased," "the judges didn't really understand our solution," "the rules of the game were not clearly explained to us," "if luck had not been against us at the one key point, we would have won," and so on. In effect, the loser's first response is to say, "We didn't really lose."
2. If the loss is psychologically accepted, the losing group tends to seek someone or something to blame. Strong forces toward scapegoating are set up. If no outsider can be blamed, the group turns on itself, splinters, surfaces previously unresolved conflicts, fights within itself, all in the effort to find a cause for the loss.
3. The loser is more tense, ready to work harder, and des-

perate to find a new positive direction (the condition of being "lean and hungry").

4. The loser tends toward low intragroup cooperation, low concern for members' needs, and high concern for recouping by working harder in order to win the next round of the competition.

5. The loser tends to learn a lot about itself as a group because its positive stereotype of itself and its negative stereotype of the other group are disconfirmed by the loss, forcing a reevaluation of perceptions; as a consequence, the loser is likely to reorganize and become more cohesive and effective, once the loss has been accepted realistically.

It is far easier to prevent reactions and feelings such as these by not arranging a competitive reward structure in the first place than to undo them once they have become established. The process consultant must find ways of bringing relevant data to the attention of the manager so he can see for himself that a motivational system that seems sound can have pitfalls.

For example, in the Apex Company there was a time when the group was considering how to organize. I was prompted to write a short memo outlining some of the costs and benefits of competition (see Appendix C) as a way of focusing the discussion on this issue. The main effect of this memo was to strengthen the position of those managers who already had misgivings about competitive relationship but needed support for that position since it is so easy to argue for competition.

If the situation is already competitive because of prior management decisions and now is becoming dysfunctional or destructive, remedial measures such as those mentioned at the beginning of this chapter may have to be tried. In the Apex Company such a condition arose when the product lines found themselves in competition with each other and with the sales department, because the product line was rewarded for how much of *its product* was sold, while sales was rewarded for *total sales.*

Consequently, sales effort was assigned not according to product line marketing plans and budgets but according to what the sales department could most easily sell. Certain products were getting too little attention, causing product line managers to become bitter at sales, while sales considered the product lines to be too autocratic and irrational.

After several years of infighting leading to a serious deterioration of relationships between the regional sales managers and the product line managers, the head of personnel (who was OD oriented) proposed to run an intergroup exercise of the type outlined above. My help was sought as the outsider who could stage-manage the process and provide the necessary theory to help groups to understand the dynamics better. The two groups met in a nearby hotel for a day and a half.

The first half day was devoted to preparing self-images and images of the other group, and sharing of these. In the afternoon the groups worked on hypotheses of why they were perceived the way they were, and in the evening they shared these and discussed far into the night how things could have gotten so out of hand. Later the groups described this night session as "getting all the garbage out of the system." It was a highly emotional evening that revealed many false assumptions and stereotypes that had grown up over the years. Just the sharing made both groups aware that they had not been serving the company's or their own interests very well by the manner in which they were dealing with each other.

The next half day was spent organizing how both sales and product lines could maximize their efforts in the future by trying to be more collaborative in a structure that made competition easier but destructive. Several new structures were invented, such as specialty salesmen for those products that required extra focusing in the marketplace, and budget reviews that allowed product lines to negotiate more effectively when they felt their products were being ignored. If sales could get information quickly to the product lines on why customers were not interested, the product lines could alter their marketing effort.

The groups agreed that they needed quarterly meetings to review the new collaborative procedures, clear new garbage out of the system, reestablish communication and trust, and redesign the structure further as needed. The new systems worked, although the quarterly meetings were indeed necessary to keep trust and communication at a high level. It proved to be far harder to undo the damage of prior competition than either group had believed possible.

Other Organizational Processes

The process consultant finds himself, through his observation of managerial behavior, witness to a variety of other organizational processes besides the ones we have reviewed. For example, he sees how managerial decisions in the areas of accounting, budgeting, and controlling will signal to the organization the degree to which subordinates are or are not trusted. The manner in which managers administer performance-appraisal plans or bonus plans also communicates a great deal about their assumptions, and therefore has an immediate as well as long-range effect on the organization. The kind of career planning that is done, the use of training or development activities, and the policies for recruitment and job placement all have implications for how people will feel, relate to each other, and carry out their work.

It is beyond the scope of this volume to treat each of these process areas in detail. For the present I merely wish to note that there are a variety of other processes to which the consultant must pay attention and which he must assess if he is to help the organization become more effective. I have deliberately concentrated on the more immediate kinds of processes that one sees in face-to-face relationships because these are the most accessible and the most likely to produce important behavior change. If organization members can change their behavior in their immediate relations, this will inevitably produce more far-reaching effects organizationally. Even more important, if managers can learn how to diagnose organizational processes better, they can continue to modify their behavior after the consultant is no longer present.

Summary

We have looked briefly at some intergroup and total organizational processes. Of special importance are the conditions that are set up for groups within organizations leading to competition or collaboration. The problems of internal competition were spelled out, and I noted how much more difficult it is to undo these effects than to avoid them in the first place. The process consultant must play an active role in encouraging managers to think through their approach to intergroup relations.

Part III

The Consulting Process in Action

We have now reviewed the major process issues that the consultant should be familiar with, and can shift the focus to the consultation activity as such. What is involved in a typical consulting project, and how should the process consultant think about its various stages and issues? The word *project* should be viewed here only in the most general sense in that PC is a very open ended activity that is usually not formalized in terms of contracts, timetables, or project definitions. Nevertheless, there are steps and stages that characterize the PC relationship that can be described and analyzed:

1. Initial contact with the client organization
2. Defining the relationship, psychological contract
3. Selecting a setting and method of work
4. Diagnostic interventions and data gathering
5. Confrontive interventions
6. Reducing involvement and termination

These stages are not easily defined in terms of periods of time. Rather, they are logically distinct areas with which the consultant must be concerned. Many of the stages, such as 2, 3, 4, and 5, go on simultaneously and involve perpetual renegotiation of the psychological contract. For purposes of exposition, however, they will be presented in the next few chapters in a linear fashion.

10

Establishing Contact
and Defining a Relationship

Initial Contact with the Client

Initial contact is made when someone from the client organization (contact client) telephones or writes me about some problem that he is experiencing or perceives in some part of his organization. Usually he comes to me for one of a number of reasons:

1. He has heard me give a talk on a topic that is related to his perceived problem.
2. He has read a paper or a book of mine.
3. He has become acquainted with me during a training program in which I was an instructor.
4. He has been referred to me by one of my colleagues.
5. He has been referred to me by another client or by someone else in his organization who is acquainted with me.

The contact client indicates that he perceives a problem that he feels is not being solved by normal organizational procedures, or he sees a lack that cannot be filled by present organizational resources.

For example, in Case A, the Apex Manufacturing Company, the contact client was a division manager one level below the president. The company is a large manufacturing concern, organized into several divisions. The contact client indicated that there were communication problems in the top management group resulting from a recent reorganization. Because the company expected to grow rapidly in the next decade, they felt they should work on these kinds of problems in preparation for their growth.

In Case B, the Boyd Consumer Goods Company, the contact client was a member of the personnel department who had known of my interests for some time, had had other contacts with professors at the Sloan School, and was interested in finding a consultant to help the newly appointed president manage the transition from traditional to more modern techniques of management in his organization.

In Case C, the Central Chemical Company, a large multidivision chemical manufacturing concern, the contact client was a fellow faculty member at MIT who had been working with the company and had learned that its management wished some additional consultation help in instituting a variety of change programs in several of their divisions. This company had originally become interested through reading the works of and hearing Douglas McGregor. They had already built a strong internal personnel staff in one of the divisions and had launched a number of very creative internal change programs. The management felt that continual contact with outside resources would help the total effort.

In Case D, the Delta Manufacturing Company, a large supplier of consumer appliances, the contact client was a member of the company's central personnel staff. He had been working in one of the divisions helping various production groups to develop strong interpersonal collaboration and team spirit. When the division director became interested in a similar activity for himself and his staff, he asked the inside man to find him a consultant who could work with the group.

In most such cases I do not know from the initial contact what the real problem is, and, therefore, only agree to discuss it further at an exploratory meeting. If I have some consultation time available, I schedule such a meeting in the near future. If I do not have time, I either ask if the problem can wait or suggest someone else who might be able to help. Occasionally I agree to an exploratory meeting with the understanding that if anything comes of it, the work will be done at a later time or by someone else.

One of the most important criteria for predicting the likelihood that a useful consultation relationship will result is the initial relationship formed between me and the contact client. I find that I evaluate the degree of openness, spirit of inquiry, and authenticity of communication of the contact client. For example, to evaluate openness, I try to assess the responses I get to some of my initial questions. If I suggest an exploratory meeting, I look for a response that indicates a genuine willingness to sit down and engage in some joint diagnosis.

If the caller seems too certain that he already knows what is wrong, or if he has me miscast as an expert in something that I am not expert in, or if he clearly has a misconception of what a consultant coming from an organizational psychology frame of reference could offer, I am cautious even in suggesting a further meeting, lest we end up wasting time. If the caller seems to want merely reassurance for some course of action he has already embarked on or wants a quick solution to a surface problem, I am reluctant to proceed.

If none of the barriers described above arises, the exploratory meeting becomes the first major step toward the establishing of a relationship. It should be noted, however, that even the suggestion of such a meeting, and the kinds of questions the consultant asks in deciding whether or not to have such a meeting, are already diagnostic interventions that will influence how the contact client perceives and thinks about his problem. The guidelines I use in deciding on questions, therefore, are the assumptions I make about what will be helpful in the here and now situation. My behavior must illustrate at all times my commitment to establishing a helpful relationship.

This philosophy also implies that the process consultant is indifferent in the immediate situation to whether or not he ends up with a client in the longer term. If in the initial meeting sufficient help is provided so that no further meetings are needed, that is effective consultation. The commercial consultant is at a disadvantage in this regard because he is trying to sell his services for longer-range projects. A process consultant must be free of the pressure to sell so that he can genuinely evaluate whether or not he can be helpful to the client. He must be free to turn down clients who would not benefit from this kind of help.

As can be seen, PC cannot start until someone in the organization accepts the assumption that relationships and interpersonal processes that accompany organizational problem solving are important targets for learning. Gaining entry to an organization in the role of process consultant is, therefore, highly contingent on one or more internal people being willing to expose their processes to scrutiny. Often such people have only the vaguest idea of what their problems actually are, but they sense that all is not as good as it could be and therefore invite observation and comment. The spirit of inquiry underlying this stance is an essential characteristic of a potentially successful client–consultant relationship.

The Exploratory Meeting

Who attends the exploratory meeting, where it is held, for what length of time, and whether or not the client will be billed for it has to be worked out jointly with the contact client. The PC philosophy requires that every intervention be jointly owned by the client system and the consultant, so the first work of the process consultant is to create a problem-solving process that will lead to a sound decision on the nature of the exploratory meeting.

The most important question is: Who should be present at such a meeting? If I have a chance to influence this decision, the kind of criteria that I use are as follows:

1. Someone high enough in the organization to be able to influence others if he is himself influenced.
2. Someone who is generally in tune with the idea of bringing in a consultant to work on organizational problems.

3. Someone who perceives a specific set of problems or symptoms that require attention.
4. Someone who is familiar with behavioral science consultants and the general notion that the client must remain active in the consultation process.

One should avoid having anyone at these early meetings who is hostile, skeptical, or totally ignorant of the kinds of service that can be offered by the consultant. If one or more such people are present and challenge me to prove that I can be of help to them, we are no longer exploring the problem. Instead I find myself seduced into a selling role, and if I permit myself to get into this role, I am already violating the PC model of helping others to help themselves. On the other hand, if the contact starts with members of the client system who are interested in trying PC, it is often possible at a later stage to design meetings or settings in which the resistant members of the system can be confronted constructively and conflicts worked through.

The exploratory meeting is usually a long lunch or a half day meeting. I usually mention to the contact client that the company should be prepared to pay a consultation fee for this meeting because the helping process really starts with the initial contact. The kinds of diagnostic questions I ask, the frame of reference from which I approach the problem, the sorts of things I observe and react to, all constitute initial interventions that, to some degree, influence the client's perceptions of his own problems. After three or four hours of exploration of his company's problems, the contact client has new perspective and new insights. At the same time I am sharing my scarcest resource — time.

The purposes of the exploratory meeting are as follows:

1. To determine more precisely what the problem is.
2. To assess whether my further involvement is likely to be of any help to the organization.
3. To assess whether the problem will be of interest to me.
4. To formulate next action steps with the client if the answers to 2 and 3 are positive.

The exploratory meeting is usually a fairly open-ended discussion during which I ask exploratory questions that are designed (1) to sharpen and highlight aspects of the presented problem, and (2) to test how open and frank the contact client is willing to be. If I feel that there is hedging, unwillingness to be critical of his own organization, confusion about his motives, and/or confusion about my potential role as a consultant, I am cautious. I suggest that nothing be decided without more exploration, or I terminate the relationship if I am definitely pessimistic about establishing a good relationship.

For example, in Case A the exploratory meeting was only with the contact client, a key manager immediately below the president. He spoke openly about his concerns that the president needed help in handling certain key people, shared his worries that the president and his key subordinates were not in good communication, and indicated that recent company history suggested the need for some stabilizing force in the organization. I asked him whether the president knew he had come to me and what the president's feelings were about bringing in a consultant. The contact client indicated that the president as well as other key executives were all in favor of bringing someone in to work with them. All saw the need for some outside help.

In Case B, the exploratory meeting was relatively perfunctory because I had already met the president at a management development session run by the company some months earlier. The meeting consisted of the personnel vice president, the president, and me, and moved rapidly toward the next stage of actually defining the goals and the setting in which to work.

In Case C, the fellow consultant who had recommended me acted as go-between and arranged a suitable set of goals and targets for my visit to the company. In Case D, the exploratory meeting was a lunch with the division manager, the inside consultant, and me. Our purpose was to determine whether the division manager and I would "hit it off together," whether we could agree on some reasonable goals for consultation, and how best to proceed if things looked promising.

In each of the above cases the initial exploration led to a

favorable response on both my part and that of the contact client. To illustrate an unfavorable outcome, in Case E, the Etna Production Company, the contact client called me to meet with him and his key personnel group to evaluate a new performance appraisal program they were planning to launch across the whole company. The contact client was the director of personnel. The exploratory meeting lasted for one day, during which time company representatives outlined the proposed program. I questioned a number of points that seemed internally inconsistent and found the client becoming obviously defensive. The further we went into the discussion, the clearer it became that the client was completely committed to his program and was seeking only reassurance from me. From the way in which he reacted to questions and criticisms, it also became clear that he was not willing to reexamine any part of his program. He did not really want an evaluation. I therefore terminated the relationship at the end of the day, saying that I did not think I could be helpful beyond the questions I had already raised.

I try to be as open and confronting as I can be during the exploratory meeting, partly as a test of how willing the client is to be open and partly to make it clear from the outset how I would define my role as consultant. The most important point to get across is that I will not function as an expert problem solver in the traditional consultant role. Rather, I will attempt to intervene directly in organizational processes as I see the opportunity. This point has to be made explicit early because the very entry of the consultant into the organization already constitutes an intervention of some magnitude. I would be deluding myself and my client if I said that I might or might not intervene, or that I would "study" the problem before intervening. I have to convince the client to accept the idea that intervention is fundamental to all stages of the consultation process, but that the nature and degree of intervention are dependent on joint diagnosis and joint decision making between the client and me.

If I feel that the contact client can accept me as an intervener in organizational processes, and if my relationship with the client is progressing comfortably during the exploratory meeting, the discussion usually moves toward defining the psychological contract.

The Psychological Contract

There are two aspects to the contract: (1) the formal decision as to how much time will be devoted to the consultation, what general services will be performed, and the form and amount of payment that will be used; and (2) the informal "psychological contract" that involves the client's implicit (and sometimes explicit) expectations of what he will gain from the relationship as well as what obligations he will accept, and the consultant's implicit (and sometimes explicit) expectations of what he will give to the relationship, what obligations he takes on, and what he expects to gain from it. It is important for both client and consultant to explore as many aspects of the contract as possible provided there is mutual understanding of what is meant. Sometimes this requires delaying the discussion until the client has experienced PC.

On the formal side, I have a simple ground rule. I work up to a certain number of days per month for a set per-hour and/or per-day fee. I do not wish the client organization to formally commit itself to a retainer or a predetermined contract of a given size, nor do I wish to promise a continuing relationship. Both parties should be free to terminate the agreement at any time if the relationship is no longer satisfactory or useful. This mutual freedom to terminate is important to ensure that the basis of the relationship is the *actual value obtained*, not the fulfillment of some obligation.

On the other hand, both the client and the consultant should be prepared to give as much time to the project as is mutually agreed on as desirable. If I have only one day per month available, and the nature of the problem is such that more time may be needed by the client, I obviously should not begin the consultation in the first place. I try to make a reasonably good estimate of how much time any given project might take if it goes well, and ensure that I have at least that much time available. For his part, the client should budget costs in such a way that if more days are needed, he has the resources to pay for them. In no case has anything of this sort ever been formalized beyond a general letter of intentions written by the client. Once we agree on the daily rate, I keep records of the amount of time spent and send monthly bills to the client.

On the psychological side, I try to assess as early in the relationship as possible all the expectations that may be deliberately or unwittingly concealed by the client. Beyond wanting to work on the presented problem, the client may expect the consultant to help in a variety of other ways, such as giving him personal evaluations of his subordinates, helping him deal with "problem people" in his organization, providing expert opinions on how certain management problems should be handled, giving support to some of the decisions the client has made, helping him to sell his decisions to others, serving as a communication channel to people with whom the client has trouble communicating, mediating conflicts, and so on. As many of these expectations as possible must be revealed early so that they do not become traps or sources of disappointment later if I refuse to go along with something that the client expects of me. On the other hand, if the client wishes to conceal certain motives, all I can do is to be diagnostically sensitive and avoid traps.

On my side, I have to be as clear as I can be about what I expect of the organization and of myself in my role as consultant. For example, I expect a willingness to diagnose and explore problem issues and to take enough time to find out what is really going on rather than rushing in hastily. I expect to be supported in my process orientation and to have organization members be committed to the process of sharing ownership of diagnostic and other interventions.

I also have to state clearly what I will do and what I will not do. For example, I have to explain fully the idea that my client is not just the *contact person* or the person of highest rank but the *entire group* with which I am working and, by implication, the entire organization. In other words, I would not support decisions that I believe would harm any given group, such as the employees, customers, or suppliers, even if I never had any contact with such groups.

This concept of the whole group or organization as the client is one of the trickiest, yet most important, aspects of PC. In observing other consultants operating in the organization in which I have been working, I have noticed that many of them essentially take the highest-level manager, typically the president, as their primary client, convince him of what the remedial intervention should be, and then proceed to help him to sell and implement the intervention even though this may be hurtful to others in the organization.

In contrast, as a process consultant, I have found myself to be most effective if I can gain the trust of *all* key parties with whom I am working so that none ever thinks of me as pushing someone else's ideas. I have found that this is quite possible to achieve across several levels of the organization. Indeed, in Case A, after many months of working with the president and his six key subordinates, I arrived at a point where all of them saw me as a potentially useful communication link. They asked me quite sincerely to report to each one the feelings or reactions of others whenever I learned anything that I felt should be passed on. At the same time they were quite open with me about each other, knowing that I might well pass on any opinions or reactions they voiced to me. They did not want me to treat everything they said to me as confidential, because they trusted me and each other enough and saw my linkage to all of them as an additional useful communication device.

This case was of great interest to me because of my own initial feelings that to serve as a carrier of this type of information was not an ideal role for me and reflected an insufficient ability on their part to tell each other things directly. Hence I took two courses of action. First, I tried as much as possible to train each of them to tell others in the group what they felt directly. At the same time, I intervened directly in their process by occasionally passing on information and opinions that they could not share when I thought this would be helpful in accomplishing their work goals.

A simple yet critical event will illustrate what I mean. Two members, Pete and Joe, did not always communicate freely with each other, partly because they felt some rivalry. Pete had completed a study and written a report that was to be discussed by the whole group. Three days before the report was due, I visited the company and stopped at Pete's office to discuss the report with him and ask how things were going. He said they were fine, but frankly he was puzzled about why Joe had not come to him to look at some of the back-up data pertaining to Joe's function. Pete felt this was just another bit of evidence that Joe did not really respect Pete very much.

An hour or so later I was working with Joe and raised the issue of the report (my unilateral decision to intervene because I thought it might be helpful). Joe and his staff were busy preparing for the meeting, but nothing was said about looking at the back-up data that Pete had available. Joe said that he was sure it was private and would not be released by Pete. Joe wanted badly to see it, but felt sure that Pete had deliberately not offered it.

I decided that it would be helpful to reveal what I knew about Pete's feelings of willingness to share the data. Joe expressed considerable surprise and later in the day went to Pete, who gave him a warm welcome and turned over to him three volumes of the data that Joe had been wanting to see and that Pete had been wanting to share. I had to judge carefully whether I would hurt either Pete or Joe by revealing Pete's feelings, and decided that the potential gains would clearly outweigh the risks.

Getting back to setting the proper expectations on the part of the client, I have to state clearly that I will not function as an expert resource on human relations problems, but that I will try to help the client to solve those problems by providing alternatives and helping to think through the consequences of different alternatives. I also need to stress my expectation that I will gather information primarily by observing people in action, not by interviewing and questionnaire surveying, unless there is a clear decision that interviewing a certain set of people is appropriate. Finally, I have to make it plain that when I am observing in meetings, I will not be very active but will comment on what is happening or give feedback only as I feel it will be helpful to the group in accomplishing its task.

The fact that I will be relatively inactive is often a problem for the group because of their expectation that once they have hired a consultant they are entitled to sit back and just listen to him tell them things. To have the consultant then spend hours sitting in the group and saying very little not only violates this expectation but also creates some anxiety about what he is observing. The more I can reassure the group early in the game that I am not gathering personal data of a potentially damaging nature, the smoother the subsequent observations will go.

Summary

All consultations start with some contact client who gets in touch with the consultant. Together they work out the next step, which often is an exploratory meeting that will involve others from the client organization. During such a meeting one begins to spell out mutual expectations.

Part of the early exploration with the contact client and any associates whom he involves is intended to establish a clear psychological contract that will govern the ongoing consultation. As I have indicated, I feel there should not be a formal contract beyond an agreement on fees and the potential number of days to be committed at the outset. Each party should be free to terminate or change this level of involvement at any time. At the level of the psychological contract it is important to get out into the open as many misconceptions as possible and to try to be as clear as possible about my own aims and style of work.

11

Settings and Methods of Work

The final issue to be addressed in the exploratory meeting or in subsequent meetings involves the selection of a setting in which to work, the specification of a time schedule, a description of the method of work to be used, and a preliminary statement about goals to be achieved. These decisions are crucial because, by implication, they define the immediate client system to which the consultant will relate himself.

The Setting

I use a number of general criteria for making decisions about the setting:

1. *The choice of what and when to observe should be worked out collaboratively with the client.* The process consultant must avoid the image of a psychologist wandering around the organization making observations about anything that strikes him as needing attention. Instead, the consultant should engage in a focused process of observation and feedback where both par-

ticipant and observer have agreed to inquire into the problem-solving process for the sake of improving it.

If the consultant feels the locus of observation should shift, he must involve the people who work in this new locus and establish a similar contract with them. Since the participants are themselves the targets of the process interventions, it is essential that they be involved in the decision to try to learn. Without this kind of psychological contract there is at best no readiness to hear what the consultant might have to say and at worst real resentment at being observed by an outsider.

2. *The setting chosen should be as near the top of the organization or client system as possible.* The reasons for beginning observations at the highest possible level are twofold. First, the higher the level, the more likely that basic norms, values, and goals can be observed in operation. The higher levels set the tone of the organization and ultimately determine the criteria for effective organizational functioning. If the consultant does not expose himself to these levels, he cannot determine what these ultimate norms, goals, and criteria are, and if he does not become acquainted with them, he is abdicating his own ethical responsibility.

Only if the consultant can personally accept the norms, goals, and criteria of the organization can he justify helping the organization to achieve them. If the consultant feels that the organization's goals are unethical, immoral, or personally unacceptable for some other reason, he can choose to attempt to change them or terminate the relationship, but this choice should be made. The consultant should not operate in ignorance of what the established authority in the organization is trying to do.

Second, the higher the level, the greater the payoff on any changes in process that are achieved. In other words, if the consultant can help the president to learn more about organizational process and to change his behavior accordingly, this change in turn is a force on his immediate subordinates which sets a chain of influence into motion. The more general way to put this point is to say that the consultant should seek that setting or group of people that he considers to be potentially most influential on the rest of the organization. Usually this turns out to be the top executive group.

3. The setting chosen should be one in which it is easy to observe problem-solving, interpersonal, and group processes. Often this turns out to be a weekly or monthly staff meeting, or some other regularly scheduled activity in which two or more members of the key group being observed transact business together. It is important to observe processes among the members, not just between individual members and the consultant. For this reason, a survey or interview methodology is only a stopgap measure. Ultimately, the consultant must have access to a situation where the organization's members are dealing with each other in their usual fashion.

4. The setting chosen should be one in which real work is going on. The consultant should avoid the situation where a group initially agrees to meet with him only to discuss their interpersonal relations. Such a meeting would be appropriate after a relationship had developed between the group and the consultant but would be premature before. The group cannot as yet trust the consultant enough to really have an open discussion of interpersonal relations, and the consultant does not yet have enough observational data to be able to help the group in such a discussion. Regular committee or work-group meetings are ideal, on the other hand, because the consultant not only sees the organization members in a more natural role but learns what sort of work the members are concerned about. At later stages, it is much easier to link observations to real work behavior, and it is much more likely that real changes will occur in members if they can relate process observations to work events.

These criteria can often not be met in an absolute fashion, but they are an important guideline. If the criteria are shared with the contact client in the process of getting joint ownership of the decision on setting, the consultant is also beginning to intervene by teaching the client something about the process of planned change.

Method of Work

The method of work chosen should be as congruent as possible with the values underlying process consultation. Thus observation, informal interviewing, and group discussions would be congruent with (a) the idea that the consultant does not already have pat answers or standard "expert" solutions, and (b) the idea that the consultant should be maximally available for questioning and two-way communication.

If the consultant uses such methods as questionnaires or surveys, he himself remains an unknown quantity to the respondent. As long as he remains unknown, the respondent cannot really trust him and hence cannot answer questions completely honestly. The method of work chosen, therefore, should make the consultant maximally visible and maximally available for interaction.

Often I choose to start a consultation project with some interviewing, but the purpose of the interview is not so much to gather data as to establish a relationship with each of the people who will later be observed. The interview is designed to reveal myself as much as to learn something about the other person. I consider the use of questionnaires only after I am well enough known by the organization to be reasonably sure that people would trust me enough to give direct and frank answers to questions.

In the Apex Manufacturing Company, the exploratory meeting led to the decision to attend one of the regular meetings of the executive committee. At this time I was to meet the president and the other key executives to discuss further what could and should be done. At the meeting I found a lively interest in the idea of having an outsider help the group and the organization to become more effective. I also found that the group was willing to enter an open-ended relationship. I explained as much as I could my philosophy of PC and suggested that a good way of getting further acquainted would be to set up a series of individual interviews with each member of the group. At the same time I suggested that I sit in on the weekly half-day meetings of the executive committee. The interviews then would occur after several of these meetings.

At the initial meeting of the group, I was able to observe a number of key events. For example, the president, Alex, was very informal but very powerful. I got the impression initially (and confirmed it subsequently) that the relationships of all the group members to the president would be the key issue, with relationships to each other being relatively less important. I also got the impression that Alex was a confident individual who would tolerate my presence only so long as he saw some value in it; he would have little difficulty in confronting me and terminating the relationship if my presence ceased to have value.

It was also impressive, and turned out to be indicative of a managerial style, that Alex did not feel the need to see me alone. He was satisfied from the outset to deal with me inside the group. Near the end of the initial meeting, I requested a private talk with him to satisfy myself that we understood the psychological contract we were entering into. He was surprisingly uncomfortable in this one-to-one relationship, had little that he wished to impart to me, and did not show much interest in my view of the relationship. I wanted the private conversation in order to test his reaction to taking some personal feedback on his own behavior as the consultation progressed. He said he would welcome this and indicated little or no concern over it. As I was to learn later, his reaction reflected a very strong sense of his own power and identity. He felt he knew himself very well and was not a bit threatened by feedback.

In the Boyd Consumer Goods Company, the consultation started in essentially the same manner. At the exploratory meeting with the president, Bill, I inquired whether there was some regular meeting that he held with his immediate subordinates. There was such a group that met weekly, and it was agreed that I would sit in on it. Bill explained to the group that he had asked me to sit in to help the group function more effectively and then asked me to explain how I saw my own role. I described PC and the kinds of things I would be looking for, stated that I would not be very active but preferred the group just to work along as it normally would, and that I would make comments as I saw opportunities to be helpful. It was decided that after a few meetings I would interview each member of the seven-man group individually.

The climate of the Boyd group was quite formal. There was not much group participation, more reliance on Bill to run the meeting, and more ambiguity about the feelings of the members for each other.

In the Central Chemical Company the pattern was entirely different, since they were geographically removed and I had contracted to spend only one week with them at a time several months hence. The person coordinating my program was quite knowledgeable about the possible uses he could make of a process consultant, and he had, as I indicated before, consulted with a colleague of mine to determine how best to use me. They decided that a workshop devoted to helping line managers improve their diagnoses and action plans for change programs that they wanted to implement was an appropriate workshop goal. Once this had been decided by correspondence, I worked with my colleague on designing the program of the week. We agreed not to freeze the plan until I was actually on the premises the evening before the workshop. We had, however, made the key decision to invite only managers who had an interest in changing some aspect of their immediate work situation, and to have each manager come with a member of the personnel staff reporting to him so that teams would be looking at the change problems.

When I arrived at the Central Chemical Company site some months later, I met with my "inside" consultant contact, his boss (who was personnel director), and one or two other personnel people who were interested in the program. We reviewed the goals and schedule of the week, decided to remain flexible until we could find out more from the participants about their change goals, and agreed that the inside consultant would work with me in implementing the program. The setting for the program was the training center of the company. All the teams (eighteen men altogether) were to meet daily at the training center for the actual workshop.

In the case of Delta, the pattern was almost identical to Apex and Boyd. The head of the division with whom I had the exploratory lunch (Dave) decided that he wanted to build his group of immediate subordinates into an effective team so that they could manage what he saw as a difficult phase involving the rapid growth of the division. He held weekly staff meetings and invited me to sit in on these regularly. After several meetings, I planned, as in the other cases, to interview each member of the seven-person group individually.

To illustrate a different kind of setting and work method, let us look at the Fairview Company. Some members of the training department had become exposed to sensitivity training several years back, introduced it into their middle and senior manager development programs, and gained a good deal of sophistication in analyzing organizational process. It became clear to a number of them that one of the major difficulties of the organization was conflict between the central headquarters and the various field units — conflicts over how much decentralization of decision-making authority there should be, conflicts concerning how much the system actually reflected earlier agreements to decentralize, and conflicts over lines of authority.

The organization had strong functional directors in the headquarters organization. As they developed financial and marketing programs, they tended to bypass the formal line organization through the executive vice president and the regional managers, instead dealing directly with the financial and marketing people in the field.

The central training group knew that there was an annual meeting of all the key executives, including headquarters and field people — fifteen in all. They consulted me about the possibility of organizing one of these meetings in such a way as to enable the entire group to work on the organizational problem. The training group was not sure how the president or vice president would respond to the idea, since there was no prior history of exposure of the group to an outside consultant. However, a number of the regional managers had attended sensitivity training groups and learned something about the potential of bringing in a "behaviorally oriented consultant." They felt strongly that something like this meeting should be tried.

A core group, consisting of the training director, two of his key staff people, and one enthusiastic regional manager, met with me for one day to plan further strategy. We decided that for such a program to work, a substantial number of the people who would eventually be at the meeting would also have to become involved in the planning and design of the meeting. This step was a crucial one, and can be derived directly from the kind of assumptions that underlie PC. A group consisting of equal numbers of head-quarters and regional managers was formed. The mission of this group was to meet for two days to plan the total meeting. The plan developed by the group was then to be presented for approval to the president and vice president.

My role as a process consultant was critical at two stages in this enterprise. First, during the two-day meeting of the planning group I had to steer them away from a traditional format in which I would make presentations about headquarters/field-type problems for them to discuss. Second, I had to take responsibility for the success of the meeting format finally chosen and find a role for myself that would make this format work.

The plan that emerged from the two days of planning had the following elements:

1. The three-day meeting would be billed as an exploration of organizational problems at the top of the organization, toward the end of improving organizational relationships.
2. The meeting would be chaired by me rather than the president of the company.
3. The agenda for the meeting would be developed by a procedure used by Richard Beckhard in which each member of the fifteen-person group would be asked to write me a letter at my home outlining what he saw to be the major organizational problems facing the group. It was then my job to put together the information from the fifteen letters into major themes and issues. These themes and issues were to be presented by me to the total group at our first session and could constitute the agenda for the three days.

The first purpose in having such letters written was to provide each person the opportunity to be completely frank without having to expose himself to the possible wrath of the boss or other members of the group. Second, it provided an opportunity to gather data from all the members before the meeting began.

Third, it involved each member in helping to set the agenda, a considerable departure from previous meetings where the agenda had been set by the vice president. It could be expected, therefore, that all the members would feel more involved in the meeting from the outset.

The letter writing had two problems connected with it: (1) it seemed a little bit gimmicky, and (2) it was difficult to know how someone would react who had not as yet met me. Would he write a frank letter to a strange professor about rather critical organizational issues? We decided that we would have to run the risk of getting no response or poor response, but that we could minimize the risk by having the members of the planning group talk to others they knew and make a personal appeal to write a frank letter.

The procedure was agreed on, was presented to the president and vice president and received enthusiastic approval, and thus became the plan for the meeting. I pointed out that the president and vice president would have to be careful in how they managed their own role. If they reverted too quickly to their power position and abandoned the role of helping to diagnose organizational problems, the group would retreat into silence and the problems would remain unsolved. I felt that both men understood the risks, were willing to take them, and had the kind of personality that would make them accept this somewhat strange meeting format.

Having agreed to go ahead, the group then decided that the vice president would send out the letter explaining the meeting format and inviting the diagnostic letters. Members of the planning group were to follow up in the districts to ensure that everyone understood the plan and the fact that the plan had come from organization members themselves, even though I had suggested many of the separate elements.

This rather lengthy procedure was essential to obtain the involvement of the members in a process-oriented meeting. Even though the ideas came from the training department and from me, the concept clearly appealed to regional and headquarters managers. Had they not become committed, it would not have been possible to hold such a meeting at all.

Summary

The choice of a setting and a method of work is highly variable. It is important that both the setting and working procedure be jointly decided between the contact client group and the consultant. Whatever decisions are made should be congruent with the general assumptions underlying PC so that whatever changes result can be self-perpetuating.

12

Diagnostic Interventions

Once the consultant is attending meetings, observing work, interviewing people, and otherwise becoming part of the ongoing organizational scene, he is engaged in a whole stream of activities that can best be conceptualized as two types of interventions — *diagnostic* and *confrontive.* In this chapter I will analyze what I mean by a diagnostic intervention and in the next two chapters take up the concept of confrontive intervention.

Gathering Data Through Diagnostic Interventions

Every decision to observe something, to ask a question, or to meet with someone constitutes an intervention into the ongoing organizational process. The consultant cannot, therefore, avoid or escape taking the responsibility for the kind of data-gathering method he uses. If the method is not congruent with his overall values, and if it does not meet the standards for an acceptable intervention, it should not be used.

The point is worth belaboring because all of the traditional consultation models, as well as the models of how to do research on organizations, make the glib assumption that one gathers data *prior* to intervening; that one observes, interviews, and surveys, then makes a diagnosis, and then suggests interventions or remedial steps.

From the point of view of PC this is an inaccurate and dangerous assumption. It is inaccurate because one can clearly demonstrate that the process of being studied influences the parties being studied. If I interview someone about his organization, the very questions I ask give the respondent ideas he never had before. The very process of formulating his own answers gives him points of view that he may never have thought of before.

The assumption is also dangerous because the various respondents who have been interviewed, surveyed, or studied may, by virtue of this common experience, band together and decide on their own what kind of action they would like to see. While the researcher-consultant is off analyzing his data, the respondents are busy changing the organization or generating demands that their boss may be quite unprepared for.

What, then, is the correct assumption, and what are its implications? The correct assumption is that every act on the part of the process consultant — even the initial act of deciding to work with the organization — constitutes an intervention. Asking for help, and having someone accept some responsibility for helping, changes the perceptions and attitudes of some members of the organization. The consultant cannot ignore these changes. He must anticipate them and learn to make them work toward the ultimate goals defined.

The main implication of this latter assumption is that the consultant must think through everything he does in terms of its probable impact on the organization. He must assume that all of his behavior is an intervention of one sort or another. Finally, he must use data-gathering methods that, at the same time, will constitute valid and useful interventions.

Methods of Data Gathering

Basically, the consultant has only three different methods by which he can gather data:

1. Direct observation
2. Individual or group interviews
3. Questionnaires or some other survey instrument to be filled out

I have already indicated that the third method is too impersonal and too much at variance with PC assumptions to be useful in the early stages of a PC project. It may become useful if the number of people to be surveyed is rather large and if the managers with whom the consultant is working fully understand the implications involved in taking a survey.

For early data gathering the choice is then reduced to observation and/or interview. In my own experience I have found that a combination of these techniques is optimal. I need a certain amount of observation in order to know what kinds of issues should be brought up in interviews, but I need some preliminary interviews in order to know whom and what to observe.

These criteria usually lead to a top-down kind of strategy. I start with the data provided by the contact client. The exploratory meeting is usually an opportunity to gather data in a group-interview setting. As the examples above have shown, the next step is often an interview of one or more of the senior people who will be involved in the project. Their consent must be obtained to do any observation of them in interaction with their group. Regular group members are usually interviewed only after one or two meetings during which I have observed what kinds of issues are being discussed and what kinds of problems exist within the group.

Once a relationship has been formed with some key group in the organization, new projects develop that involve new settings, but the methods of gathering data in the new settings are essentially the same. For example, one of the managers of the original group may want to know how the members of his own staff group feel about the organization and the work setting. He and I may then plan a series of interviews of his subordinates, leading to a series of feedback meetings. This procedure will not be initiated, however, until the manager has obtained the support and consent of his subordinates and until they too feel that I can be trusted. If it is not convenient for me to meet all of them and/ or observe their meetings, a relatively greater burden falls on the manager to persuade his subordinates to participate. But the project cannot proceed until the subordinates genuinely agree.

In this connection, an important criterion for extending a data-gathering method is that the manager who would like to use it should himself have participated in an earlier project. If the manager has been interviewed by me and has heard what kind of feedback I give after a series of interviews, he is in a much better position to decide whether such a technique would be useful in his group, and he is better equipped to explain to his subordinates what the procedure will be like.

No data-gathering method is right or wrong in the abstract. Whether or not it is appropriate and useful can be judged only from earlier observations and interviews. In a way the entire PC project must always be viewed as an unfolding series of events where subsequent events can only be predicted from earlier events. The project should be planned in a general way, but the issues that come up in the flow of work, and the new behaviors that are generated by the earlier interventions, are hard to predict, and some of the most important ones are those for which the least planning was done.

What should be the content of interviews or surveys? I have discussed in Part II of this book the kinds of things the consultant looks for when he observes a group in action. These general categories of organizational and interpersonal process should always be on the consultant's mind as things to be sensitive to, but I have found that to ask directly about them is not useful. Instead what should guide an interview or survey is the presented problem and the goals of the consultation.

For example, in the Apex Manufacturing Company, part of the initial mandate was to help the group to relate to the president. In the interviews that I conducted with group members, I concentrated quite heavily on what kinds of things went well in the relationship, what kinds of things went poorly, how relationship problems with the president were related to job performance, in what way the group members would like to see the relationship change, and so on. I did not have a formal interview schedule but held an informal discussion with each member around issues of the sort I have just mentioned.

In contrast, when I began to interview group members in the Boyd and Central companies, I concentrated much more on what kind of job each member had, with whom he had to work in the performance of that job, what kinds of problems existed in any of these relationships, what organizational factors aided or hindered effective job performance, what the company climate was like, and so on.

In the case of the Delta Manufacturing Company, I gathered no data until the evening before the workshop, and subsequently within the workshop itself. In the Fairview Company, on the other hand, I gathered written data by means of the letters. In this case, each respondent was invited to write down whatever he saw as problems existing in the relationships between the headquarters organization and the various regional centers.

The common theme in all these data-gathering approaches is a concern with organizational relationships and perceptions of organizational processes. The specific questions vary, but the general area is the same. The other common thread is a concern with organizational effectiveness. I always attempt to determine what factors are helping to make the person, group, or unit more effective, and what factors are undermining or hindering effectiveness. My assumption is that both sets of factors are always present in any organization.

Intervention Style

Having identified the kinds of content areas that I explore in interviews, I would like to close the discussion by describing some of the aspects of style, or how the consultant presents himself. For example, in the interview itself, my method of asking questions and the content of what I ask project a certain image of me. If I want to establish a collaborative, helping relationship with the person being interviewed, I must behave in a manner congruent with such a relationship. This means I cannot play the role of the psychologist who asks obscure questions upon which I then place "secret" interpretations or the like.

The content of the questions should be self-evidently relevant. If I am concerned about improving organizational effectiveness, then I should ask about it. If I am concerned with improvement, I should ask about those things that are going well in addition to those which are going poorly.

The questions can push the respondent into areas he might not ordinarily think to mention, provided that they are relevant and that the consultant senses a willingness on the part of the respondent to enter into those areas. For example, in all of the cases mentioned, I asked quite probing questions about how the decision was made to use a consultant, the attitudes expressed by members toward my coming in, what they thought were my particular qualifications for the job, where there might be tension over having a consultant in, and so on. As I mentioned earlier, if the contact client is unwilling to deal with these areas openly in the early discussions, I am likely to be cautious about becoming involved. Once working within the organization, I would interpret unwillingness to deal with such areas as caution on the respondent's part, and it would be up to me to try to determine the reasons for the caution.

The kind of question one asks also puts new ideas into the head of the respondent. For example, I often ask what kind of career planning a person has engaged in with others in the organization. The answer often is "None," but a new issue often comes up later in the interview in the form of "I wonder why no one has sat down with me to talk about my career," or "Maybe I should go have a talk with my boss about my future in the company." If I ask a person to describe the network of others with whom he must deal in order to get his job done, he often realizes for the first time what this network is like and why he has problems keeping up with his job. In other words, the interview can be a powerful tool of influence and education, and the process consultant must consider when and how to use it for influence purposes.

If I have reason to believe that the interviewee may be defensive or want to present a socially desirable picture, I ask factual and historical questions. Direct questions about values or opinions are the most likely to come back biased and thus are typically avoided.

Summary

There are basically three kinds of data-gathering methods: observation, interview, and questionnaire. Because any one of the methods is some kind of intervention into organizational process, the consultant must choose a method that will be most congruent with the values underlying PC and with the general goals of the PC project. The way he gathers data and the kinds of questions he asks give the consultant an opportunity to intervene constructively. In the next chapter I will take a closer look at other kinds of intervention to explore more fully the options available to the consultant.

13

Influencing Process Through Confrontive Interventions: Agenda Management

Deliberately Altering Process
Through Confrontive Intervention

As I have shown, one cannot completely separate the stages of diagnostic data gathering and intervention. Both occur simultaneously: how one gathers data constitutes an intervention, and the kind of intervention one chooses will reveal new data derived from the reaction to the intervention. The separation of these two processes is, therefore, basically a matter of point of view or frame of reference. In the last chapter I focused on those interventions that are primarily designed to elicit diagnostic information. In this and the next chapter I will focus on interventions that are specific attempts to change organizational process by deliberate actions on the part of the consultant.

The interventions that a process consultant might make cannot be rigidly classified, but a broad categorization can be suggested:

A. Agenda-managing interventions
    1. Questions that direct attention to process issues

2. Process-analysis periods
3. Meetings devoted to process issues
4. Conceptual inputs on process-related topics
B. Feedback of observations or other data
    1. Feedback to groups during process analysis or regular work time
    2. Feedback to individuals after meetings or after data gathering
C. Coaching or counseling of individuals or groups
D. Structural suggestions
    1. Pertaining to group membership
    2. Pertaining to communication or interaction patterns
    3. Pertaining to allocation of work, assignment of responsibility, and lines of authority

The outline is arranged in terms of a descending likelihood of use of the particular intervention. In other words, the kind of intervention I am most likely to make pertains to the group's agenda; the kind I am least likely to make is a structural suggestion. Actual solutions to management problems are not even listed because they would not be considered valid interventions in a PC model. If I permitted myself to become interested in a particular management problem in sales, marketing, or production, I would be switching roles from that of process consultant to that of expert resource. Once I have become an expert resource, I find I lose my effectiveness as a process consultant.

Agenda-Managing Interventions

Process-oriented Questions and Process-Analysis Periods

The basic purpose of this type of intervention is to make the group sensitive to its own internal processes, and to generate on the part of the group some interest in analyzing these processes. In the early stages of a project, I often find myself suggesting to a group that they allocate fifteen minutes or so at the end of their meeting to review the meeting. I may suggest some dimensions such as how involved they felt, how clear communications were, how well member resources were used, and so on. If the group is willing, I have them fill in a postmeeting reaction form (see pp. 57–58) and tabulate their own data for further discussion.

If the group agrees to some period of time for process analysis, no matter how short, I can further stimulate their interest by asking them questions that direct their attention to process issues. In addition, I will usually have observed particular events that have been important during the meeting.

For example, in a number of meetings I have observed the chairman making decisions hastily and without full commitment from the group. My question during a process-review period then might be: "How did you all feel about how the decision was made?" I have to resist answering the question with my own feelings. First of all, my feelings might be irrelevant or atypical; and second, I want the group to learn to gather its own data and draw its own conclusions. If I am pressed, I will answer with my observation or my own feeling, but my preference is usually to turn the question back to the group.

Out of process-analysis sessions there often arise two further issues, leading to further interventions. The group sometimes discovers that it has a variety of dissatisfactions with the manner in which it arrives at and processes its work agenda. I find myself at this point suggesting various ways by which the group can evaluate what to put on the agenda, how much time to allocate to each item, how to sort items in terms of importance or type of problem, and so on.

The other issue pertains to the matter of interpersonal process itself. The more interested the group becomes in its own workings, the more time it devotes to discussing this topic and the less time there is for its regular agenda. To deal with this dilemma I often suggest that process work could perhaps be done in depth by periodically allocating a whole meeting or some set block of time just to processes in the group.

Meetings Devoted to Process Issues

Such meetings are often held away from the office at a motel or some other detached location to permit the group to really work on group issues. I do not suggest this kind of meeting, however, until I believe the group is emotionally ready to handle a larger dose of process analysis. One of the frequent mistakes I have observed in colleagues' efforts to help organizations is an initial suggestion of holding a meeting to explore "relationships" and "interpersonal issues." Such a meeting should not be scheduled without firsthand knowledge that members want it and are ready to deal emotionally with whatever issues might come up.

Conceptual Inputs

The final subheading under agenda-managing interventions concerns the matter of presenting relevant elements of theory about individuals, groups, and management process. I do not have a set pattern of what I offer a group or when I offer it, but some examples may make clear the use of this intervention.

In the Apex Manufacturing Company, I found that the treasurer consistently made the operating managers uncomfortable by presenting financial information in an unintentionally threatening way. He wanted to be helpful, and he felt everyone needed the information he had to offer, but it often had the appearance of an indictment of one of the other managers: his costs were too high, his inventory control had slipped, he was too high over budget, and so on. Furthermore, this information was often revealed for the first time in the meeting, so that the operating manager concerned had no forewarning and no opportunity to find out why things had gone out of line. The result was often a fruitless argument about the validity of the figures, a great deal of defensiveness on the part of the operating manager, and irritation on the part of the president because the managers could not deal more effectively with the treasurer.

As I observed this process occurring repeatedly over several weeks, I decided that merely drawing attention to the pattern would not really solve the problem because everyone appeared to be operating with constructive intent. What the group needed was an alternative way to think about the use of financial control information. I therefore wrote a memo (see Appendix A) on control systems and circulated it to the group. When this came up for discussion at a later meeting I was in a better position to make my observations about the group, since a clear alternative had been presented. My feeling was that I could not have successfully presented this theory orally because of the amount of heat the issue always generated, and because the group members were highly active individuals who would have wanted to discuss each point separately, making it difficult to get the whole message across.

In working with the Apex group I found the written "theory memo" a convenient and effective means of communication (see samples in the Appendix). With other groups I found different patterns to be workable. For example, if the group gets away for a half day of work on group process, I may insert a half hour in the middle (or at the end) of the session to present whatever theory elements I consider to be relevant. The topics are usually not selected until I observe the particular "hangups" that exist in the group. I therefore have to be prepared to offer, on short notice, input on any of a variety of issues.

A final method of theory input is to make reprints of relevant articles available to the group at selected times. Often I know of some good piece of theory that pertains to what the group is working on. If I suggest that such an article be circulated, I also try to persuade the group to commit some of its agenda time to a discussion of the article.

The key criterion for the choice of theory input is that the theory must be relevant to what the group already senses is a problem. There is little to be gained by giving "important" theory if the group has no data of its own to link to the theory. On the other hand, once the group has confronted an issue in its own process, I am always amazed at how ready the members are to look at and learn from general theory.

Agenda-managing interventions may strike the reader as a rather low-key, low-potency kind of intervention. Yet it is surprising to me how often working groups arrive at an impasse on simple agenda-managing issues. In a way, their inability to select the right agenda for their meetings and to discuss the agenda in a constructive way is symbolic of other difficulties that are harder to pinpoint. If the group can begin to work on its agenda, the door is often opened to other process discussions. Let me provide some case examples.

Case Examples

In the Apex Manufacturing Company I sat in for several months on the weekly executive committee meeting, which included the president and his key subordinates. I quickly became aware that the group was very loose in its manner of operation: people spoke when they felt like it, issues were explored fully, conflict was confronted fairly openly, and members felt free to contribute.

This kind of climate seemed constructive, but it created a major difficulty for the group. No matter how few items were put on the agenda, the group was never able to finish its work. The list of backlog items grew longer and the frustration of group members intensified in proportion to this backlog. The group resonded by trying to work harder. They scheduled more meetings and attempted to get more done at each meeting, but with little success. Remarks about the ineffectiveness of groups, too many meetings, and so on became more and more frequent.

The group was obviously overloaded but did not know how to cope with this condition. Their agenda was too large, they tried to process too many items at any given meeting, and the agenda was a mixture of operational and policy issues without recognition by the group that such items required different allocations of time. I suggested to the group that they seemed overloaded and should discuss how to develop their agenda for their meetings. The suggestion was adopted after a half hour or so of sharing feelings. It was then decided, with my help, to sort the agenda items into several categories, and to devote some meetings entirely to operational issues while others would be exclusively policy meetings. The operations meetings would be run more tightly in order to process these items efficiently. The policy questions would be dealt with in depth.

Once the group had made this separation and realized that it could function differently at different meetings, it then decided to meet once a month for an entire day. During this day they would take up one or two large questions and explore them in depth. The group accepted my suggestion to hold such discussions away from the office in a pleasant, less hectic environment.

By rearranging the agenda, the group succeeded in rearranging its whole pattern of operations. This rearrangement also resulted in a redefinition of my role. The president decided that I should phase out my attendance at the operational meetings but plan to take a more active role in the monthly one-day meetings. He would set time aside for presentation of any theory I might wish to make and for process analysis of the meetings. He had previously been reluctant to take time for process work in the earlier meeting pattern but now welcomed it.

The full-day meetings changed the climate of the group dramatically. For one thing, it was easier to establish close informal relationships with other members during breaks and meals. Because there was enough time, people felt they could really work through their conflicts instead of having to leave them hanging. It was my impression that as acquaintance level rose, so did the level of trust in the group. Members began to feel free to share more personal reactions with each other. This sense of freedom made everyone more relaxed and readier to let down personal barriers and report accurate information. There was less need for defensive distortion or withholding.

After about one year the group decided quite spontaneously to try some direct confrontive feedback. We were at one of the typical monthly all-day meetings. The president announced that he thought each group member should tell the others what he felt to be the strengths and weaknesses of the several individuals. He asked me to help in designing a format for this discussion. I first asked the group members whether they did in fact want to attempt this type of confrontation. The response was sincerely positive, so we decided to go ahead.

The format I suggested was based upon my prior observation of group members. I had noticed that whenever anyone commented on anyone else, there was a strong tendency to answer back and to lock in on the first comment made. Hence, further feedback tended to be cut off. To deal with this problem I suggested that the group discuss one person at a time, and that a ground rule be established that the person being described was not to comment or respond until all the members had had a chance to give all of their feedback. This way he would be forced to continue to listen. The ground rule was accepted, and I was given the role of monitoring the group to ensure that the process operated as the group intended it to.

For the next several hours the group then went into a detailed and searching analysis of each member's managerial and interpersonal style, including that of the president. I encouraged members to discuss both the positives and the negatives they saw in each person. I also played a key role in forcing people to make their comments specific and concrete. I demanded examples, insisted on clarification, and generally asked the kind of question that I thought might be on the listener's mind as he tried to understand the feedback. I also added my own feedback on points I had observed in that member's behavior.

At first it was not easy for the group either to give or to receive feedback, but as the day wore on the group learned to be more effective. The total exercise of confrontation was considered highly successful, both at the time and some months later. It deepened relationships, exposed some chronic problems that now could be worked on, and gave each member much food for thought in terms of his own self-development. It should be noted that the group chose to do this spontaneously after many months of meetings organized around work topics. I am not sure they could have handled the feedback task effectively had they been urged to try sooner, even though I could see the need for this type of meeting some time before the initiative came from the group.

In the Apex case, my intervention tended to help the group move from chaotic meetings toward a differentiated, organized pattern. In the end, the group spent more time in meetings than before, but they minded it less because the meetings were more productive. The group has also learned how to manage its own agenda and how to guide its own processes.

In the Boyd Consumer Goods Company, a similar situation was present but the direction of learning was different. I found that the executive group was strangling itself with formality and trivia. Agendas were long and detailed, meetings were highly formal, and members were responsible for reporting to the group on various operational issues on a carefully planned monthly schedule. If anyone tried to make comments on a report, he was quickly reminded that he knew less about the topic than the reporter. Consequently most of the talk during meetings was of a reporting, attack, or defense variety. Little open-ended problem solving took place. Most members looked (and acted) passive and bored. When interviewed, they confirmed that they felt this way during meetings; yet, surprisingly, they tended to defend their meetings as necessary.

My own feeling was that the members were caught up in their own traditions. They had always run meetings this way; hence they felt that boredom and lack of involvement were the "normal" subjective feelings for participants in a meeting. Those who felt a little more frustrated and rebellious did not know what methods to follow for livelier, more productive meetings. Hence there were widespread feelings of apathy, resignation, and frustration.

I tried a whole series of interventions over a period of several months, most of them unsuccessful from my point of view. First, I asked the group to review its own agenda and share feelings about it. Some members revealed feelings of frustration but still staunchly defended the agenda pattern as necessary. Second, I tried to help the group to differentiate policy from operational decisions. It seemed to me that whenever they tried to discuss policy, operational problems would intervene and preempt a major portion of the time. I also felt that the group tended to hold too limited a concept of policy. The group verbally agreed with me but failed to change its pattern of operation in any substantial way. Third, I tried being directly confrontive about the apathy and frustration I saw in the members. The group accepted my confrontation like "good soldiers," defended itself a little bit, told me I had been very helpful, and then resumed its discussions in the old pattern.

A partial breakthrough came some months later. The president of the company had in the meantime attended a sensitivity-training lab and had come back with a somewhat greater enthusiasm for group-process work. He realized that the group could be more productive and recognized the need to make it so. We agreed to devote some time to discussion of what the group's agenda and pattern of operations should be. In the meantime, another event had taken place: the company had reorganized, putting responsibility for many of the day-to-day operational problems clearly on the shoulders of certain key individuals. To make the reorganization work, it was decided not to have as much group time devoted to reporting out and monitoring members' work areas.

When the group met to discuss its own future, some of the same depression I had previously observed was still in evidence. After about twenty minutes of general discussion, I said in a rather exasperated tone that I never saw this group have any *fun*. What would it take to make people want to come to the meeting because the meeting would be *fun*? This comment released a burst of laughter, as if some kind of inner dam had burst. The group had really been operating on the assumption that work could not be fun, and was just silently taking its painful medicine.

Once this issue had been brought out into the open, members agreed that meetings could be more fun. In the subsequent discussion, members delineated several key requirements for better meetings: a climate of greater acceptance in the group which would permit members to share ideas, plans, and problems with each other, without feeling that they would be attacked by other members; more concentration on sharing information and problems, and less on trying to make decisions in the group; and more effective use of group time by better agenda control.

The group spent an hour or more discussing how it might operate in the future and, more important, agreed on the use of a process-analysis session at the end of each meeting, to review whether it was hitting its own targets. It was decided that one member of the group should be the process recorder and give feedback to the group at the end of the session. This decision was especially good since the members needed practice in observing group process. Shortly afterward, my participation in the meetings was curtailed by other commitments, but at a later time I had an opportunity to discuss the group's progress with the president, and he felt that the meetings improved, that the climate became more open, and that the process-observer role has been very helpful to the group in monitoring its own functioning.

This case illustrates for me the trial-and-error nature of intervention. I could not really have predicted which of my various efforts to loosen the group up would work. Indeed, if there had not been related changes, such as the reorganization and the president's experience at the training laboratory, maybe none of my efforts would have worked. Merely helping the group to identify its process does not automatically produce a change in that process, even if the group is quite frustrated and knows a change is needed.

Summary and Analysis

Agenda-managing interventions are one category of confrontive interventions that are designed to deliberately influence the group's process. Such interventions are confrontive because they draw the client's attention to process issues that cannot be evaded. Everyone has witnessed the events that are the focus of the intervention. The group can react defensively or ignore the intervention, but it has been confronted and at least its consciousness of the events has been heightened.

I emphasize the confrontive nature of such interventions, even if they are mildly stated questions, because if they are based on observed events they draw attention irrevocably to something that has happened. It is for this reason that the process consultant should take care about the timing and wording of such interventions. In diagnostic interventions the consultant can claim ignorance when he asks an embarrassing question. But a question about some shared events in a meeting has much more potency because the group knows that the consultant has witnessed the events.

Agenda-managing interventions are only mildly confrontive, however, because they only draw attention to certain events and minimize a sharing of the observations and evaluations of the consultant. Such "feedback" from the consultant is addressed in the next chapter.

14

Confronting Through the Use of Feedback

Feedback of Observations or Other Data to Groups

There are basically two types of circumstances that call for this type of intervention. Case 1 is the situation where some group has agreed to a meeting in which interpersonal processes would be discussed, and has further agreed to have the consultant survey the members of the group for their individual reactions and feelings. The feedback of the survey results then serves as the opening agenda for the meeting. Case 2 is the situation where a group has already learned to discuss interpersonal process and has developed a need to supplement such discussion with more personal kinds of feedback. The meeting described in the previous section in which Apex executives gave each other feedback with the help of the consultant is a good example of the latter type of situation.

In both types of situation, there must be some readiness for feedback and some consensus that feedback of observations or interview results would be a legitimate activity for the group to undertake. There is nothing more tempting for the process consultant than to leap in with his own observations as soon as he has picked up some data on an interesting issue. If the consultant is to maintain congruence with the PC model, however, he must resist the temptation lest he put the group immediately on the defensive or undermine his own position by reporting something that does not make sense or is unpalatable to group members. The issue is not whether the observation is valid. The issue is whether the group is able and ready to understand and learn from the observation. Such ability and readiness must be built up before feedback can be useful.

The first type of intervention — reporting back data gathered from individuals — is a useful way to orient the group as to what its process issues may be. The previously cited case of the Fairview Company illustrates the use of this device as a way to open a discussion. By having group members write to me about the major organizational issues that they perceived, I was able to construct an agenda that would maximize the probability that the group would confront issues of importance to the members. At the first meeting of the group I presented the major categories of issues that the letters had revealed and tried to illustrate each issue by paraphrasing from one or more letters. The group was thus getting feedback, but the identity of the individual information source was protected.

I noticed during the three days of discussion that as the members became more comfortable with each other, they were increasingly able to make their own points and identify themselves openly with the various issues; they leaned less and less on me as the source of input. If the senior people in the group had reacted punitively to any of the issues brought up, the group would no doubt have avoided talking about those issues and there would have been less revelation of personal feelings. Fortunately the senior people were receptive, willing to listen to the issues, and able to work on them constructively.

In one of the divisions of the Apex Manufacturing Company, I followed a different procedure. After getting to know the top-management group through several group meetings, I suggested that it might be useful to interview and give feedback to the next level below the vice president. There was some concern on the part of the senior group that there might be a morale problem at this level. Initially I was asked merely to do an interview survey and report back to the top group. I declined this approach for reasons already mentioned: gathering data to report to a higher group would violate PC assumptions because it would not involve the sources of the data in analyzing their own process. I suggested instead that I conduct the interview with the ground rule that all my conclusions would first be reported back to the interviewee group, and that I would tell top management only those items that the group felt should be reported.[1]

The group would first have to sort the items and decide which things they could handle by themselves and which should be reported up the line of authority because they were under higher management control. The real value of the feedback should accrue to the group that initially provided the data; they should become involved in examining the issues they had brought up, and consider what they themselves might do about them.

The above-mentioned procedure was agreed upon by the top management. One vice president sent a memorandum to all members who would be involved in the interview program, informing them of the procedure, his commitment to it, and his hope that they would participate. I then followed up with individual appointments with each person concerned. At this initial appointment I recounted the origin of the idea, assured the interviewee that his *individual* responses would be entirely confidential, told him that I would summarize the data by department, and told him that he would see the group report and discuss it before any feedback went to his boss or higher management.

In the interview I asked each person to describe his job, tell what he found to be the major pluses and minuses in the job, describe what relationships he had to other groups, and explain how he felt about a series of specific job factors such as challenge, autonomy, supervision, facilities, salary and benefits, and so on. I later summarized the interviews in a report in which I tried to highlight what I saw to be common problem areas.

---

[1]This procedure was first brought to my attention as a method by Mr. Richard Beckhard.

All the respondents were then invited to a group meeting at which I passed out the summaries and explained that the purpose of the meeting was to examine the data, deleting or elaborating where necessary, and to determine which problem areas might be worked on by the group itself. We then went over the summary item by item, permitting as much discussion as any given item warranted.

The group meeting had its greatest utility in exposing the interviewees, in a systematic way, to interpersonal and group issues. For many of them, what they had thought to be private gripes turned out to be organizational problems that they could do something about. The attitude "Let top management solve all our problems" tended to be replaced with a viewpoint that differentiated between intragroup problems, intergroup problems, and those which were higher management's responsibility.

The interviewees not only gained more insight into organizational psychology but also responded positively to being involved in the process of data gathering itself. It symbolized to them top management's interest in them and concern for solving organizational problems. Reactions such as these are typical of other groups with whom I have tried the same approach.

Following the group meeting, the revised summary was then given to top management, in some cases individually, in others in a group. My own preference is to give it first individually, to provide for maximum opportunity to explain all the points, and then to follow up with a group discussion of the implications of the data revealed in the interviews. Where the direct supervisor of the group is involved, I have often supplemented the group report with an individual report, which extracts all the comments made by interviewees concerning the strengths and weaknesses of the supervisor's style of management. These focused feedback items have usually proved of great value to the manager, but they should be provided only if the manager initially asked for this type of feedback.

In giving either individual or group feedback from the interview summary, my role is to ensure understanding of the data and to stimulate acceptance of it so that remedial action of some sort can be effectively undertaken. Once the expectation has been built that top management will do something, there is great risk of lowering morale if the report is merely read, without being acted upon in some manner. Incidentally, it is the process consultant's job to ensure that top management *makes this commitment initially* and that high-level officials understand that when the interviews are completed there will be some demands for action. If management merely wants information without willingness to do something about the information, the consultant should not do the interviews in the first place. The danger is too great that management will not like what it hears and will suppress the whole effort; such a course will only lead to a deterioration of morale.

The results of interviews (or questionnaires) do not necessarily have to go beyond the group that is interested in them. One of the simplest and most helpful things a group can do to enhance its own functioning is to have the consultant interview the members individually and report back to the *group as a whole* a summary of its own members' feelings. It is a way of hauling crucial data out into the open without the risk of personal exposure of any individual if he feels the data collected about him are damaging or that the analysis of such data will result in conclusions that are overcritical of his performance.

Feedback to Individuals

A more detailed analysis of how to give feedback can be found in Chapter 8, "Appraising Performance and Giving Feedback," but some comments should be made in this context about the circumstances of when and how the process consultant can and should get involved in feedback to clients. Feedback from the consultant to an individual is an appropriate intervention when (1) some data have been gathered about the individual (by either interview or direct observation), and (2) the individual has indicated a readiness to hear such feedback.

In the case where a number of subordinates have been interviewed, some of the comments they make will deal with their reactions to the boss's behavior. If the superior has agreed beforehand to listen to the others' reactions, it is quite appropriate for the consultant to describe the range of comments to him and to assist in interpreting the comments. If the consultant feels that the manager is interested and shows a readiness to listen and learn, it is entirely appropriate for the consultant to share these observations.

In order for feedback to be effective, the consultant must be able to ask the right questions, observe the relevant behavioral events, and give the feedback in a manner that will facilitate learning on the part of the recipient. The behavior asked about or observed must be relevant to the task performance of the group and to the goals of the total consultation project. The manner in which the feedback is given must reflect sensitivity to the blind spots or areas of defensiveness of the recipient. Feedback must be concrete, descriptive, verifiable, timely, and specific.

The consultant must be prepared for defensiveness or too facile verbal acceptance, both of which imply a denial of the feedback. He must know how to impart potentially threatening information without demeaning the recipient. As I think back over my various consulting experiences, unquestionably the ones with the most disastrous results were those where I fed back "facts" without any concern for the feelings of the recipient. The facts were then denied, and I was politely but firmly invited to terminate the relationship.

The giving of individual feedback can be illustrated from several cases. In the Apex Manufacturing Company I met with each of the vice presidents whose groups had been interviewed and gave them a list of comments that had been made about their respective managerial styles. I knew each man well and felt that he would be able to accept the kinds of comments that were made. In each case we scheduled at least a one-hour session so we could talk in detail about any items that were unclear and/or threatening.

These discussions usually become counseling sessions to help the individual overcome some of the negative effects that were implied in the feedback data. Since I knew that I would be having sessions such as these, I urged each interviewee to talk at length about the style of his boss and what he did or did not like about it. In cases where the boss was an effective manager, I found a tendency for subordinates to make only a few vague generalizations that I knew would be useless as feedback. By probing for specific incidents or descriptions, it was possible to identify just what the boss did that subordinates liked or did not like.

In the Delta Manufacturing Company I was invited by the division manager to observe and comment on the regular staff meetings. In addition I held discussions periodically with the manager and was invited to comment on any aspects of his behavior that I had observed. He had formulated fairly specific goals for his meeting and was interested in the degree to which he was meeting those goals in his role as chairman. He asked for feedback from group members at the end of meetings but also sought my observations.

In the workshops run for the Central Chemical Company, I concentrated primarily on the co-trainer, the member of the company who was working with me but wanted to learn how to run workshops like these on his own. After each session I would give him feedback on his participation in it and, incidentally, solicit his feedback on my participation. As we learned to reciprocate with our observations, the feedback process became more meaningful to both of us.

As a rule I do not hesitate to ask members of the client organization to give me feedback on my own behavior as a consultant. Although they are usually reluctant to do so early in the relationship, I find that as we get to know each other they become comfortable in telling me where I was effective or ineffective with them or with others. The ability to give me feedback in the two-person setting is, of course, an important skill that should transfer as an ability to be more open and direct with others in authority positions. The ability to give me feedback is also an important indicator of how well the problem of dependence on the consultant has been solved.

Summary

A major category of confrontive interventions that are designed to influence process are the various kinds of feedback that the process consultant gives to individuals or groups, or that they give to each other with the aid of processes designed in part by the consultant. The most important issue in deciding whether and when to engage in such feedback processes is how ready the group or individual is to deal with feedback, and how much the client has been involved in the decision to get some feedback. It rarely works out for the process consultant to decide unilaterally to give feedback, even though he may have observed events that are dramatic in their learning potential.

15

Coaching, Counseling, and Structural Suggestions

The last two categories of confrontive intervention are coaching/counseling and structural suggestions. As was stated before, I find these to be relatively rare compared to the other categories discussed, and they are in principle more powerful. It is therefore all the more important either that the client have a voice in when these types of interventions are made, or that the consultant take great care to ensure that the client is ready for them if he makes them unilaterally.

Coaching or Counseling

The giving of feedback to individuals or to groups almost invariably leads to coaching or counseling sessions. The manger may learn that he somehow fails to hear certain members of the group, that he does not give enough recognition for good performance, or that he is too unapproachable when the subordinate needs help. Inevitably his next question is "How can I change my behavior to achieve better results?" Similarly, a group may learn that its members see the meetings as dull or unfruitful; inevitably the members then ask, "How can we make our meetings more interesting and productive?"

There are two cautions that the consultant must keep uppermost in his mind before answering the above questions:

1. Don't respond until you are sure that the group (or individual) has really understood the feedback and has been able to relate it to concrete observable behavior.
2. Don't respond until you are sure that the group member (or manager) has begun an active process of trying to solve the problem for himself.

If the consultant is not sure on point 1, he should continue to ask such questions as "What does that comment mean to you in terms of how you see yourself?" "Can you think of anything you do that might give people that impression?" Or "What do you think the giver of the comment was trying to get across to you?"

If the consultant is not sure on point 2, he can ask such questions as "Do you see anything in your own behavior that you could change?" "What might you do differently to create a different reaction?" Or "Do you really want to change your behavior?"

If the consultant receives a response like "I'm paying *you* to give me advice," he must reassess the state of the relationship and the readiness of the recipient of the feedback to work on the problem area. If the feedback has been sincerely sought and has been understood, most likely the recipient will have ideas and share these with the consultant. The consultant's role then becomes one of adding alternatives to those already brought up by the client and helping the client to analyze the costs and benefits of the various alternatives that have been mentioned.

I do not wish in this short volume to go into the theory and practice of counseling, but I do wish to underline the basic congruence between theories of counseling and the theory of process consultation that I am presenting here. In both cases it is essential to help the client improve his ability to observe and process data about himself, to help him accept and learn from feedback, and to help him become an active participant with the counselor/consultant in identifying and solving his own problems.

In all of the companies with which I have worked, there have arisen multiple opportunities to coach and counsel individuals or groups. There does not seem to be any particular pattern of timing to such sessions. Rather, I have had to be ready to sit down with people when *they* were ready to examine some of their own behavior and consider alternatives.

The major difference between being only a counselor and being a process consultant has been the fact that my data gathering has given me information and perspectives that a counselor often does not have. I have usually observed my client in action and heard what other people have said about him. This additional knowledge, when fed into the counseling sessions, enriches the choice of alternatives that can be considered and opens up many of the problem areas to more concrete discussion.

For example, I have spent some hours with a manager who sees himself as a very progressive force in a rather conservative organization. My observations, and what others say about him, would suggest that he himself is rather conservative in his behavior. His *ideas* are progressive, but his actual behavior tends to be stultifying to others. Our individual sessions are most productive when we can examine his self-image against what others say and what I have observed. As this manager learned to view his conservatism in action, he realized that he undermines some of his own progressive ideas. This realization has led to some marked changes of behavior and an increase in his effectiveness.

There is a close similarity between interventions that draw the group's attention to certain kinds of process issues and what I choose to call counseling (or coaching) types of interventions. One of the most common opportunities to coach or counsel is to intervene when a particular event has occurred that is typical of some problem the group is trying to overcome. At these times the consultant can be most effective by pointing out what has just occurred and inviting the group to examine the consequences. He is giving feedback at a timely moment in order to help the group to become more effective.

Case Examples

The first case illustrates both the issue of feedback and how that leads to counseling. In one company's executive committee meetings I noticed that the group seemed to have low confidence in one of its members, the marketing manager. This lack of confidence was evident in the degree to which others ignored him, argued with him, and denigrated him outside the meetings. Every time this man attempted to explain any of his actions, decisions, or plans in the meetings, one of the more aggressive members would interrupt him and either answer for him or elaborate on what he thought the marketing manager had said.

The group seemed to expect this person to be weak and passive, and confirmed their expectation by preventing him from being anything else. I decided to intervene at the point where the behavior was most visible (just after the marketing manager had been ignored or interrupted on some issue) and tell the group that I observed the pattern repeatedly (confrontive feedback).

The group then expressed some interest in hearing whether the marketing manager did indeed feel cut off. He expressed some rather strong feelings confirming my observations. Once these feelings were known to the other members, they began to listen more attentively to him. As they did so, they discovered that he had a lot to contribute and was anything but "weak" and "fuzzy-headed," as they had believed. Group members then began to trust his decisions more and became more comfortable in delegating authority to him.

After each meeting both the chairman of the group and the marketing manager asked to see me privately. The chairman wanted me to advise him on how he could run the meeting better so that this kind of thing would not happen again, and to give him feedback after each meeting on how he was doing as a chairman.

The marketing manager asked me how he could learn to be more assertive and not collude with the aggressive members by allowing himself to be shut down. In both cases I set up a series of meetings right after the formal meeting to counsel each of these managers (note that the agenda for the counseling was their own).

In another group, the difficulty was initially related to the manner in which the boss of the group interacted with the members. The boss wanted the group members to be strong, self-reliant, confident decision makers. He said this explicitly and his behavior implied it. I observed on repeated occasions that if any group member showed weakness in any form (not knowing what he wanted, having unclear plans, being unable to answer a critical question from another member), the head of the group would become angry and belabor the person for many minutes on end. The more the head of the group pressed, the more silent, embarrassed, and unsure the target person became.

In talking to such persons later, I often found that the only feeling they sensed in the head of the group was blind anger, and this made them so defensive that they could not hear what he really wanted of them. In each such conversation I found myself counseling the individual member to try to listen for the feelings other than anger. For example, I wondered whether the boss was anxious that things were out of control and that this showed up as anger. I urged members to try to reassure the boss rather than to defend themselves.

On several occasions I tried to interrupt the process in midstream and collect feelings both from the person being belabored and from other members of the group (agenda managing and controlling). In addition I gave direct feedback to the group head, both in front of the group and later privately, concerning the impact his behavior was having *on me*. I expressed puzzlement and asked the boss what he was actually feeling, and advised him to try to be more accurate in communicating what he really felt.

This led to some self-analysis on his part and the request to have me counsel him between meetings. His behavior in the group gradually shifted away from communication of anger toward communication of anxiety and disappointment, which in turn made it possible for the group to home in on the issue that was really bothering them.

Finally, I had occasion to attend one of the group meetings when the boss was absent. The group used the opportunity to inquire what I thought they should do in managing their boss's feelings better, and I found myself in a counseling role to the entire group. We then spent over an hour analyzing what was going on, examining options, and deciding how to behave differently in the future, with my role being primarily that of a coach.

Structural Suggestions

As I indicated at the outset of this chapter, this kind of intervention is rare, largely because it violates some of the basic assumptions of the PC model. The consultant is rarely in a position to suggest how work should be allocated, or how communication patterns should be altered, or how committees should be organized. The most he can do is help the manager to assess the consequences of different alternatives or suggest alternatives that have not been considered.

For example, when the Apex Manufacturing Company went from a functional to a product-line organization, I noticed that communication among the functional people (for example, in marketing and engineering) decreased markedly. During group meetings there were complaints and some recriminations about the possible error of having reorganized.

My intervention was designed to draw attention to the fact that *any* form of organization has both strengths and weaknesses. Hence the manager needs to make an effort to create informal structures to compensate for the weaknesses created by the formal structure. I embodied this point in a short memo (see Appendix B) and asked for time on the agenda to discuss the point.

The company eventually adopted a committee structure that brought the functional specialists together on a regular basis and thus reduced the communication gap that had resulted from the reorganization.

The consultant must make it quite clear that he does not propose any particular solution as the best one. However frustrating it might be to the client, the consultant must work to create a situation where the client's ability to generate his own solutions is enhanced. The consultant wants to increase problem-solving ability, not to solve any particular problem.

In my experience there has been only one class of exceptions to the above "rule." If the client wants to set up some meetings specifically for the purpose of working on organizational or interpersonal problems, or wants to design a data-gathering method, then the consultant indeed does have some relevant expertise that he should bring to bear. From his own experience he knows better than the client the pros and cons of interviews or questionnaires; he knows better what questions to ask, how to organize the data, and how to organize feedback meetings; he knows better the right sequence of events leading up to a good discussion of interpersonal process in a committee. In such matters, therefore, I am quite direct and positive in suggesting procedures, who should be involved in them, who should be told what, and how the whole project should be handled.

For example, recall that in the Apex Manufacturing Company the president decided at one of their all-day meetings to try to give feedback to all the members. He asked me to suggest a procedure for doing this. In this instance I was not at all reluctant to suggest, with as much force and logic as I could command, a particular procedure that I thought would work well. Similarly, when it was proposed to interview all the members of a department, I suggested exactly how this procedure should be set up. I explained that all the members had to be briefed by the department manager, that a group feedback meeting would have to be held, and so on. I have not been at all hesitant to refuse to design a questionnaire study if I thought it was inappropriate, or to suggest canceling a meeting on interpersonal process if I thought the group was not ready.

In conclusion, the process consultant should not withhold his expertise on matters of the learning process itself; but he should be very careful not to confuse being an expert on *how to help an organization to learn* with being an expert on the *actual management problems* that the organization is trying to solve. The same logic applies to the evaluation of individuals: I will under no circumstances evaluate an individual's ability to manage or solve work-related problems; but I will evaluate an individual's readiness to participate in an interview survey of his group or a feedback meeting. If I feel that his presence might undermine some other goals that the organization is trying to accomplish, I will seek to find a solution that will bypass this individual. These are often difficult judgments to make, but the process consultant cannot evade them if he defines the *overall health of the organization* as his basic target. However, he must always attempt to be fair to both the individual and the organization. If no course of action can be found without hurting either, then the whole project should probably be postponed.

I can give two further examples of structural interventions. In Company G, not previously referred to, I have worked for some time with a member of the corporate management-development group. I have functioned primarily as an adviser, counselor, and sounding board on various programs being developed by the group. The organization does not have major aspirations in the organizational development direction, although there is a growing interest in this kind of activity. Sometime last year, the inside manager was requested to consider a training program for all of the key marketing people in the various divisions of the company.

I was called in to help design this program and to function as a staff member in it. My responsibilities included the recruiting of another staff member, helping members of management formulate their hopes and needs for the program, and then helping to design the actual program. This required a shift in my role from process consultant to an expert resource on the design and execution of a management-training program.

In my relationship with Company G, I find myself making this switch from time to time. The role switching works because I have worked with this client company for a number of years and the client contact is himself comfortable in playing and adapting to different roles in the relationship. The primary contact also functions as a point of communication with other groups in the organization where process consultation is needed from time to time. For example, I have worked with a sales group in one of the divisions of the company on an interview-feedback project, in determining how the members of the operating sales force in one region were viewing their job and in helping management to reassess the overall style of operation in the sales function.

The second example comes from the Boyd Consumer Goods Company. My primary work in this organization was to meet with the top-management group and to counsel individual members of the group. Last year I was asked by the personnel director to become involved in the annual manpower survey and to help the organization design a more coherent overall approach to management development. To accomplish this task I asked to be a part of the manpower committee. During the meetings I attempted to assess the needs of the organization and the kind of program that would meet these needs. In doing this I was beginning to shift toward being an expert resource and abandoning the process consultant role.

It seemed to me, as I listened to the discussions, that the group would fall short of generating a clear concept of a program in the time it had allotted for itself; hence I intervened structurally and suggested a multicomponent program of self-development, systematic use of internal and external training, and a revision of policies of recruiting and utilizing people in the organization. All of the points were extrapolations of what members of the committee wanted to do, but I put them together into a total framework and made some effort to "sell" it to the group. The group adopted the program and made a proposal of it to other members of management and the board.

In looking back on this intervention, I have wondered whether the structural nature of it was indeed warranted and whether my own goals were truly accomplished. There is some evidence that the program has been bought in principle and that everyone agrees to it intellectually, but there has been relatively little move to implement it. At least one possibility as to why it has not been more systematically implemented is that I went too far beyond the group with my intervention — somehow the group lost ownership of the program and hence felt no real commitment to implement it. If this hypothesis is correct, it illustrates nicely the fine line between process and expert consultation and the inherent dangers of structural interventions.

Summary

In the past several chapters I have tried to draw attention to the varieties of intervention that the process consultant uses.

I hope it is clear to the reader that the essence of the PC model is to continuously rediagnose and to act accordingly. Therefore, one cannot specify particular recipes for intervention or particular sequences that should be used in any given project. A sequence that may work in Company A may be all wrong in Company B. Instead, the consultant must be ready to intervene in a variety of ways as opportunities arise and as his judgment tells him certain actions are appropriate. He must be flexible enough to take advantage of opportunities based on his own judgments.

The following are kinds of intervention that were reviewed:

1. Agenda managing through questions, through process-analysis periods, through meetings devoted to interpersonal and group process, and through theory inputs on various process issues.
2. Various kinds of feedback sessions to individuals or groups, based either on observed data or on data obtained in interviews.
3. Coaching or counseling, which occurs either in specific sessions devoted to that purpose or as part of an ongoing interaction in a group.
4. Structural suggestions pertaining to process-oriented meetings or other parts of the consultation project.

A more refined analysis of intervention types can be found in volume 2 of *Process Consultation* (1987).

16

Evaluation of Results and Disengagement

So far in this book we have examined in some detail the thinking and activities of a process consultant. We have not concentrated on the big picture: what kinds of outcome or result does the process consultant look for over a period of time, how does he measure these outcomes, and how does he decide at some point to reduce his involvement with the client system?

These questions are not easy to answer because the goals of PC cannot be stated in simple measurable terms. The ultimate goal of any organization-development effort is, of course, improved organizational performance. Organization-development efforts as I have defined them always involve activities that are carried out with the philosophy and attitudes of PC and, therefore, one would expect to achieve effectiveness by changing some of the *values* of the organization and by increasing the *task and interpersonal process skills* of key managers. Performance is, in turn, related to these value changes and increases of skill. In the short run, then, the consultant looks for evidence that certain values are changing and that certain skills are increasing.

Values to Be Changed
Through Process Consultation

Task Versus Interpersonal Concern

The single most important value to be changed in any OD effort concerns the relative attention given to task versus human concerns. Most managers start with the value that the most important concerns of management are efficient task performance primarily, and human relations secondarily (or as time permits). The problem for the process consultant is to change this value — make the manager feel that human relations and the management of interpersonal and group events are at least as important as immediate task performance.

The logic behind this value is that for the manager his task can be accomplished only through other people; hence effective interpersonal relations become a prime means to the end of efficient task performance. Organizations in the end are nothing more than networks of human relationships. If these networks do not function effectively, there is nothing with which to perform the tasks to be accomplished.

Content Versus Process Focus

A second value that has to be changed in any OD effort concerns the relative attention given to the content of the work and the structure of the organization versus the process by which work is done and the structure of that process. Managers tend to focus much more on the content of decisions, interactions, and communications. They tend to devalue the importance of "personality," of "feelings," and of "how things are done," or they attempt to dodge such process-related issues by perpetual redesign of the formal structure of the organization.

The process consultant faces the problem of showing managers that processes in the organization follow patterns that can be studied and understood, and that have important consequences for organizational performance. Most important, processes can be rationally changed and adapted to increase the effectiveness of performance. Therefore, one should attempt to improve the organization through a joint consideration of the content and formal structure, on the one hand, and of the processes of the organization, on the other hand.

Short-run Output Versus Long-range Effectiveness

A third value concerns the relative attention given to short-run output versus long-range effectiveness. Most managers feel that every hour of every day should be occupied with activities that have an immediate output. The process consultant knows from his experience that the diagnosis of process events often involves periods of slow and calm analysis that may at first appear to be a terrible waste of time. He must change the manager's value system so that he becomes tolerant of such periods, realizing that the time invested in building effective task processes and interpersonal relations leads to much quicker and more effective ultimate task performance.

Instant Solutions Versus Perpetual Rediagnosis

A fourth value that the process consultant must inculcate is the acceptance of the need for perpetual diagnosis as an alternative to insistence on instant solutions or generalizations and principles by which to operate. I assume that the rate of change in the environment (and, therefore, within organizations) will increase, and that this in turn will require an increase in the organization's ability to diagnose both the environment and itself. A principle that holds up for the next six months may be invalid within a year.

The manager must accept perpetual diagnosis of process as a way of life if he is to avoid obsolescence and organizational failure. Ideally, the manager would not merely accept this value grudgingly but would discover that perpetual diagnosis can be fun and lead to perpetually better day-to-day task performance. I am not advocating what so many managers seem to fear — that if they do too much diagnosis they will be unable to be decisive when an occasion demands it. I am advocating that decisions be made, within the time constraints imposed by the task requirements, but that they be made in terms of a *diagnosis*, however short, rather than a policy or general principle that may no longer have any validity.

In summary, the process consultant attempts to change the manager's attitudes and values in the direction of more concern for human problems, process issues, long-run effectiveness, and the diagnostic process itself as a way of achieving organizational adaptability. By implication, one major way to assess the results of a PC effort is to gauge the degree to which these values have taken hold in key managers. Such an assessment cannot be made formally or through some kind of specific measuring tool. It must be made by the consultant through observation of the activities of managers in the organization, or by the managers themselves.

Skills to Be Learned

As I have been repeating throughout this volume, the most important skill to be imparted to the client is the *ability to diagnose and work on his own problems in the task, interpersonal, group, and organizational area.* Initially the process consultant has more knowledge and skill than the client. As the PC effort progresses, he should be able to observe an increase in the knowlege and skill of the various managers who have been involved.

One of the best indicators of the growth of such skills is the willingness of various groups or teams to tackle process-analysis periods or agenda-review periods by themselves. How willing are they to assign an observer role, and how skillful are they in picking out key group events, in sharing feelings, in reviewing group action?

It should be clear that a willingness to engage in activities that initially have been the consultant's reflects a change in values. Even if a given manager were able to engage in more self-diagnostic processes, he might resist such an activity if none of the values cited above had changed. On the other hand, willingness reflecting a value change is not enough if there has not been a corresponding development of skill.

The assessment of the skill of the client system in diagnosing and working on its own problems must, as in the case of values, be made by observations on the part of the consultant and/or by the client system itself. It is important that managers feel confident in solving their own problems, and solving them effectively. Even if the consultant doubts that the level of skill reached is sufficient, he must be prepared to back off if members of the client system themselves feel they are able to go ahead without his help.

Case Examples

In the Apex Manufacturing Company, considerable value change and skill growth occurred over the course of the first year. During this period I spent a great deal of time in two major activities: (1) sitting in on various meetings of the top-management group, and (2) conducting interview and feedback surveys of various key groups, as managers decided they wanted such interviews done. In addition there were periods of individual counseling, usually resulting from data revealed in the interviews.

I have already given examples of the kinds of specific activities that occurred in the group meetings, interviews, and feedback sessions. It was clear that with increasing experience, the group was learning to tune in to its own internal processes (skill), was beginning to pay more attention to these and to give over more meeting time to analysis of interpersonal feelings and events (value change), and was able to manage its own agenda and do its diagnosis without my presence (skill).

The group first discovered this from having to conduct some of its all-day meetings in my absence. Where such meetings used to be devoted entirely to work content, the group found that even in my absence they could discuss task and interpersonal process with profit. The members themselves described this change as one of "climate." The group felt more open and effective; members felt they could trust each other more; information was flowing more freely; less time was being wasted on oblique communications or political infighting.

During the second year, my involvement was considerably reduced, although I worked on some specific projects. The company had set up a committee to develop a management-development program. I was asked to sit in with this committee and help in the development of a program. After a number of meetings, it became clear to me that the kind of program the group needed was one in which the content was not too heavily predetermined. The problems of different managers were sufficiently different to require that a formula be found for discussing the whole range of problems.

One of the reflections of the value change that had taken place in the managers was their recognition that they should be prime participants in any program they might invent. If a program was not exciting or beneficial enough to warrant the committee's time, it could hardly be imposed on the rest of the organization.

We developed a model that involved a series of small-group meetings at each of which the group would set its own agenda. After every third meeting or so, a larger management group would be convened for a lecture and discussion period on some highly relevant topic. Once the first group (the committee plus others at the vice president level) had completed six to eight meetings, each member of the original group would become the chairman for a group at the next lower level of the organization. These ten or so next-level groups would then meet for six to eight sessions around agenda items developed by themselves. In the meantime the lecture series would continue. After each series of meetings at a given organizational level, the model would be reassessed and either changed or continued at the next lower level with the previous members again becoming group chairmen.

My role in this whole enterprise was, first, to help the group to invent the idea; second, to meet with the original group as a facilitator of the group's efforts to become productive; third, to serve as a resource on topics to be covered and lecturers to be used in the lecture series; and fourth, to appear as an occasional lecturer in the lecture series or as a source of input at a small-group meeting. As this procedure took form, my involvement was gradually reduced, although I still meet with the original committee to review the overall concept.

In subsequent months I met occasionally with individual members of the original group and with the group as a whole. My function during these meetings was to be a sounding board, to contribute points of view that might not have been represented among the members, and to help the group assess its own level of functioning. I was able to provide the group with some perspective on its own growth as a group because I could more easily see changes in values and skills.

It has also been possible for the group to enlist my help with specific interpersonal problems. A measure of the growth of the group has been its ability to decide when and how to use my help, and to make those decisions validly from my point of view in terms of where I felt I could constructively help. This relationship of being called in from time to time as new issues arose continued for many years, and I considered my work with this organization to have been generally successful in terms of getting values and skills across.

In the Boyd Consumer Goods Company, my participation was initially similar, but for a variety of reasons changes in the organization occurred much more slowly. The top-management group accepted many of the values at an intellectual level but has not really committed itself to trying to make them work. Some members of the group have worked much harder at this than others. At the level of skill development, the group has experimented with a variety of techniques, such as having a member of the group be an observer and then report back. These activities have had a noticeable (although not a great) impact.

Part of the problem in this company is that they have had to fight a number of traditions that are, in varying degrees, out of line with the kinds of values I espoused. They have also faced a number of crises that required immediate action and that eroded efforts to concentrate on increasing diagnostic and interpersonal skills. This case illustrates that if the basic culture of the organization involves assumptions that are out of line with the values underlying PC, it is difficult to achieve clear-cut changes. For the culture itself to change, a more intensive organization change program would have had to be launched (Schein, 1985).

Over a period of months I continued to meet both with individuals and with the group as a whole. My activities involved counseling members of the group and keeping a gentle but firm pressure on members of the system to become more open, trusting, and, thereby, effective. Recently the group decided on its own to hold a two-day meeting at which some strong personal feelings were shared by members of the group. Although the experience was traumatic for one or two members, the feeling of most was that it had been constructive and they looked forward to more of the same at some later time. My role in the meantime was to help them to understand the emotional experience they had been through and show them how to turn it into a constructive experience. After some months our contact was reduced, and I have since lost touch with what is going on. In looking back on this experience, I feel that not much was accomplished, given the amount of effort, but the group could move only as fast as its culture would allow.

In the Central Chemical Company, I worked in a more discrete fashion around projects that were scheduled well in advance and that were evaluated right after each workshop by the inside consultant and me. The initial workshops were done within a single division, and the decision whether to continue depended on whether other divisions would decide to hold some kind of planned change activity. Two other divisions decided to go ahead, so I became involved in planning, executing, and evaluating these particular programs while periodically visiting with the corporate inside consultants on overall strategy.

When the workshops were over some several years later the emphasis in the overall effort shifted to more use of inside consultants, so my work was terminated. The overall effort was considered to be highly successful in that it got a process started that could then be taken over by internal resources, but a great deal of change had been accomplished already by the externally influenced workshops.

In the Delta Manufacturing Company, I found the key group to be from the start relatively high in its acceptance of OD values and in its level of skill. After a dozen or so meetings the group and I reviewed the project and decided that for the moment nothing more was needed.

As problems developed, the group would resume contact with me. Some months later the group had to be expanded because the whole division that was involved was to be expanded. With the expansion came some potential new problems. Because the diagnostic skill of the group was already high, I was called in again to make some plans for a longer meeting at which some of the new problems would be explored in depth.

I continued to work sporadically with this organization for a number of years, always with a sense of effectiveness because they had learned when and how to use external help.

Conclusion

Process consultation is an emergent process. To put simple boundaries on it would be difficult. Similarly, it is difficult to give overall evaluations. One can look at gradual changes that occur in the culture of the client organization; one can look at the results of specific projects, such as an interview-feedback cycle; and one can assess the immediate impact of an intervention in a group. But one cannot measure specific indicators, however, much this might be desirable. In the end, the outcome of a period of PC must be judged jointly by members of the client system and the consultant. Both must make a judgment of whether to continue the relationship and in what manner to continue it.

If, in the judgment of either party, there should be a reduction of involvement, how is this process accomplished?

Disengagement: Reducing Involvement with the Client System

The process of disengagement has, in most of my experiences, been characterized by the following features:

1. Reduced involvement is a mutually agreed upon decision rather than a unilateral decision by consultant or client.
2. Involvement does not generally drop to zero but may continue at a very low level.
3. The door is always open from my point of view for further work with the client if the client desires it.

I would like to comment on each of these points, and give some examples.

1. Joint Decisions

In most of my consulting relationships there has come a time when either I felt that nothing more could be accomplished and/or some members of the client system felt the need to continue on their own. To facilitate a reduction of involvement, I usually check at intervals of several months to see whether the client feels that the pattern should remain as is or should be altered.

In some cases where I have felt that a sufficient amount had been accomplished, I have found that the client did not feel the same way and wanted the relationship to continue on a one-day-per-week basis. In other cases I have been confronted by the client, as in the Apex Manufacturing Company, with the statement that my continued attendance in the operational group meetings was no longer desirable from their point of view. As the president put it, I was beginning to sound too much like a regular member to be of much use. I concurred in the decision and reduced my involvement to periodic all-day meetings of the group, although the initiative for inviting me remained entirely with the group. Had I not concurred, we would have negotiated until a mutually satisfactory arrangement had been agreed on.

I have sometimes been in the situation of arguing that I remain fully involved even when the client wanted to reduce involvement, and in many cases I was able to obtain the client's concurrence. I have also been involved frequently in arguing for a reduction of involvement either because I felt that nothing more could be accomplished or that the client was becoming too dependent on me.

The negotiation that surrounds a reduction of involvement is, in fact, a good opportunity for the consultant to diagnose the state of the client system. The kinds of arguments that are brought up in support of continuing (or terminating) provide a solid basis for determining how much value and skill change has occurred.

The reader may feel that since the client is paying for services, he certainly has the right to make unilateral decisions about whether to continue the services. My point is that if the consultation process has even partially achieved its goals, there should develop sufficient trust between consultant and client to enable both to make the decision on rational grounds. Here again, it is important that the consultant not be economically dependent on any one client, or his own diagnostic ability may become biased by his need to continue to earn fees.

2. Involvement Not Zero

If the client and consultant agree on a reduced involvement, both should recognize that this does not necessarily mean a complete termination. In fact, a complete termination is not desirable because the diagnosis on which reduced involvement is based may not be accurate enough to warrant termination. A more desirable arrangement is to drop the level to perhaps a half day every three or four weeks, or attendance only at certain kinds of special meetings, or an interview with key members of the client system once every two or three months. Through this mechanism the client and the consultant can reassess periodically how things are going.

In the Boyd Consumer Goods Company, there was a period where I felt that a plateau had been reached. At this point I suggested that I reduce my involvement to a half day every other week, and even then only if specific individuals wanted to have some time to talk over problems with me. After a few months at this reduced level, a number of events made it more important than ever for the top-management group to increase their level of effectiveness. The group decided to have more meetings and asked me to become reinvolved at an increased level. This decision was much easier to negotiate from a reduced involvement than it would have been from a situation where I had terminated the relationship completely.

In my relationship with the Apex and Fairview companies, there were long periods where I did not pay any visits, but it was understood that as problems or issues came up the client was free to call on me with the expectation that I would respond positively. The only problem with this kind of arrangement is that it becomes difficult for the consultant to plan his time. Obviously, if several clients decide to increase their involvement all at the same time, it may be impossible for the consultant to respond. If this occurs, the consultant has to be open about his dilemma and determine from the various clients whether they can wait for a month or so. I have found from experience that I can carry about four clients at any given time, with two of them being more active (one half day every week), while two others are dormant (an occasional visit every three weeks to a month).

3. Reinvolvement Is Always Possible

This point is closely related to the previous one, but I want to separate it to bring out a special aspect of the obligation of the process consultant. In any process consulting relationship with a client, I think the consultant should make it clear that the door is always open to further work once the relationship has begun. The reason for this obligation is that a good relationship with a consultant is difficult for a client to develop. Once both the consultant and the client have invested effort in building such a relationship, it does not terminate psychologically even if there are prolonged periods of no contact. I have had the experience with a number of clients of not seeing them for many months and yet being able to tune in on the group very quickly once contact has been reestablished.

As a general rule it should be the client who reestablishes contact, but I would not advocate sticking to this rigidly. I have, after some period of no contact, called a client and asked if I could talk with him to find out what was going on. In several cases such a call was welcomed and served as the basis for some additional counseling or process observation. The consultant must be careful not to violate his role by selling himself back to the client. It must be an honest inquiry that can comfortably be turned down by the client should he desire to do so. I have been turned down often enough to know that there is nothing inherent in the situation to force an artificial contact. Rather, it sometimes helps a client who wanted help anyway to ask for it in a face-saving way.

Summary

I have spelled out several values and skills that the process consultant desires to pass on to the client system. The values are a more balanced concern for human issues along with task issues, process along with content, long-range effectiveness along with short-run efficiency, and perpetual diagnosis along with seeking rules, principles, and generalizations.

In the skill area it is primarily the ability to diagnose and work on task and interpersonal processes that is crucial, in that the ultimate goal of PC is for the client to be able to recognize and solve his own problems.

Evaluation of progress can be judged by both the consultant and the client, but since PC is an emergent unpredictable process, evaluation itself becomes a perpetual activity rather than a set activity or stage.

If either the consultant or the client feels that involvement should be reduced, a process of disengagement is desirable, but the reduced involvement should be jointly decided, should not be psychologically permanent, and should allow for either the consultant or the client to feel free to call for the consultant's reinvolvement.

17

Process Consultation in Perspective

Why Process Consultation?

This book will, I hope, serve several purposes. First, I want to introduce a model of the consultation process that I believe describes what the typical consultant does (or should do) in an organization-development effort. Many of the volumes written on OD give an overview of the OD effort but do not give a detailed view of the consultant's day-to-day operation. This revised volume 1 with the more detailed and elaborated volume 2 should provide the kind of detail that is often missing.

Second, I want to explain as clearly as I can what has gone on between me as a consultant and a number of clients I have had over the years. I have found that some of my colleagues have entertained some remarkable misconceptions about what I do when I visit a company. I want to clear away some of these misconceptions.

Third, I want to contribute to the general theory of organizational consultation by illustrating clearly one style of working with an organization. In view of the increasing amount of research and consultation in complex organizations, it is important to know clearly what one is doing. I hope I have clarified some of the issues by laying out the concept of process consultation.

I should like to close this volume by making a few general comments about process consultation in relation to other kinds of activities, as a way of giving some perspective to this procedure. Process consultation, first of all, is *a way of studying organizations.* I believe very much in Lewin's dictum: "If you want to understand something, try to change it." Much of the consultant's satisfaction comes from the combination of exercising diagnostic and intervention skills while being constantly exposed to organizational process from which one learns what goes on in organizations. This exposure has enriched and sharpened my teaching and research skills and has led me to attempt to articulate this way of clinically studying an organization (Schein, 1987b).

As I mentioned in my original preface, one of my colleagues once asked me why I "wasted" time teaching managers elementary psychology when I could be doing research that would influence thousands. The first answer is that PC is anything but the teaching of elementary psychology. For me it is a complex process of producing changes in the organization that are not achievable by any amount of good writing. The change process is one not merely of transmitting ideas but of changing values and of teaching skills. I derive far more satisfaction from improving an organization's effectiveness than I would from teaching a few managers some psychology that they might not know how to apply anyway.

The second answer is that research done on organizations by people who do not get close to organizational processes has, to me, a kind of unreal quality about it — unreal because in focusing on concepts that are so far removed from the immediate experiences of members of the organization, one does not know how to generalize from the results. On the other hand, the kind of diagnosis that occurs when one conducts a series of interviews or observes groups in action brings organizational phenomena to life. For me consultation has been one important way to do research.

The third, and perhaps most important, answer is that my

teaching would be sterile without the kind of "feel" one gets from close contact with organizations. I could, of course, periodically immerse myself completely by taking a job in an organization. Apart from the fact that I would not like the dislocation involved, I am not sure that such a complete transition is necessary to get the kind of feel I am talking about.

Does Process Consultation Have Analogues?

The process consultant often operates in organizations in much the same way as a general practitioner does in medicine; he is, in a sense, an organizational internist and often an organizational psychiatrist. The analogy holds if one thinks of the consultant as helping the organization to arrive at a diagnosis before deciding on some specialized treatment. The analogy breaks down, however, if one considers that the internist is the prime expert in the diagnosis. He runs tests, asks questions, pokes about, and then delivers a diagnosis and advice. The process consultant, in contrast, attempts to involve the organization in self-diagnosis and enables the organization to give itself sound advice.

A better analogy is to think of the process consultant as a sociotherapist for a system that varies in size and composition from time to time. The concepts of "diagnosis" and "helpful intervention" derive directly from concepts of therapy, especially small-group therapy or training. The major difference between helping a group and consulting for an organization lies in the complexity of the task.

To be an effective process consultant, the person needs diagnostic and intervention skills that are quite different from those used in training or therapy groups. The consultant does not have the environmental supports of a training or therapy setting; he cannot count on the intensive involvement that training groups generate; he cannot even assume a commitment to learning comparable to that of patients or trainees. Through his own interventions, from an ambiguous power base, and in the midst of ongoing work, he must build involvement and commitment, and gain acceptance for the importance of looking at process.

The sociotherapist model suggests itself if one considers

that the consultant is primarily dedicated to helping the system help itself in terms of whatever pathology he may find there. Once an initial contract has been established, the consultant must be prepared to work with whatever he finds, and he must, like the individual therapist, be very careful not to suggest things that will be resisted and not to fall into the trap of thinking he is an expert on that particular organization. All he is expert at is giving help. On the other hand, the sociotherapist model also has limitations in that it suggests pathology. In my experience it is the healthy organization that knows enough to expose itself to help now in order to ensure even greater health in the future. Sick organizations tend to resist help and, alas, PC has no better chance of being introduced in such organizations than any other kind of help.

As a final thought, I would like once again to contrast PC with more standard kinds of consultation models. The standard model is one in which the consultant gives expert advice on how to solve a particular problem that the organization has identified: how to improve production scheduling, how to determine costs, how to obtain marketing information, how to increase productivity, how to select and train certain kinds of personnel, and so on. Even if initial work with the consultant leads to a redefinition of the problem, the consultant's task remains the same: to help develop an expert solution.

The process model, in contrast, starts with the assumption that the organization knows how to solve its particular problems or knows how to get help in solving them, but that it often does not know how to use its own resources effectively either in initial problem formulation or in implementation of solutions. The process model further assumes that inadequate use of internal resources or ineffective implementation result from process problems. By this I mean that people fail to communicate effectively with each other, or develop mistrust, or engage in destructive competition, or punish things that they mean to reward and vice versa, or fail to give feedback, and so on.

The job of the process consultant is to help the organization to solve its own problems by making it aware of organizational processes, the consequences of these processes, and the mechanisms by which they can be changed. The process consultant helps the organization to learn from self-diagnosis and self-intervention. The ultimate concern of the process consultant is the organization's capacity to do for itself what he has done for it. Where the standard consultant is more concerned about passing on his knowledge, the process consultant is concerned about passing on his skills and values.

Appendix A:
Memo I Some Comments on Internal Auditing and Control Programs

A. Some Ideas Why Internal Auditing Is Seen As Nonhelpful or As a Source of Tension:

1. Auditors often feel primary loyalty to auditing group rather than company as a whole; they tend, at times, to feel themselves outside of the organization. Managers, on the other hand, feel primary loyalty to organization.
2. Auditors are typically rewarded for finding things wrong, less so for helping people get their work done. Managers, on the other hand, are rewarded for getting the job done, whether things were wrong or not.
3. Auditors tend to be (a) *perfectionists*, and (b) focused on *particular* problems in depth. Managers, on the other hand, tend to be (a) *"satisficers"* rather than maximizers (they tend to look for workable rather than perfect or ideal solutions), and (b) *generalists*, focusing on getting many imperfect things to work together toward getting a job done, rather than perfecting any one part of the job.

4. The auditor's job tempts him to *evaluate* the line operation and to propose solutions. The manager, on the other hand, wants *descriptive* (nonevaluative) feedback and to design his own solutions.

B. Some Possible Dysfunctional Consequences of Tension Between Line Organization and Auditing Function:

1. Members of the line organization tend to pay attention to doing well, primarily in those areas which the auditor measures, whether or not those are important to the organizational mission.
2. Members of the line organization put effort into hiding problems and imperfections.
3. Management tends to use information about their subordinates in an unintentionally punishing way by immediate inquiries, which gives subordinates the feeling of having the boss on their back even while they are already correcting the problem.
4. Members of the line organization are tempted to falsify and distort information to avoid punishment for being "found out," and to avoid having their boss "swoop down" on them.
5. *Detailed* information gathered by the auditing function tends to be passed too far up the line in both the auditing function and the line organization, making information available to people who are too far removed from the problem to know how to evaluate the information.

C. Some Tentative Principles for the Handling of Auditing:

1. *Line involvement:* The more the line organization is involved actively in decisions concerning (a) which areas of performance are to be audited, and (b) how the information is to be gathered and to whom it is to be given,

the more helful and effective the auditing function will be.

2. *Horizontal rather than vertical reporting:* The more the auditing information is made available, *first* to the man with the problem (horizontal reporting), then to his immediate boss only if the problem is not corrected, and then only to higher levels in either the line or the auditing group if the problem is still not corrected, the more likely it is that auditing will be effective (because line organizations will be less motivated to hide or falsify information and less likely to feel punished).

3. *Reward for helping rather than policing:* The more the managers in the auditing group reward their subordinates for being *helpful* (based on whether they are being perceived as helpful by the line) rather than being efficient in finding problem areas, the more effective will be the auditing function. (Auditing people tend to be undertrained in how to use audit information in a helpful way; an appropriate reward system should be bolstered by training in how to give help.)

4. *Useful feedback:* The more the auditing information is *relevant* to important operational problems, *timely* in being fed back as soon after problem discovery as possible, and *descriptive* rather than evaluative, the more useful it will be to the line organization.

Appendix B:
Memo II Organization

1. The organization (any organization) can be thought of as having the following components:
   A. *Permanent Systems*
      Examples: product lines, product groups, manufacturing, finance, sales, executive commitee
   B. *Temporary Systems*
      Examples: task forces, review committees, ad hoc problem-solving groups
   C. *Coordinating Systems* (may or may not be permanent)
      Examples: project groups that deliberately cut across product lines (for example, standardization group); production engineering groups that coordinate between some product group and manufacturing; committees charged with functional responsibilities (for example, engineering committee, salary committee, and so on)

This kind of classification focuses on the issue of whether you put any given function or group, such as marketing, engineering, or programming, into a permanent, temporary, or coordinating role.

The other point about the classification is the identification of weakness in the product line organization as the permanent system, and then the strengthening of the total organization by building appropriate temporary and coordinating systems to offset the weaknesses. For example, if lack of standardization is one of the weaknesses of the product line organization, you build special groups to worry about this, *but they can be temporary groups.*

The basic long-range question, then, is what kind of temporary and/or coordinating systems you need in order to make the product line organization work well.

Appendix C:
Memo III Erosion of Rationality: One Hazard of Internal Competition on Product Planning

1. One major alleged gain of competition is that it increases motivation to win. There is nothing in the ethic of competition, however, that guarantees rationality or concern for high quality (unless you can assume that you need rationality and quality in order to win, an assumption that is often untenable).
2. A second major alleged gain of competition is that several independent problem solvers may produce better solutions than those same problem solvers working together.
3. A major hazard of competition is that, in the desire to win for one's product, one may begin to exaggerate the virtues of one's own product and exaggerate the weaknesses of the competing product. If two or more competitors each begin this process of subtle distortion, it becomes harder and harder to determine the true strengths and weaknesses of each product.
4. A second major hazard of competition is that in the process of selling one's own product solution one becomes emotionally committed to it. This commitment is one reason for the tendency to exaggerate (mentioned

above). A further problem with commitment and loyalty based on competition is that they create an attack-defense type of interaction. One is either selling, advocating, or defending. These types of interaction do not necessarily lead to effective problem solving, because they force both advocate and defender to play up only the good things in their project and to try to hide the weaknesses. In other words, a debate does not encourage true, open communication. Yet can you solve problems rationally without true, open communication?

5. If during the process of competition one or more parties become personally threatened (for example, their own job is threatened by the product decision), the danger arises that the inter*product* competition becomes an inter*personal* competition. If this happens, it becomes harder to make a rational product decision because it implies rejecting one *person*, not merely one *plan*. The issue is not whether this is actually true, but whether or not the participants *feel it to be true.*

6. Once competition becomes inter*personal*, participants increasingly become motivated to play politics and win by behind-the-scenes lobbying, undercutting the adversary, hiding information, making the other person look bad, and so on. Once competition gets to this stage, it is very hard to undo, to get people to work together collaboratively.

7. How can these negative features be avoided while still gaining the advantages of competition?
   A. *Be aware* of the hazards.
   B. *Think through* at what point to switch from competition to collaboration *before* the competitive process has undermined rationality.
   C. *Agree beforehand* at what point you will switch from competition to collaboration. Don't wait until you see the negative symptoms. By that time it may already be too late.
   D. *Make sure everyone knows the ground rules and is willing to play the game that way.*

E. *Keep checking people's feelings* as to whether or not they are beginning to feel threatened. *Build this kind of checking into meetings.* Don't let it become merely "conversation around the water-cooler."

F. *Learn to be flexible;* be able to switch back and forth from competition to collaboration and use each strategy when appropriate.

References

Allen, T. J. *Managing the Flow of Technology.* Cambridge, Mass.: MIT Press, 1977.

Ancona, D. G. Groups in Organizations: Extending Laboratory Models. In C. Hendrick (ed.), *Annual Review of Personality and Social Psychology: Group and Intergroup Processes.* Beverly Hills, Cal.: Sage, 1988.

Bales, R. F. *Interaction Process Analysis.* Reading, Mass.: Addison-Wesley, 1950.

Bales, R. F., and Cohen, S. P. *SYMLOG.* New York: Free Press, 1979.

Bennis, W., and Nanus, B. *Leaders.* New York: Harper & Row, 1985.

Birdwhistell, R. L. "Paralanguage: Twenty-five Years After Sapir." In H. Brosin (ed.), *Lectures on Experimental Psychiatry.* Pittsburgh: University of Pittsburgh Press, 1961.

Blake, R. R., and Mouton, J. S. "Reactions to Intergroup Competition Under Win–Lose Conditions." *Man. Sci.,* 1961, 7, 420–435.

———. "Overcoming Group Warfare." *Harvard Business Review,* Nov.–Dec. 1984, no. 6, 98–108.

Bradford, L. P.; Gibb, J. R.; and Benne, K. D. (eds.). *T-group Theory and Laboratory Method.* New York: Wiley, 1964.

Carter, L.; Haythorn, W.; Meirowitz, B.; and Lanzetta, J. "A Note on a New Technique of Interaction Recording." *J. Abn. Soc. Psych.*, 1951, 46, 258–260.

Chapple, E. D. "Measuring Human Relations: An Introduction to the Study of Interaction of Individuals." *Gen. Psych. Mono.*, 1940, 22, 3–147.

Dalton, M. *Men Who Manage.* New York: Wiley, 1959.

Hall, E. T. *The Silent Language.* Garden City, N.Y.: Doubleday, 1959.

Harvey, J. B. "The Abilene Paradox: The Managment of Agreement." *Organizational Dynamics*, summer, 1974.

Lewin, K. "Frontiers in Group Dynamics." *Human Relations*, 1947, 1, 5–41.

Scheflen, A. E. "Quasi-Courtship Behavior in Psychotherapy." *Psychiatry*, 1965, 28, 245–255.

Schein, E. H. *Organizational Psychology.* Engelwood Cliffs, N.J.: Prentice-Hall, 1965. Third edition, 1980.

——. *Organizational Culture and Leadership.* San Francisco: Jossey-Bass, 1985.

——. *Process Consultation: Volume II.* Reading, Mass.: Addison-Wesley, 1987a.

——. *The Clinical Perspective in Fieldwork.* Newbury Park, Cal.: Sage, 1987b.

Schein, E. H., and Bennis, W. G. *Personal and Organizational Change Through Group Methods.* New York: Wiley, 1965.

Sherif, M.; Harvey, O. J.; White, B. J.; Hood, W. R.; and Sherif, C. W. *Intergroup Conflict and Cooperation.* Norman: University of Oklahoma Book Exchange, 1961.

Tannenbaum, R., and Schmidt, W. H. "How to Choose a Leadership Pattern." *Harvard Business Review*, 1958, 36, 95–101.

White, R., and Lippitt, R. "Leader Behavior and Member Reactions in Three Social Climates." In D. Cartwright and A. Zander (eds.), *Group Dynamics.* White Plains, N.Y.: Row-Peterson, 1953.

Process Consultation
Volume II

Foreword

The Addison-Wesley Series on Organization Development originated in the late 1960s when a number of us recognized that the rapidly growing field of "OD" was not well understood or well defined. We also recognized that there was no one OD philosophy, and hence one could not at that time write a textbook on the theory and practice of OD, but one could make clear what various practitioners were doing under that label. So the original six books by Beckhard, Bennis, Blake and Mouton, Lawrence and Lorsch, Schein, and Walton launched what has since become a continuing enterprise. The essence of this enterprise was to let different authors speak for themselves instead of trying to summarize under one umbrella what was obviously a rapidly growing and highly diverse field.

By 1981 the series included nineteen titles, having added books by Beckhard and Harris, Cohen and Gadon, Davis, Dyer, Galbraith, Hackman and Oldham, Heenan and Perlmutter, Kotter, Lawler, Nadler, Roeber, Schein, and Steele. This proliferation reflected what had happened to the field of OD. It was growing by leaps and bounds, and it was expanding into all kinds of organizational areas and technologies of intervention. By this time many textbooks existed as well that tried to capture the core concepts of the field, but we felt that diversity and innovation were still the more salient aspects of OD today.

The present series is an attempt both to recapture some

basics and to honor the growing diversity. So we have begun a series of revisions of some of the original books and have added a set of new authors or old authors with new content. Our hope is to capture the spirit of inquiry and innovation that has always been the hallmark of organization development and to launch with these books a new wave of insights into the forever tricky problem of how to change and improve organizations.

We are grateful that Addison-Wesley has chosen to continue the series and are also grateful to the many reviewers who have helped us and the authors in the preparation of the current series of books.

Cambridge, Massachusetts   Edgar H. Schein
New York, New York   Richard Beckhard

Preface

When I wrote the first volume of *Process Consultation* in 1969, I was writing more in anger than with perspective. I was trying to explain myself and to clarify what seemed to me to be a great deal of confusion around the concept of consultation and helping. In the last fifteen years I have had many opportunities to test the ideas laid out in the original book, and have found that many have stood the test of time. At the same time, I have observed that some of the ideas as originally expressed need at the minimum clarification and, in some cases, modification.

The goals of this new book, then, are 1) to reaffirm the concept of process consultation as a viable model of how to work with human systems, 2) to clarify the concept where needed, and 3) to introduce some modifications and new ideas that elaborate on the original ideas.

My original intention had been simply to revise the 1969 book. However, as I began to write, I realized that most of what I was saying was an elaboration and that the new ideas were intended for a much different audience. Whereas my original book was a primer for consultants, the present book is much more a new approach for experienced consultants and a prescription for effective management. I have kept duplication of material to a minimum so that both the original book and the present one would be useful to the reader who is coming upon these ideas for the first time.

Who Is My Audience?

When I first wrote about process consultation in 1969, I had in mind my fellow scholars and practitioners. I was trying to explain to them what a social psychologist can and should do when working with an organizational client. However, I found that a lot of line managers were interested in the book, particularly the sections describing and explaining human processes in organizations.

I started to assign the book to my middle-level executive classes and found that it was perceived by them as very relevant to their understanding of management. Line managers often have to function as process consultants vis-à-vis their subordinates, peers, and bosses. In fact, one of the most powerful insights that managers obtained was that they could influence situations without the direct use of power and formal authority. So the present version is written with this broader audience in mind. I believe that all managers can become more effective if they adopt some of the concepts of process consultation and learn some of the skills associated with that concept.

Acknowledgments

Over the years the person who has influenced my understanding of process consultation most has been Richard Beckhard. He put into practice many of the seminal ideas of Doug McGregor, my original mentor at the Massachusetts Institute of Technology, and one of the founders of the National Training Laboratories, where I really learned how to work with people and groups. I will always treasure the opportunities to work with Dick and to watch him in action. He also went over the first draft of this book and made many helpful suggestions.

Three other people were particularly helpful in the preparation of this book. My student and colleague Gideon Kunda went over the entire first draft with a fine-tooth comb pointing out all the dilemmas, unanswered questions, and theoretical inconsistencies. Gideon is a talented consultant and his advice and feedback were, therefore, immensely helpful. My colleague of many years, John Van Maanen, carefully read the first draft and noted from his more anthropological perspective how the ideas could be improved upon and how the writing could be clarified. I have had many productive debates with both Gideon and John that have sharpened my ideas and forced me to think more clearly.

The third person who helped greatly was Steve Jenks, who reviewed the manuscript carefully for the publisher and made many helpful suggestions on how it could be improved. My only regret is that I could not take all the suggestions of these three people since they were all so valuable, but I found that I had to be consistent with my own style and priorities of what I was trying to get across. So the final result, while enriched by their efforts, is entirely my own responsibility.

My clients over the years were my real teachers. Though the case materials used in the book are all disguised, I would like to acknowledge a number of companies with whom I have worked extensively and from whom I learned a great deal about life in organizations and how to be helpful to organizational clients. Analog Devices, British Petroleum, Essochem Europe, Exxon, Digital Equipment Corporation, General Foods, Guaranty Trust Company, ICI, Polaroid, Shell, W. R. Grace, Ciba-Geigy, Procter and Gamble, the Internal Revenue Service, ALCAN, ALCOA, the Northrop Company, Motorola, General Electric, Steinbergs, H. P. Hood & Company, The Carlson Corporation, and many others provided consulting opportunities from which I could learn. I am grateful to them for the opportunity.

I am also grateful to my students and to participants in Process Consultation workshops that I have conducted over the years. Their questioning and probing sharpened my understanding. As has been my experience with other writing projects, I have needed the support of my wife to keep at them and get them done. She has, as usual, provided this support and I am grateful for it.

Cambridge, Massachusetts   E. H. S.

Contents

Process Consultation
Volume II

Part I

Introduction and Overview

This book argues that consultants and managers have a common problem: how to influence situations toward desired goals in the human systems in which they intervene. They attempt to improve things in organizations by a process that, in its broadest sense, can be thought of as "helping." In other words, not any intervention is desirable, only those interventions that help to accomplish desired ends.

To think of themselves as "helpful interveners" is not uncommon among consultants. It is less typical of managers to think of themselves as helpers because they exercise authority and have accountability that is fundamentally different from consultants. Managers think of themselves as results oriented, and it is tempting to slip into the fallacy that the end justifies the means, and hence that any intervention that will get you there is OK.

But observe effective managers in their day-to-day behavior. You will notice that a great deal of what they do resembles strikingly what consultants would advocate as helpful interventions. So I argue that effective managers can and should operate in a manner similar to consultants, and that they can learn much from consultants on how to intervene helpfully to achieve desired results.

It is not clear whether managers recognize that helping is one of their most important functions, and even if they do, there are so many models of how to intervene helpfully that it would be easy for a manager to get confused about this critical role. This part of the book therefore presents several models of helping that draw on different kinds of expertise; I will explore in detail both the assumptions that underlie the models and the implications of using them.

The first chapter shows in greater detail how the helping interventions of consultants and managers are similar, and how, therefore, each can learn from the other. In particular, managers can learn to be more effective if they emulate some of the activities of effective consultants.

In the second chapter I examine in detail several models of consultation and make the argument that the process-consultation model not only works best for consultants as interveners but also is the model potentially most useful for managers. Since the focus in this model is on managing the "process," the third chapter goes into some detail on what is meant by this term, what one can contrast it with, and how one can best focus one's interventions on the right kinds of process issues.

Part II examines a number of simplifying models of important human processes that are essential to understand if one is to intervene effectively. I examine what goes on inside the person, what goes on between people that is culturally determined, and what goes on during change in a human system. This part of the book is relevant theory and could be read before or after the other parts of the book.

Part III examines in detail the strategy and tactics of intervention — what the consultant or manager can actually say or do to accomplish some of the goals of process consultation. I also provide categories of types of interventions and examine some of the dilemmas that arise in the consultation process. Some readers may wish to read this section first because it is the most concrete.

The concepts of this book are laid out in a sequence because one can only present material in a linear fashion in written form. But in fact everything refers to everything else, and intervention is cyclical. One needs theory and concepts to think of what to do, and as one acts one learns more about what is going on that enriches theory and concepts. One needs general principles from which to derive specific behavior, but the specific behavior must be examined in order to test the principles. So the reader is invited to skip around, to find an order of reading that makes sense to him or her, and not be bound by the linear format of the chapters.

1

Managers and Consultants as Helpers

On the surface it would seem that management and consultation are totally different processes. Managers are usually thought of as having formal responsibility for defined organizational outcomes; they have line bosses; they have specific resources at their disposal with which to exercise the authority they have been given; they are expected to be committed to the organizational mission; they have subordinates; and they are "inside" and part of the organization, in the sense that they cannot evade certain kinds of difficult decisions and situations. They are accountable, and this accountability cannot be delegated.

Consultants, on the other hand, are typically thought of as outsiders. Even so-called inside consultants who work full time for a given company are typically thought of as outsiders to the particular department they are working in at any given time. They are typically thought of as being free to negotiate their areas of responsibility with others who are defined as clients; they work on a contract basis; they have the power that derives from being an "independent outsider" and being perceived as an expert in certain areas; and they have the freedom to leave a difficult situation except where professional responsibility dictates "hanging in." They are not expected to display the loyalty and commitment usually associated with being a manager.

How then can it be true that common skills and concepts apply to both managers and consultants? To make that argument one must look a bit beneath the surface. People who are perceived by their colleagues, bosses, and subordinates to be *effective* managers and *effective* consultants have in common that, when they relate to others whom they are trying to influence, they both take the stance of trying to *help*. Even though they have different sources of power and influence, the effective practitioners seem to gravitate toward a more common role definition vis-à-vis others with whom they are working — *the helping role*.

The Helping Orientation as Common Ground

For most consultants the concept of being helpful is central to their understanding of the role. What is less obvious is that effective managers view themselves in the same way. They are trying to accomplish their goals by being helpful to subordinates, peers, superiors, customers, suppliers, and any others with whom they have regular dealings.

Remember, I am speaking of managers who are judged to be *effective*, who are perceived to be the kind of people who get the job done and who are able to build their human organization at the same time so that jobs continue to get done. We all know of managers who do not behave like helpers at all, who misuse their authority, issue unilateral commands and decisions in areas where others know more, control the allocation of resources in a coercive manner, make and announce decisions without consultation, and generally keep their subordinates confused about who is responsible for what. They tend to view subordinates as replaceable resources to be exploited rather than developed, and they tend to use any means to accomplish goals, even if some of these means are costly to the human organization.

Effective managers, on the other hand, seem to conceptualize their role and structure their relationships with others very differently. They behave in such a way that *subordinates, peers, and supervisors get the help they need in order to get things done,* to succeed, to achieve the goals that have been set.

Let me give a few examples. Most managers accept the concept of "delegation." Once targets have been set, whether jointly negotiated or imposed from on high, the manager's problem is how to *help* the subordinate to achieve those targets. The manager cannot do the job himself;[1] he must create a situation in which the subordinate will do what he can, and he must help the subordinate in whatever way he can to do it.

Most managers accept the responsibility for developing their subordinates, if only to ensure that they have trained their own successors so that they can move on themselves. Any teacher or coach knows that you cannot really train or develop people without giving them opportunities to try things, to practice, and then *helping* them to improve their performance by various means. Terms such as *coaching* and *mentoring* reflect this kind of definition of the developmental task.

Most managers who deal with customers have learned that it is best to think of a sales relationship as a situation in which the salesman/manager is trying to *help* the customer to solve his problem. The salesman who feels that to *appear* helpful is all that is needed soon discovers that the customer sooner or later will see through this and then become more resistant. The best salesman is the one who really can and does solve the customers' problems and who has trained himself to think in those terms. Genuine commitment to customers, something that we hear being advocated more and more today as a key to organizational success, is not at all unlike the commitment of a consultant to a client.

Most managers have to create groups and run meetings. They soon learn that if they want the group to be effective, the role they must play as leader or chairperson of the group is to help the group work through its emotional issues before it can

---

[1] In the interests of smoother and more concise writing I will use the generic masculine pronoun for both male and female managers or consultants when general concepts are discussed; in specific examples I will draw on both male and female examples.

work on tasks effectively, and then to help the group to accomplish that task. Helping the group on both the emotional and the task level continue to be managerial responsibilities throughout the life of the group if the group is to remain effective.

As for *general* managers, whose responsibilities cut across the various business functions and who manage complete organizational units, in many functions the subordinates are often each more expert than their boss. It is in such situations, where the boss's job is to integrate, coordinate, and blend the expertise of others for coherent decisions, that the skills of helping become most relevant. Such decision processes often occur in groups or involve the interaction of a number of people whose contributions must be orchestrated. What consultants often do in their role as helpers to management can be effectively done by managers themselves once they learn to pay attention to and manage process events.

Finally, if the boss calls the manager in to help him with a problem, the manager must know how to adopt a helping stance vis-à-vis a higher-up in the organization. In other words, managers spend a great deal of their interpersonal time in the process of helping others. Therefore, if they are to be effective managers, they must learn how to help effectively, something that most consultants also have to learn.

Process Consultation as the Key to Effective Helping

In this book I will present several models of helping — the expert model, the doctor–patient model, and the process consultation (PC) model. I will try to show that at various times all human beings find themselves having to help others and thus must make an instant choice as to which model to adopt, which helping role to be in. My argument is that the key to effective helping, both for the manager and the consultant, is the ability to be a process consultant and not to succumb to the temptations of being the expert or the doctor except where that is appropriate.

Process consultation puts the emphasis on helping others to help themselves, not on solving their problems for them or giving them expert advice. The reasons for advocating the relevance of PC are both theoretical and practical. On the practical level we have all had our share of disastrous experiences where our "expert" advice was refused, misunderstood, or actually sabotaged. On the theoretical level, PC is more developmental. If the person being helped just accepts expert advice, he may solve his immediate problem but he may not learn anything about how to solve problems of this nature, skills that would enable him to solve a similar problem in the future.

Knowing how to be an effective process consultant is probably more relevant in today's complex world than it might have been in times past. In a technologically complex society neither managers nor consultants can really give commands or tell others what to do. Even in medicine, specialists and surgeons are finding themselves in complex relationships with their patients where they are *helping* those patients to make a beneficial decision rather than just "ordering" a given procedure. This point appears paradoxical, because, one might reason, the more complex the world, the more dependent we become upon experts to tell us what to do since we do not understand ourselves how things work. The problem is that, because we do not understand, when the expert tells us what to do, we often misunderstand or mistrust what we are told, and then either do it wrong or are afraid to do it at all. So the expert learns the hard way that just having expertise does not guarantee that one can influence others.

A more realistic model of management as well as consulting is to see the process as one of *intervening facilitatively* to accomplish agreed upon goals. The concepts, strategies, and tactics to be discussed in this book are, therefore, directed to both line managers and consultants, and the examples are drawn from both what consultants do and what managers do. Managers reading this book may find at first that the ideas seem less applicable to them, but the more they think about the managerial role, the more they will come to recognize how much of their own behavior resembles that of consultants, and, therefore, how much they might increase their own effectiveness if they learned some of the philosophies, concepts, and skills that consultants, especially process consultants, use.

These points can best be illustrated from some of my own

work with organizations. To remain objective in analyzing the case materials while protecting the identities of the clients with whom I have worked, I have constructed the case materials to be composites and have disguised identities wherever necessary. However, I have tried to characterize individual behavior accurately within these composite portraits in order to bring out what really happened in these situations. Several of these composite cases will be referred to throughout the chapters of the book, so a certain amount of background information will be provided as needed.

The Allen Financial Service Company

This composite case illustrates the elements common to my work with my client and my client's relationship with his organization and, therefore, reinforces my argument that consultants and managers often have similar problems and that managers often can accomplish their goals best by doing some process consulting with their own subordinates. What I mean by a "client" is itself complex, as we will see in Chapter 7, but for present purposes I will refer to the "primary client" as the person who sought my help and is paying for my services.

Fred Ralston, my primary client, was the head of an international operations and data processing division of a large, multinational financial service organization. I first got to know him during an executive development program, when I observed that he took a great interest in how to improve the organization. About one year after he had taken over the division he called to explore a consulting relationship with me and some other faculty members at MIT's Sloan School of Management. He expressed interest in bringing into the organization some ideas that attracted him; outside consultants would help with his various programs. My initial response was limited by the fact that I only had one day per month available, but Ralston felt that would be enough to get started, so I agreed to an exploratory meeting.

I learned from Ralston and from a long explanatory letter written by his personnel manager, Bob Ryan, that Ralston had taken over an organization that had been through several very tough years during which new technology had been introduced, costs had been cut very sharply, and many people had been replaced. Ralston's immediate predecessor had swung the pendulum back toward more concern for people, but costs were beginning to rise again, so Ralston saw his mandate as being to introduce a more effective overall management process that would put the emphasis equally on 1) keeping costs under control, 2) continuing to introduce the most advanced technology possible in order to make the organization efficient, 3) creating a climate of participation and teamwork in the organization to ensure that motivation, commitment, productivity, and high quality would be achieved, 4) starting a strategic planning process to prepare for an uncertain future, and 5) introducing a marketing orientation to the operations people so that they could expand the business and contribute to profits for the total company.

He was very taken with many of the concepts of process consultation and he believed strongly in the importance of developing the organization under him. He asked me whether I would help him to implement some of his ideas on how to run the division and to build an effective management team. I indicated that since I already knew him, I was ready to sit down with him at his office in a nearby city. I told him that I would bill him either at an hourly or daily rate and that we should let the goals and amount of time to be devoted to the consultation evolve naturally. We agreed by phone to an initial one-day meeting at his office.

What is important is what I learned during this first day about Ralston's managerial style and what implications this had both for my working with him and for his relationship to his organization. Our first meeting consisted of a face-to-face discussion that lasted most of the day. Ralston reviewed for me how he planned to institute various programs and ideas he had for improving productivity, reducing costs drastically, and getting the division to provide effective low-cost service and to do so in a way that it would truly help the sales and marketing effort of the company. He wanted to redesign the work of the service clerks so that they could have more direct customer contact, provide broader rather than highly specialized services, and adopt a marketing orientation so that when they were dealing with customers on service issues they would also find ways of selling additional services.

Ralston had already instituted a strategic planning process and had hired a consultant to run seminars for the department heads and their subordinates. He had launched a communications program involving regular meetings of groups of lower-level employees with senior management. He had hired a consulting firm to do a major survey of the whole division with the goal of redesigning jobs, and had instituted a productivity program that required each manager to report at least ten new productivity ideas for his group every month.

These new programs were imposed on top of a very tightly structured set of cost-reduction targets that involved as well a systematic effort to reduce the number of managers and employees in the organization by a certain percentage in each of the next several years. Ralston knew from conversations with his boss and from having worked in the Allen Company for a long time that his long-range success depended upon keeping costs flat while increasing productivity, quality, and the amount of business the division was doing, and he had obtained the approval of his boss to impose even tighter targets on his own division than had been requested of the entire company. Ralston reported that his boss was delighted with the results that had already been obtained in the first year. The boss was a hands-off delegator who kept encouraging Ralston to do even better but did not want to know too much about how these goals were being achieved.

To make sure that cost targets were met, Ralston used a series of quantitative indexes to monitor various operations on a daily and weekly basis. If there were too many errors, cost overruns, or other indicators that the program was off target, Ralston immediately and decisively reprimanded the responsible manager under him. I learned later from conversations with others in the division that his immediate subordinates resented the tone of these reprimands more than the fact of having the data brought to their attention. They had accepted the cost-reduction targets as a valid divisional program and felt that they were meeting them.

I also learned later that Ralston's immediate subordinates, the department heads, and various lower levels of employees of the division were proud of what they were accomplishing and felt completely behind Ralston. He was a charismatic leader who produced real results and everyone knew that higher management was proud of the division's accomplishments.

What Then Was the Problem? From what Ralston told me it appeared that he wanted reassurance and confirmation that his programs were on the right track, and he wanted a sounding board on how best to accomplish his results. But it sounded to me from what he said that there might be too many programs, that they were not in any priority, and that maybe his group had trouble juggling so many programs all at once. It also occurred to me that they might feel overworked, tense, and resentful at having so many things thrust at them.

As Ralston reviewed for me the various goals he was trying to accomplish, it became obvious to me that he was trying to do too many things all at once and was not seeing the connections among the various activities that he himself was launching. Each time he launched a new program he hired an outside consultant or assigned an inside person to administer it, attended the first session or two if it involved special meetings, but then went on to other matters. He seemed not to realize that for his subordinates each of these programs were "extras" on top of what they were already doing, while for him they were only activities to be monitored. I guessed from how he described matters that his subordinates must be in a state of panic and chaos trying simultaneously to keep all of the cost indicators in line while launching major new productivity, job redesign, strategic planning, and communications programs.

My Process Interventions. In the first several hours of our meeting I mostly listened and recorded on a chartpad each of the activities that Ralston was telling me about so that we could begin to build a road map of where this was all going. I decided that it would be helpful to reflect back to Ralston all the activities he was launching and help him to begin to see that they could be ordered and that priorities could be assigned to each program. Illustrating the activities by recording them on a chartpad for both of us to view also provided me an opportunity to begin to confront Ralston with the sheer volume of what he was doing.

At lunch Ralston introduced me to the personnel manager,

Bob Ryan, who had briefed me by mail on the general nature of the organization, its charter, its organization chart, and the broad purpose of the consultation project "to help Ralston implement the various programs he had launched." I also met Ralston's personal assistant, who managed various of his appointments and program activities. After lunch I had a half hour with each of them while Ralston attended a meeting and made some phone calls. I observed that he himself was frantically busy and seemed to be overloaded.

Other Perspectives. During the private meetings with the personnel manager, Bob Ryan, and the assistant, Joan Smith, I was told that the division was indeed floundering from being overwhelmed by too many programs, that the department heads under Ralston were stretched to the breaking point and so were neglecting some of the important priorities, such as the productivity program and the job redesign survey. Worst of all, they were confused about Ralston's goals. They felt that they had been enormously successful in bringing the various daily indexes under control and that the division was performing beautifully on the basic cost-containment program, but that Ralston was not giving them enough credit or enough breathing space to keep going. They saw him as piling up more and more programs to the point where they had no choice but to subvert or ignore some of them, realizing full well that if Ralston discovered this he might lose his temper and be very punishing.

There seemed to be an ambivalence developing between Ralston and some members of his group. They were thrilled to have a strong leader who had made the division effective, but he was overloading them without sharing his own vision and priorities in a way that could be implemented. No one quarrelled with any of the activities singly, but together they constituted an overload. Both Ryan and Smith said that they had attempted to give Ralston feedback on what was happening, but he either did not hear it or chose to ignore it. They were glad that Ralston had sought my counsel because they thought an outsider might provide some help in a situation that was getting very tense. At this point I had no information from others so had to take these various points of view as differing perspectives without knowing for sure what was actually going on.

Further Interventions. Later during the day I again met Ralston for a final two-hour session in which I asked him what relationships he saw among the various activities that he had launched, and what he thought the impact of all of these programs might be on his subordinates. My goal was simultaneously to help him to develop a road map and to determine how much insight he had into the impact of his managerial style. What came through in his answers was his tremendous enthusiasm for all of his programs, how much support he had obtained from his boss, and how much he believed he could now teach his subordinates. He clearly saw himself as a visionary with a record of success, who would pass on his vision to his division and make it a model of how to run such a service division.

At the same time he seemed to need reassurance that he was on the right track and was more than willing to discuss with me how he might accomplish his goals better. He also acknowledged his own personal overload, an area that I immediately focused on as a primary objective for our consultation. It seemed to me that the best motivator toward change might be Ralston's own fatigue and stress level.

Next Steps. At the end of the day we agreed that at least one concrete next step (suggested by me) was to build an overarching framework for all of the programs that had been launched so that Ralston himself could articulate his vision in a more coherent way. I defined my goal as being to help him with his own sense of overload and fractionation, while learning gradually what else might be going on in the departments. After all, it was possible that Ralston's assessment that the group could do more and that he could show them how was correct. I could not automatically assume that what Bob and Joan had told me was an accurate assessment.

We agreed to meet in a month and, at that time, to review the various programs and put them into a coherent structure that would make it possible to put priorities on them in case too much was being done all at once. This schedule was determined both by the fact that Ralston was very busy and that at this point one day per month was all I could spare. How this case evolved will be discussed in later chapters.

Some Lessons. A number of lessons, insights, and issues emerged from this first day. As a consultant I had learned a good deal about how Ralston expected to structure his relationship to me. He wanted reassurance that he was on the right track, he wanted to fine-tune his ideas and get help in getting them organized into a coherent program, and he wanted personal counsel on how he could be a more effective manager because he sensed that his subordinates were ignoring or sabotaging some of his programs. He clearly viewed me as an expert on management and asked me point-blank to give him advice. Whenever I did offer thoughts he wrote them down very seriously in a notebook that he had brought to the meeting.

But I had an uneasy feeling that there was a mixed message in his request. I was not really sure what was going on except that a conflict had apparently developed between Ralston and some of his subordinates, and that so far Ralston saw no connection between that conflict and his own behavior as a manager. I saw the need to 1) learn more about what was really going on in this division; 2) help Ralston to see for himself how his chosen role as a leader, visionary, and expert might be undermining his own goals; and 3) help him to design the implementation of some of his programs such as the job redesign survey to ensure that his goals could be achieved.

Ralston's targets were sound, but his methods of implementation clearly were not producing the desired results, and it was not clear whether he had the process insights to manage simultaneously a stringent cost-reduction program, a new strategic planning process, a participative communications program, a productivity improvement program, and a major employee survey leading to job redesign and reorganization of the division.

This case illustrated for me the points I am trying to make about how managers and consultants have similar problems, and how a process orientation toward such problems is not only desirable but essential. Ralston was seemingly doing everything right. He had the right goals, the support of higher management, the support of his own department heads, a record of phenomenal success in reducing costs while building business, yet too many things were not working, and Ralston feared that if he let up on the pressure even slightly, all the indicators would immediately go out of control again. In fact he pointed out to me how this had happened just a few months before when he had been on an extended trip. When he returned he had to be Mr. Tough Guy for a while to get things back under control.

Ralston sometimes sounded like a parent who had an unruly bunch of children whom he loved but had to teach how to behave properly. At other times he sounded very insecure and in need of reassurance that his ideas were on the right track. Bob Ryan, the personnel manager, and Joan Smith, Ralston's personal assistant, implied that the subordinates were more than able to do what Ralston wanted but things slipped because they were overloaded. So the minute he was away, they used the time to catch their breath, hence the slippage in the indicators. When I asked Ralston at one point whether it was possible that the subordinates were overloaded, he shrugged this off as being just an excuse. He had seen groups like this who could do it all, but he would have to show them how.

Conclusion

The situation in the case just described is a prototype of what I run into often. The client needs some help from me on a managerial issue, but, as the scenario unfolds, I realize that one of the problems the client has is that he is not acting sufficiently like a process consultant with his own subordinates, peers, and supervisors. If he could learn to take more of a process orientation, learn to manage human processes better, he would not be generating some of the problems that led him to call for help. In other words, many of Ralston's goals were valid and accepted, but the manner in which he chose to implement them, the process of monitoring, and his style of supervision caused unanticipated problems that, in the end, made the accomplishment of the goals difficult. Both consultants who have to help managers and managers themselves can learn from Ralston's mistakes and can add to their managerial repertoire the concepts and behaviors of effective consultants.

2

What Is Process Consultation?

The Helping Dilemma

One of the persistent dilemmas that faces any manager or consultant is how to be helpful in a situation in which there is a genuine choice between

- giving advice, telling others what to do, playing the role of an expert, and
- helping "clients" to figure out the solution for themselves, facilitating their own problem solving, even if that involves withholding what may seem to the consultant an obvious solution.

This dilemma is so common because once we are asked for help, there is an automatic tendency to assume that we "know" something that the asker is seeking. It is psychologically difficult to resist taking advantage of the situation and to become the instant expert that the other person is seemingly assuming us to be. But we have also noticed that when we do share what we know, when we give advice, when we attempt to get others to do what we think they should do, people resist, point out how we have missed the point, invent reasons why the suggested solution will not work, offer new information that makes the advice irrelevant, and in other ways manage to subvert what we have offered.

If we are very observant, we will also notice that one reason for this resistance is that the person seeking help or advice often resents being in that role. Just as the helper may feel "one up" in being asked for help, the person with the problem may well feel "one down" for not being able to stay on top of things. The troubled person needs help, but, at the same time, does not like to be in the position of having to ask for it.

If we are to be influential and genuinely helpful, we must learn when and how to be in the role of expert advice giver and when to be in the role of facilitator and catalyst. We need to develop diagnostic criteria to aid in making a valid choice among the possible modes of helping.

To begin to develop such criteria I will first lay out three different models of consultation and explore the assumptions that underlie each model (see Schein, 1969). To think of these as models of consultation implies that any manager or consultant *must be able to play each of these roles at the appropriate time.* In my own experience as a consultant and in various administrative roles, the most important choice I had to make in confronting any given situation was whether to be the expert or the process consultant, and when to switch roles as the situation shifted. Not only must the consultant be able to switch roles when need be but he must do so in a way that is minimally confusing or disruptive to the relationship with the client, just as a manager must be able to switch from "orders giver" to "friendly helper" as the occasion and the task demand.

Confusion About "Consultation"

Before examining the models and their underlying assumptions a few more words need to be said about the concept of consultation and how it has come to be used in much of the management literature. What is a consultant to an organizational client supposed to do? What functions does he fulfill? For example, consultants vis-à-vis their clients and managers vis-à-vis their subordinates might do any of the following things.

1. *Provide information* that is not otherwise available.
2. *Analyze information* with sophisticated tools not available to clients or subordinates.
3. *Diagnose* complex organizational and business problems.
4. *Train* clients or subordinates to use diagnostic models that permit them to make better decisions.
5. *Listen and give support, comfort, and counsel* during troubled times.
6. *Help to implement difficult or unpopular decisions.*
7. *Reward and punish* certain kinds of behaviors, using status as an "outsider" as a special source of authority.
8. *Carry information* that is not moving up the normal chain of command to higher levels or that does not move laterally as needed.
9. *Make decisions and give commands* on what to do if line management for some reason cannot do so.
10. *Take responsibility* for decisions, *absorb the anxiety* that may attend the uncertainty of how things will come out, and, in other ways, *provide the emotional strength* to help others through difficult situations.

It should be noted that these many functions that a consultant might fulfill also apply to the managerial role. It is because of the multifunction aspect of these roles that clients or subordinates — people who need help — are often bewildered and unable to figure out what kind of help they need. They are often advised not even to seek help unless they can determine exactly what they want their helper to do. Subordinates are similarly advised not to go to their bosses unless they know exactly what kind of help they need, lest they appear to be confused and not on top of their jobs.

The paradoxical fallacy of this advice is that consultants and bosses are often *most helpful* when the person in need of help is most bewildered and does *not* know what kind of help or advice to seek. What I have called "process consultation" fits best precisely those situations where people are troubled but neither know what the problem is nor what kind of help they should be seeking. It is at those times, and, consequently, when the person in difficulty may be most upset and potentially defensive, that PC becomes most relevant.

People often sense that all is not well or that things could be better, but they do not have the tools with which to translate their vague feelings into concrete action steps. Process consultation does not assume that the manager or the organization knows what is wrong, or what is needed, or what the consultant should do. All that is required for the process to begin constructively is some *intent* on the part of someone in the organization to improve the way things are going.

The consultation process itself then helps the client to define diagnostic interventions that lead to the right problem-solving steps; the client thus learns how to solve problems on future occasions without the help of the consultant. The goals of the process consultant are to pass on some of his or her skills, perspectives, and broad insights to the client.

In this sense PC is very similar in assumptions to many kinds of clinical and psychiatric counseling that put the emphasis on clients figuring out for themselves what their problems are and what they should do about them. Such assumptions also underlie many theories of supervision and delegation in the sense that the "developmentally" oriented boss will structure situations for subordinates in which they can learn to solve problems for themselves. The boss functions as a process consultant to the subordinates, rather than giving orders or advising them what to do.

Focusing on these similarities is crucial because I have discovered over and over again in my own consulting and teaching that the process consultant's role is a general role that applies across a very wide range of life situations. It applies to parent–child relationships, to friendships, to marital relationships, to superior–subordinate relationships, and to any other kind of interpersonal situation in which one party is seeking some kind of help. In a sense, then, I am trying to lay out some of the assumptions that would underlie any *general theory of "helping,"* regardless of the context in which this occurs. My examples are drawn primarily from organizational contexts, but the general assumptions underlying the role of the helper have broader implications.

Three Models of Consultation

In order to highlight the particular assumptions that underlie PC, I will contrast it with two other major consulting models: the *purchase of information or expertise* model and the *doctor–patient* model. The time to become aware of the choices among models is at that moment in a relationship when one party says to the other: "Can you give me some advice?" or "I need some help," or "I don't know what to do with this problem I've got," or, simply, "What should I do?" I will examine each of the models in the consulting context and at the end of the chapter show how they apply to the manager.

The Purchase of Information or Expertise

The core of this model is that the client has made up his mind on what the problem is, what kind of help is needed, and to whom to go for this help. The buyer, an individual manager, or some group in an organization determines that more knowledge is needed on some matter or that some activity needs to be carried out, concludes either that he does not have the capability to gather the information or perform internally or that it is economically or politically more expedient to have it done by outsiders, and hence goes to a consultant for the service.

The most extreme and purest cases would be the hiring of a systems analyst to write a computer program, the hiring of a lawyer to assess the legal implications of a given course of action, or an architect to design a new building. Less extreme versions would be a manager wishing to know how a particular group of consumers feel, or how to design a plant, or how to get the accounting system converted to a new computer. Or, a manager may wish to find out how to more effectively organize some function such as research and development, or how to redefine a set of jobs after the introduction of information technology in a given department, or to conduct a survey of morale in a unit of an organization. Or the chief executive officer or a division head may wish to find out what the competition is doing in a given area, what the market possibilities are for a new product line, how to assess the potential benefits and hazards of a given new strategy; in such cases the information purchased is the equivalent of "intelligence" and therefore must be obtained in part by covert means, and preferably by outsiders.

The essence of the message from the client to the consultant is "Here is my problem; bring me back an answer and tell me how much it will cost." Psychologically the message is "Please take the problem off my shoulders and bring me back a solution," which permits the client to relax and concentrate on other matters, secure in the knowledge that the expert is now handling the situation — "owning the problem." If the solution does not work or the information turns out to be useless, the consultant can easily be blamed.

If this model is to work effectively the following assumptions must be met:

1. *The client has correctly diagnosed the problem.* If the client has misdiagnosed the problem, the consultant in this model feels no particular obligation to help in rediagnosing it. If the client wants a consumer survey, the survey expert will provide it, even if the real problem may be a power struggle between the marketing and the R&D departments.

2. *The client has correctly identified the consultant's capabilities to provide the expertise.* If the client has correctly determined that a survey is needed but then goes to someone who is not expert enough to do the survey, the poor outcome is the client's problem. Unless the consultant is governed by a personal code of ethics and professionalism, there is nothing in this model that obligates the consultant to do anything other than sell his or her services. To evaluate the expertise is the client's obligation and burden.

3. *The client has correctly communicated the problem and the nature of the expertise or information that is to be purchased.* If the client wanted to focus the survey on how employees felt about their supervisors, but only communicated that he wanted an "employee survey" done, it is possible that the information gathered will turn out to be irrelevant to the problem that motivated it in the first place. The client–consultant interaction is often faulty in this area because the client does not check carefully whether what the consultant "heard" accurately mirrors what the client was trying to get across. The consultant then

charges off to solve the problem that he assumes, and only later is it discovered that the consultant was working the "wrong" problem.

4. *The client has thought through and accepted the potential consequences of obtaining the information or the service.* If the survey reveals a serious problem, is the client manager prepared to deal with it? If not, the situation may deteriorate even further because the employees now know that the problem has been investigated and surfaced. If nothing is done, they may feel that management is deliberately ignoring it. Consultants who operate primarily in the purchase of expertise or information role report over and over again that clients become angry and disillusioned if the information or service they are given does not fit their prior expectations. Yet clients will rarely acknowledge that they may be responsible for one or more of the above assumptions not having been met.

In summary, this model of consultation is appropriate only when clients have diagnosed their needs correctly, have correctly identified consultant capabilities, have done a good job of communicating their needs to the consultant, and have thought through the consequences of the help they have sought. The irony of this model is that the expertise is attributed to the consultant, but in fact a tremendous load falls on the client to do things correctly if the problem is to be solved.

When the assumptions clearly cannot be met because the problem is too complex, too difficult to diagnose, or too hot to handle, the client will most likely turn to one of the next two models.

The Doctor–Patient Model

This model is a variant and elaboration of the previously described expert model in that it gives the consultant the additional power to make a diagnosis and recommend what kind of information and expertise will solve the problem. The client experiences some pain or observes some symptoms of pathology but does not really know what is wrong or how to fix it. The consultant is called in and given the mandate to "find out what is wrong, and recommend how to fix it."

From the client's point of view these are the same conditions that would initiate a PC process, so it is the consultant's choice whether to accept the mandate to be the doctor or to develop the role of process consultant. It is essential, therefore, for the consultant to understand clearly the consequences of the choice of model.

The doctor–patient process might begin with the president or senior managers of an organization hiring a consultant or team of consultants to "look the firm over" or do an "audit," much as a person might go to an internist for a physical. The consultants are supposed to find out what is wrong with any part of the organization and prescribe a therapeutic program, which often involves changing key people or reorganizing.

Often the manager who hires the consultant is not the one who is directly experiencing the problems. A department may be perceived to be in trouble, and the division or corporate level manager may "order" a consultant to investigate that department to find out what is wrong. Managers sometimes create a comparable situation internally when they ask a subordinate to go to some other part of the organization to "find out what is going on" and to return with a recommendation on what should be done.

The essence of this model is that the client delegates to the consultant not only locating a remedy but, first, diagnosing the disease. The client becomes very dependent on the consultant until the consultant is ready to offer a prescription. As in the expert model, the consultant takes the problem onto his own shoulders and permits the client to relax, secure in the knowledge that someone else is looking into it.

If the doctor–patient model is to be helpful the following assumptions must be met:

1. *The diagnostic process itself will be seen as helpful.* In most organizational situations involving human systems one cannot separate diagnosis from intervention, hence the very process of calling in a doctor to do a diagnosis already constitutes an intervention with unknown consequences. Unless the client is willing to run the risks of perturbing the organization by having a consultant observe, ask questions, study data, and so on, he should be cautious about using this model at all. One cannot bring a consultant into an organization without stirring up all kinds of

questions and feelings, even if the mandate to the consultant is "only to do a diagnosis." On the other hand, when the client *wants* to perturb the organization, to stir up a lot of self-analysis, and possibly to expose a lot of "dirty linen," this model becomes highly appropriate.

2. *The client has correctly interpreted the organization's symptoms and has located the sick area.* Not only may clients misperceive what is going on, but they may use incorrect criteria for defining what is pathological. They may define certain financial indicators, productivity levels, turnover, morale statistics, or levels of griping as symptoms of ill health, whereas, in reality, such symptoms may reflect only temporary conditions or may be a normal response to what is happening to the organization.

Frequently senior managers have made up their minds that they have a problem in marketing, finance, manufacturing, or administration, have asked for expert help in that area, and have implemented various prescriptions, only to discover much later that the problems persist because the original assumption about what was wrong was incorrect.

It is very easy for clients and consultants to get caught up in a vicious circle of incorrect diagnosis because the client is anxious to get help and the consultant is anxious to sell his services. It is easy for the consultant to be persuaded by the client's complete dependence to prescribe those remedies that fit the consultant's area of expertise rather than what may really be the problem.

Of course, if the assumption holds and the sick area is correctly identified, then the organizational equivalent of surgery may be the right treatment, such as when a company analyzes its various divisions or product lines in terms of profit contribution and decides to sell those units that are not contributing appropriately. The difficult questions arise when the diagnosis involves parts of the human system where the data may not be as clear-cut as financial or sales data. In those instances the client may need the equivalent of the organizational internist whose job is to help the client decide upon and find a specialist. And the internist will, in all likelihood, rely initially more on a process consultation model in order to get the best information on what is wrong.

3. *The person or group defined as "sick" will reveal the pertinent information necessary to make a valid diagnosis; that is, they will neither hide data nor exaggerate symptoms.* One of the most obvious difficulties with the doctor–patient model is that it assumes that the person or organization defined as the "patient" will be cooperative in revealing information relevant to a diagnosis. In my own experience I have found several sources of systematic distortion of information. The direction of the distortion depends upon the organizational climate and the underlying assumptions of the organizational culture.

If the climate is full of mistrust and insecurity, respondents are likely to hide any damaging information from the consultant because they fear punishment for revealing problems that might reflect badly on the boss. If, on the other hand, the climate is trusting and open, respondents may view the contact with the consultant as an opportunity to unload all their grievances, small and large, leading to an exaggeration of the problem.

Unless the consultant spends time actually *observing* the department, he is not likely to get an accurate picture of what is going on. The picture is likely to be equally clouded for the consultant who just shows up and starts observing, if the group to be observed has not invited the consultant to do so. When a contact client asks me to "visit" or "come and talk to" a group in which there is allegedly a problem, I tend to resist until I have a much clearer idea of what is going on in that group *from the contact client's perspective.* If we then agree that I should visit, that decision has to be owned and implemented by the contact client.

The issue here, as in the first model, is how much the consultant is willing to allow the client to become dependent by being willing to take the problem onto his own shoulders. Such dependence is initially comfortable for the client and makes the consultant feel very powerful, but often leads to trouble because the next assumption to be discussed does not hold up.

4. *The client will understand and correctly interpret the diagnosis provided by the consultant, and will implement whatever prescription is offered.* When the "doctor" begins to work out what is wrong, both parties to the relationship feel comfortable because the process of diagnosis is moving things forward, but neither can anticipate what will be found and whether or not

the client will accept the diagnosis, will understand the implications, and will do what the doctor says in order to "get well."

Sometimes the consultant is deliberately obscure, technical, or otherwise esoteric in order to impress the client and to ensure that further services will be purchased. There is nothing in the implicit contract that obligates the "doctor" to worry about how well the client understands the diagnosis and its implications except norms of professional conduct. In medicine these norms are reasonably clear and enforced through licensing, peer review, and professional associations. In the field of management consulting the norms are much less clear, and there are few practical ways of enforcing them because more of the contact between client and consultant is hidden from view.

An even bigger problem is that the diagnosis may be correct and understood, yet the client will not or cannot implement the prescription. For example, the consultant may recommend reorganization, which may be an entirely correct prescription in the abstract but may not fit some prior assumptions that the client has about the organization or the employees, or some prior political deals he has made with some managers, or his own values. Such hidden aspects of the organization — in effect its culture — may not have been revealed to the consultant.

If the client is now displeased with the prescription or feels he has "wasted money," it is entirely his own fault for having entered into a doctor–patient model without considering all of its consequences (unless, of course, the consultant failed to spell out these consequences in the initial contacts). If the consultant cares sufficiently about implementation, he will discourage the use of this model, knowing in advance how likely it is to lead to unanticipated and undesirable consequences.

5. *The client can remain healthy after the consultant leaves.* If the client already knows how to solve problems of the sort that may be discovered in this model, then it may be useful. But if the diagnosis and prescription involves further implementation by the consultant, then the problem itself is likely to recur, because the client will not have learned any problem-solving skills.

For example, if the client hires the "doctor" to find out

what is wrong with a particular division and it is discovered that the manager of the division has problems that require some professional counseling, the client can hire the consultant to provide the counseling, but if the problem recurs the client will have to call in the doctor all over again.

In summary, the doctor–patient model is appropriate only when the client is experiencing clear symptoms, knows where the sick area is, is willing to intervene in the organization's systems by bringing in a consultant, and is willing to become dependent on the consultant for both diagnosis and implementation. It implies that the patient is willing to "take his medicine" and thereby cure the ills, but he will probably not learn how to take care of himself better or do his own diagnosing and healing in the future. And the power relations among members of the organization may be changed permanently by the very process of bringing in a doctor.

The Process Consultation Model

The major distinction of the PC model lies in how the consultant structures the relationship, not in what the client does. The process can start with any of the kinds of examples that I have given above for the other models. Clients may ask for information, invite the consultant to do a diagnosis, or ask for help in some other way, but the consultant is not obligated to respond literally to the client's overt request.

The consultant operating by the PC model starts with very different assumptions about the nature of the client system and the goals of the consultation process. The most central premise of PC is that the *client owns the problem* and *continues to own it* throughout the consultation process. The consultant can help the client to deal with the problem, but the consultant never takes the problem onto his own shoulders. This premise has to be emphasized strongly because all of the forces when someone asks for help are pulling in the direction of the helper to "take the monkey off the client's back." It is very easy for the consultant to get seduced into saying something like "I'll take care of it *for you,*" rather than communicating the message, "It's *your problem,* but I'll help you work on it and help you solve it."

I am not saying that in the expert or doctor model the client automatically abdicates. It is possible in any of the models for the client to continue to feel that he owns the problem yet needs help from a doctor in working on it. However, the PC model makes it a central concern that the consultant communicate clearly the expectation that he will *not* take over the problem, should the client wish to take the more dependent stance.

Even if the consultant feels he or she knows exactly what is wrong and what to do about it, such diagnostic and prescriptive ideas should probably be withheld early in the process for three basic reasons: 1) the consultant is most probably wrong to some unknown degree because of the likelihood that there are hidden cultural, political, and personal factors operating; 2) even if the consultant is right, the client is likely to be defensive, to not listen or deny what is being said, to argue, or to misunderstand and thereby undermine the possibilities of solving the problem; and 3) even if the client accepts the consultant's diagnosis he probably fails to learn how to do such diagnoses in the future himself.

It is a key assumption of process consultation that the client must share in the process of diagnosing what may be wrong (or learn to see the problem for himself), and must be actively involved in the process of generating a remedy because only the client ultimately knows what is possible and what will work in his culture and situation.

The process consultant can play a key role in sharpening the client's understanding of what is wrong and how to deal with it, and may provide ideas and alternatives to consider that may not have occurred to the client. But he strongly encourages the client to take ultimate responsibility for deciding what to do, how to intervene in the situation. Not only does this approach increase the likelihood that the immediate problem will be solved, but, even more important, the client learns the skills of problem solving so that he or she can continue to solve problems after the consultant leaves.

It should be emphasized that the consultant may or may not be an expert in solving the client's particular problems. Such expertise is less relevant than are the skills of involving the client in self-diagnosis and teaching intervention skills to the client. The consultant must be an expert on human relations, particularly the processes of establishing and maintaining a helping relationship. If it is then discovered that special expertise in marketing, finance, or other aspects of business is needed, the consultant should help the client to locate a specialist to provide that expertise.

Another major premise of PC is that diagnosis and intervention cannot be separated in practice. To the extent that the consultation entails actively working with the contact client and others who may become involved, the consultant is intervening by asking certain kinds of questions and raising certain kinds of issues. Even the consultant's presence is an intervention in that it sends a message to the organization that someone there has perceived a problem that warrants the presence of a consultant.

The major criteria that govern what the consultant does, therefore, derive from intervention theory, not diagnostic theory. Consultants take into account the kinds of diagnostic *interventions* they are willing to make. This often limits what kinds of questions can be asked, of whom they can be asked, what terminology is used in asking them, and so on. It is this premise, that diagnosis and intervention are inseparable, that makes the tactics of PC most different from the tactics of the other two models of problem solving.

It is also this premise that makes it most clear how consultation and management begin to blend into each other. Managers learn that asking questions that appear to be purely diagnostically oriented in fact becomes a powerful intervention, and that such "diagnostic" interventions are often more helpful than telling others what to do. Effective managers learn that they do not have to be experts or doctors to be influential, and that they can often have more influence by judiciously playing the process consultant role. But in this learning is embedded the fundamental idea that the manager or consultant is *never* just diagnosing. He is always intervening to some degree, even if he is just sitting quietly listening to a subordinate talk.

Given these general premises, we can say that PC is most appropriate when the following assumptions are met:

1. The client is hurting somehow but does not know the source of the pain or what to do about it. I am referring here to the actual state of affairs, not necessarily how the client might initially present the problem. I have often been told that the problem is exactly such-and-such, only to discover after asking a few questions that the client is, in fact, unsure *what* the problem is but hesitant to admit it.

2. The client does not know what kind of help may be available and which consultant can provide the kind of help that may be needed. The process role is one that the consultant works himself out of, either by helping the client to find a specific expert or doctor if needed, or, more typically in organizations, by helping the client to figure out for himself what to do next.

3. The nature of the problem is such that the client not only needs help in figuring out what is wrong but would benefit from participation in the process of making a diagnosis. Most problems in organizations that produce generalized pain, in the sense that managers know that something is wrong but are not sure what is wrong, are nontechnical. Such problems typically involve one or more other people, have group or organizational components, involve cultural assumptions, political issues, personal attitudes and values, and, most important, involve the client's own perceptions, feelings, and judgments to an unknown degree.

Such information is deeply embedded in the system and would not be easily elicited by the consultant working as an outsider. Only by a collaborative process of the outsider working with the client and other insiders can the relevant issues be identified and the correct information elicited about what is going on, why it is going on, and what it means. What the consultant must bring to the surface is information that illuminates what the problem really is, why it is a problem (maybe the client's pain should be viewed as "normal"), why it is a problem right now (what is actually happening that motivated calling the consultant), and what might be done about it (maybe the situation should be left alone).

4. The client has "constructive intent," is motivated by goals and values that the consultant can accept, and has some capacity to enter into a helping relationship. Much more will be said about this later, but it is critical to note now that PC will not work if the client has hidden motives and goals that the consultant does not accept, or if the client is determined to be dependent or destructive (in terms of the consultant's basic value system). One of the most important tasks of the early relationship with the client is for the consultant to examine possible hidden agendas in order to determine whether or not he can accept them.

I have frequently been asked to visit companies to help in the making of a diagnosis only to discover that my visit was motivated by the contact client's need to involve me in a political power struggle of his own. Or I am asked to make an educational intervention, only to discover that the contact client's real motive is to convince his boss to pursue a particular course of action that I may not agree with at all.

The consultant must also determine through various kinds of diagnostic questions how much constructive intent and capacity to receive help is present, and be prepared to terminate or redefine the relationship if it does not feel congruent. The tactics of how to make this determination will be discussed in the later chapters. Because the PC orientation is more likely than other problem-solving approaches to reveal such lack of congruence, it is typically most appropriate for the early stages of a helping intervention.

5. *The client is ultimately the only one who knows what form of intervention will work in the situation.* Often an outsider, the consultant cannot possibly know the ultimate constraints that may be operating in a problem situation. That should not prevent the consultant from offering alternatives and stimulating the generation of alternatives in the client, however. The consultant can then help the client to think through the consequences of different interventions in the decision process.

If the consultant is an insider, this constraint is less severe, but an equally important psychological factor may be at work that still argues for caution in giving advice unilaterally. "Advice" generally does not work even if it is asked for, because 1) clients' psychological defenses prevent them from hearing or accepting certain kinds of advice, 2) many clients prefer to figure things out for themselves, and 3) clients often resent being given a solution because it reminds them of being at a disadvantage in having to admit a problem.

On the other hand, giving advice *as a diagnostic intervention* may be highly appropriate at times in order to elicit further information about what may be going on. The client's resistance then becomes new diagnostic information to be interpreted, and the tension that may arise between client and consultant becomes direct data to be worked on.

6. *The client is capable of learning how to diagnose and solve his own organizational problems.* The nature of life in organizations is such that there is no correct solution to problems that will last forever. Conditions will change, requiring new diagnoses and new solutions. Management is a perpetual coping process of solving problems to improve situations and/or to keep them from getting worse. If the client is not capable of learning how to learn, how to continue to solve problems, then the PC model is not appropriate.

However, it is my conviction that unless organizations are staffed with people who are capable of such learning, they will not survive in the long run. Therefore I believe it is essential for managers to become themselves effective process consultants vis-à-vis their subordinates, peers, and bosses. This use of the consulting process to pass on problem-solving skills then becomes one of its most important developmental aspects, guaranteeing future problem-solving capacity.

Process Consultation Defined

PROCESS CONSULTATION IS A SET OF ACTIVITIES ON THE PART OF THE CONSULTANT THAT HELP THE CLIENT TO PERCEIVE, UNDERSTAND, AND ACT UPON THE PROCESS EVENTS THAT OCCUR IN THE CLIENT'S ENVIRONMENT.

The process consultant seeks to help the client gain insight into what is going on around him and teaches him how to intervene in those events in such a manner as to increase that insight and to improve the situation to meet the client's goals. The events to be observed and intervened in are the various human actions that occur in the normal flow of work, in the conduct of meetings, and in the formal and informal encounters between members of the organization. Of particular relevance are the client's own actions and their impact on other people.

The Manager as Consultant

When should a manager be an expert, a doctor, or a process consultant? The formal authority of a manager makes it easy for him to fall into the expert or doctor role, especially when help is being sought by a subordinate. But if the goals of the manager are to teach the subordinate problem-solving skills and to ensure that the solutions developed will be the right ones and will be implemented correctly, then being a consultant is by far the preferable way to begin to help.

The manager has all the same problems that the consultant has of having people give him incorrect information, make incorrect diagnoses of their own problems, attribute to him expertise he may not have, want him to take over their problems, resent his giving them advice even when it is correct, misunderstand prescriptions, and so on. Therefore, the effective manager will start out in the PC role and remain in it until he is convinced that stepping into the situation as an expert or doctor really makes sense.

Obviously, if the boss is asked to be the doctor to a department below him, he has the formal power to implement whatever solutions he decides on, but it is not always clear that the members of the department will understand or accept what someone who is normally one or two levels removed from them imposes on them. There is thus the risk that the boss as doctor will think he has solved the problem, when, in fact, the group fails to implement, implements incorrectly, or even sabotages the solution.

On the other hand, if the boss has expertise or information that subordinates clearly lack and need, then it would be foolish not to play the content expert role, just as the consultant would play that role when it is appropriate — for example in designing meetings or conducting a survey. In other words, the most important thing for the manager to learn is that he has the choice among helping roles and must learn to assess situations quickly to make the right choice. My preference for always starting in the process consultant role is based on the fact that this role preserves the maximum flexibility and is the most consistent with the developmental goal of teaching clients to be effective in solving their own problems.

The Allen Company Revisited

If we apply some of the above points to the case of Fred Ralston, the division manager, cited in Chapter 1, we can see some of the dilemmas. Ralston viewed himself as an expert compared to his subordinates. He had learned a lot in his career, had had an undisputable success, and had academic training to bolster many of his own practical theories. He respected expertise and was willing to grant even greater expertise to me as a professor and consultant. On the other hand, he seemed less willing to treat the members of his organization as experts in their own right.

What Ralston seemed not to understand, as became evident from data I later obtained by getting to know Ralston's subordinates, was that some of his department heads felt genuinely insulted and maligned by the level and type of direction they were given. They also felt that they had expertise and experience. They felt they knew better than Ralston what was really going on in some of the departments and how to fix it. They felt they knew which solutions and programs would work and which ones would not. But they did not feel that they could be totally honest with Ralston because he would just lecture at them and make them feel even more frustrated and misunderstood.

So the most serious consequence of Ralston's overusing of the expert role was that he began to operate on somewhat incorrect assumptions about what was really going on. And he did not realize that his stance sometimes forced his subordinates to manipulate him in order to protect themselves.

One of the most important roles I developed as Ralston's consultant was to begin to get him to think about the consequences of his own managerial style, and to think about the possibility that he could accomplish his own goals much better by acting as a process consultant himself. I asked him frequently why he did what he did and asked him to speculate on the probable consequences of his own behavior on his subordinates. I asked him to think clearly about his goals and to reexamine the means he was using to accomplish them. In order to keep the financial indicators in line, did he need to monitor them *daily*, and if they went off, did he need to send punishing notes to his subordinates? I speculated out loud on how I might react if I were one of his subordinates, and asked him to imagine how he would react to a boss like himself.

I reinforced the idea that he could continue to set tough targets because it was clear that his success depended on his clarity and determination around these targets. He clearly was not going to compromise on that. But he could begin to give his subordinates more freedom in how to achieve those targets and create processes where genuine diagnosis could be engaged in by the department heads and their subordinates if and when the targets were not met.

For example, if errors were made vis-à-vis customers, it was the practice to pay the customer a penalty fee to show the organization's concern for high-quality, error-free performance. Ralston had the habit of asking during his weekly staff meeting for individual reports on *all* errors and what was being done about them, a practice that was boring and impractical because so many errors occurred that none of them could be analyzed in enough detail to learn anything useful from the discussion. By getting Ralston to examine alternative processes I gradually got him to change to a system of quality control in which an investigation would tackle only those errors of great consequence, do a thorough analysis of them, and then report findings to the staff meeting in detail so that everyone could learn from the experience.

Instead of writing punishing notes to his subordinates regarding drop-offs in cost indicators that he reviewed daily, Ralston was able to redesign his monitoring, making it into a weekly or monthly review, and he began to ask questions and engage in genuine dialogue with his subordinates, who were the parties responsible for the cost data.

These small changes in managerial behavior reflect fundamental changes in Ralston's view of his own relationship with his subordinates. As he began to trust them more, he was able to give up being the expert. As he gave them more freedom, he discovered that they knew more than he had assumed and that they could meet his targets without his detailed daily "help." In some measure he began to see himself not only as the target-setter for the group, but also as the consultant to the group, helping them to achieve the targets that he had set.

Conclusion

The three models of consultation highlight the complexity of the helping process. Each of these models is relevant at times, if the assumptions that underlie the model can be met. Most problems that I have encountered in the human parts of organizations do not fit the expert or doctor model. I generally start a consultation process, therefore, wearing my process consultant hat and switch to the other models only when I am sure that they are appropriate.

Everything a consultant does to a client from the moment the client makes contact with the consultant is an intervention of some sort. Therefore it is most appropriate to start with a model that emphasizes intervention as central. This is not to say that I can afford to ignore diagnostic issues, but rather to argue that I must make my diagnosis as I begin to intervene. There is no period of diagnosis "prior to intervention," though most consulting models claim one. The consultant must accept the responsibilities that accompany the activities involved in diagnosing a situation.

The line manager faces the same problem as the consultant. How the manager intervenes with subordinates and other members of the organization sets the tone. Although the manager may have to serve as expert or doctor at times, that role is often inappropriate for supervising and monitoring the group. It is desirable for the manager to learn how to be a process consultant in order to give genuine help to subordinates, and, not only to achieve the organization's goals better, but also to help those subordinates grow and develop.

3

What Is "Process"?

The concept of process is central to an understanding of consultation and management. In its broadest sense "process" refers to *how* things are done rather than *what* is done. If I am crossing the street, that is what I am doing, but the *process* is how I am crossing: walking, running, dodging cars, asking someone to help me across because I feel dizzy, or some other way.

Process is everywhere. In order to help, intervene, and facilitate human problem solving, one must focus on communication and interpersonal processes. The processes we need to learn to observe and manage are those that make a demonstrable difference to problem solving, decision making, and organizational effectiveness in general.

Understanding of human interpersonal and group processes is critical for the *manager* because effective managers spend far more time intervening in *how* things are done than on *what* is done. An effective manager must be able to create situations that will ensure that good decisions are made, without making those decisions himself and without even knowing ahead of time what he might do if he had to make the decision alone. Managing the decision process in this way becomes more necessary as technological complexity and the rate of change in the environment increase. The primary job of line managers will eventually be to create and manage the processes that ensure effective decision making.

How to Focus on Process

How does a consultant or manager know what to focus on when trying to intervene to improve a situation? Imagine yourself to have been invited to a staff meeting to see if you can be helpful in making that group more effective. If you are the manager who has called the meeting, imagine yourself trying to make the meeting as effective as possible. What should you be paying attention to? What kinds of interventions should you be considering?

Table 3–1 presents a simplifying model of the possibilities. The cells in the table overlap and, in reality, the distinctions are not as clear-cut as the descriptions imply, but we need simplifying models if we are to make any sense at all of the complex data that typically confront us in human situations.

First, we have to differentiate a situation's content from its process and its structure. Second, we have to differentiate, for each of the three aspects of a situation, whether we are focusing on the *task* issues or the *interpersonal* issues.

Table 3–1
The Foci of Observation and Intervention

	Task	**Interpersonal**
Content	1. Formal agenda, goals	4. Who is doing what to whom
Process	2. How the task is done	5. How members relate to each other, communicate, etc.
Structure	3. Recurrent processes— "standard operating procedures"	6. Recurrent interpersonal relationships, roles

Task Content (Cell 1). The most obvious thing to focus on in the meeting is why the group is there in the first place. What is its task? What are the goals of the meeting? Why does the group exist at all? Every group, every organization has an ultimate function, a reason for existence, a mission, and its goals and tasks derive from that ultimate function.

A group may not be aware of its ultimate mission or may not agree on its goals. In fact, one of the main functions of the consultant or manager may be to help the group to understand its task and function. This subject is something that the consultant or manager should then focus on explicitly, because if there is misunderstanding or disagreement at this level, the group will have a hard time functioning effectively.

The most observable aspect of task content is the actual subject matter that the group talks about or works on, what would typically be labeled its formal agenda. If the group has a secretary and keeps minutes, the content of the discussion is what will appear in the minutes. One of the choices you have as a helper, whether in the role of consultant or manager, is to keep close track of the task content to make sure that it stays "on track," to ensure that the group achieves its goals.

Task Process (Cell 2). Even if you pay close attention to and actively manage task content, the group may develop communication problems. People may not listen to one another or may misunderstand one another, people may interrupt one another, arguments and conflicts may develop, the group may not be able to agree, too much time may be spent on what you might regard as trivial issues, disruptive side conversations may develop, and other behavior may be displayed that gets in the way of effective task solution.

If you have been in a variety of groups you may also become aware that different groups working on the very same task may approach it very differently. In one group the chairperson calls on people to give their input; another group's chairperson invites anyone to speak who cares to. In one group there is angry confrontation and arguing; in another group there is polite, formal questioning. In one group decisions are made by consensus, in another they are made by voting, and in a third they are made by the manager after listening to the discussion for a while.

In other words, groups may have the same task and same content yet engage in drastically different processes of working on the task. *Task process*, then, is the way in which the group works, how it solves problems, gathers information, makes decisions, and so on. Task processes are elusive. It is easy to experience and to observe them but hard to define and clearly segregate them from the content that is being worked on. Group members learn that they can partially control the content outcomes by controlling the process, as senators do when they filibuster or as debaters do when they destroy an opponent's argument or composure by ridicule, changing the subject, or in other ways diverting the process from what has been said. One of the toughest tasks for the intervener is not to get seduced by the content, not to get so caught up in the actual problem the group is working on as to cease to pay attention to *how* it is working.

Task Structure (Cell 3). You will notice if you observe a group for some period of time that certain patterns recur, that some kinds of events happen regularly and some kinds of events never happen. For example, one group always uses parliamentary procedure, while another one refuses to vote on any issue even if they cannot resolve the issue by any other means. One group always has an agenda and follows it slavishly, while another waits until the meeting begins before generating a list of topics.

If the group contains more than one level of management you may notice some people interrupt others consistently while others never interrupt each other, and the pattern you may observe is that higher ranking people interrupt lower ranking ones but never the reverse. You might also note that if you are the chairman of the group that members will look to you for guidance and direction, and that if members of the group have been assigned particular roles or tasks, they will behave consistently with those assignments. Such regularities in the work of the group can best be thought of as the *task structure* of the group, relatively *stable, recurring processes* that help the group or organization to get its tasks accomplished.

In large organizations we think of the structure as being the formal hierarchy, the defined chain of command, the systems of information and control, and other stable recurring processes that are taught to newcomers as "the way we work around here." But it is important to recognize that the concept of structure is only an extension of the concept of process in that it refers to those processes that are stable, recurring, and defined by members in the group as their "structure."

All groups require such regularities and stability to make their environment and working patterns predictable and, thereby, manageable. The assumptions that develop over time as the underlying premises of those patterns can then be thought of as part of the culture of the group. They become shared and taken for granted, and the structures that we can observe can be viewed as artifacts or manifestations of the culture of the group (Schein, 1985a).

The culture itself is not immediately visible because it is best thought of as the taken for granted underlying and unconscious assumptions that have evolved over time to deal with the various external and internal issues that the group has had to face (Schein, 1985a). But the culture will be reflected in the overt behavior that is visible and can be searched out through a joint process of inquiry between the outsider and members of the group. For purposes of this model it is useful to focus on the manifest artifacts, the visible behavior, always bearing in mind that they reflect important underlying assumptions that will eventually have to be taken into account.

The task structure that evolves in a group is composed of regularities that pertain specifically to the group's survival in its external environment. All groups face at least five basic survival problems:

1. *Defining the fundamental mission that justifies its existence—its primary task.* The structural elements dealing with this issue are usually company charters, statements of philosophy or mission, formal agenda statements, and other efforts to document members' implicit understanding about the role of the group.

2. *Setting specific goals derived from the mission.* The structural elements are written goal statements, formal planning procedures and their outcomes, publicly defined targets and deadlines.

3. *Deciding what means to use to accomplish the goals.* The structures for accomplishing goals are the defined formal organization, assigned task roles, and recurring procedures for solving problems and making decisions.

4. *Measuring and monitoring whether or not goals are being accomplished.* Formal information and control systems are set up, and managerial planning, budgeting, and review processes are formalized.

5. *Getting back on course by fixing problems once they are identified (when the group discovers it is off target or not accomplishing its goals).* A group needs processes for remedying situations, fixing problems, getting itself back on course. Often solutions are invented ad hoc, but any group or organization has to be able to regularize remedial and corrective processes and thus make them part of the structure of the group.

In a young group, the task structure processes will not be very stable; the young group is not very structured. As the group evolves, it develops assumptions about itself. If those assumptions lead to success, they eventually become the culture of the group. They then become visible and may be formally described in organization charts, manuals of procedure, rules of order, and other artifacts of the culture.

Interpersonal Content (Cell 4). We have now defined all the cells that deal with the group's task, its problems of survival in its environment, but, of course, the consultant or manager observing the group will note immediately that many of the salient events that occur in the group have to do with what the members are doing to one another, much of which may have relatively little to do with the task at a manifest level.

We will see that Joe seems to always get into fights with Joan, and that Mildred consistently supports Jim, almost no matter what he says, and that Rudy dominates the conversation and tries to control all the other members, while Paul speaks up rarely, and only when asked a direct question. We will note that some people interrupt others; that some people increase the tension in the group by being divisive, while others reduce tension by cracking a joke at just the right moment when things were getting too tense. We will see that some members are good initiators and energizers of the group, while others are good summarizers and are able to test consensus in the group.

Just as we can track the content agenda of the group, we can also track "who does what to whom," "who plays what roles in the group," and construct a picture of the group in terms of the actual members and their relationships to one another and to the task. Whereas the focus in cell 1 is on the task content, the focus in cell 4 would be on the relationships among the members of the group, regardless of what the group is actually working on.

Interpersonal Process (Cell 5). Separating process from content is difficult in the task area because people consciously and unconsciously manipulate both process and content. But just as it is possible to observe a group at work and abstract the methods it uses to accomplish that work, so it is possible to abstract the interpersonal processes evident in a group independent of the actual people involved in these processes.

Thus, for example, one group may exhibit frequent confrontation and arguing among members, while another group's members may always be very polite and agree with one another. In one group people may listen to each other intently and try to build on each others' ideas, while in another group they may constantly vie for one another's attention, paying more attention to how they present their own view than to what others may have said.

It is important to observe interpersonal process because group outcomes result from a complex interaction of what goes on at the task (cell 2) and interpersonal (cell 5) level. For example, you may notice that different members have different definitions of the task, and this leads to various kinds of communication breakdowns interfering with task performance. You may also notice that some members systematically seem not to listen to other members, resulting in imperfect accumulation of information relevant to the task.

Or you may notice that, while some members are working on generating alternative solutions, others are busy advocating or attacking one of these solutions, and it may strike you that certain members are always attacking what certain other members bring up no matter what the task content. Such interpersonal conflicts obviously get in the way of effective decision making. Or you may notice that a great many good ideas have been proposed but that the group has lost track of them because no one has put them on the board. Yet whenever anyone offers to be the recorder some other members strongly resist the idea with jibes about grabbing the chalk as being a power ploy.

All of these behaviors also involve task processes as previously defined in that they affect directly the efforts of the group to work on its task. But, at the same time, each of these processes also involve aspects of members' relationships with and feelings about one another, their roles, and mutual influence patterns that do not directly affect the task. These then would be examples of *interpersonal process* that seem more motivated by the feelings people have toward each other than by task concerns. One of the toughest choices for the intervener is deciding when to intervene around such processes and when merely to note them and leave them alone.

Interpersonal Structure (Cell 6). In order to develop structure — that is, stable, recurring processes — the group needs to develop a culture that will solve its problems of survival in the external environment. Similarly, any group or organization needs to develop stable, recurring processes to manage its internal affairs, to enable members to work together and to feel secure as a group. Recurring and stable processes are necessary to make the internal group environment safe and predictable so that members can relax enough to put their emotional energy into working on the survival tasks (Schein, 1985a).

Part of the culture of the group, then, can be thought of as the stable perceptions, thought processes, feelings, and communication rules that permit the group to function as a group. What are the internal problems for which such stability is required? For any group to function it must develop a stable solution for each of the following problems:

1. *How to communicate with each other — developing a common language.* The observable structure will be the actual language the group evolves as it works together: special termi-

nology, special meanings attached to certain words and concepts, and special symbols that only insiders will understand.

2. *How to define its own boundaries — developing rules of inclusion and exclusion.* The observable structure will be the policies and practices of recruitment, who is given symbols of membership such as uniforms or badges, policies about rehiring people who may have left, policies toward temporary members or contract workers, rules about whom one tells things and from whom one must keep secrets, and so on.

3. *How to allocate power and authority — developing criteria for who can influence whom and on what issues.* In this area what is formally structured and how things work out in practice have often been noted to be different. It is possible to publish organization charts and to have rules about the chain of command, but observers often note that even on a regular basis some of these rules are ignored and alternate structures will develop that often get labeled the "informal" structure.

4. *How to define appropriate peer relationships — developing criteria for openness and intimacy, appropriate levels of cooperation and competition.* This area is often the least structured and, therefore, the source of most anxiety until new members have learned the implicit rules of the game. But in observing indoctrination programs or mentoring discussions, one notes structure expressed by such remarks as "Around here teamwork is the name of the game," "Never get caught playing politics," "We always address the boss by his title here," "We are very informal and on a first name basis here," "You always better tell exactly what you think, even if you feel it might get you into trouble," or "You always have to be careful not to contradict the boss in public," and so on. Such rules do not get embedded as readily as more explicit rules in the visible formal structure, but they always exist in the culture (Van Maanen, 1979).

5. *How to allocate status and rewards.* The formal reward system, the performance appraisal system, the ratings of potential, and the actual recurring procedures for promoting and otherwise rewarding and punishing people are usually observable. As in item 4, however, the structures embodied in written policies and procedures do not always match the recurring regularities that may be observed — the informal reward system.

6. How to deal with unexplainable, unmanageable, and threatening events. This area is the least likely to be formally structured, though every group will evolve rituals and procedures for dealing with those unpredictable and stressful events that cannot be easily controlled. It may develop superstitions, myths, or symbolic rituals like rain dances. Such processes may become stable in that they are passed on and taught to new generations of members.

As it interacts, the group evolves stable perceptions and relationships to deal with each of the above areas, and these gradually become assumptions about itself and come to constitute a major part of the group's culture. Once again, the underlying assumptions will not be visible in the overt workings of the group, but the process observer will see the effects in the political alliances, in the communication patterns, in the recurring patterns of expressed feelings of members toward each other, and in the deference and demeanor they display toward each other.

The immediate intervention focus should be on the dynamic processes that are visible because then members can see the same things that the observer sees. Eventually, as the group itself becomes more sophisticated in analyzing its own processes, less visible structural and cultural elements can increasingly become the focus of intervention.

In summary, as the consultant or manager, you would note events in all six cells of Table 3–1. The key question to consider, then, is which of these events are most relevant to increasing the effectiveness of the group.

The Primary Task as the Basis for Intervention

The most important criterion for deciding what to observe and where to intervene is your perception of what the *primary task* of the group is. By primary task I mean that set of goals which justify the existence of the group, the reason for which it was called together, its basic mission, the perceptions that relate the group to its external environment and that will ultimately determine its survival as a group. The primary task will not always be immediately obvious but can generally be inferred or even asked about. If the timing of the question is premature, one may not get an accurate answer, so further observation and checking may be required.

In a new relationship with an individual client or when managing a new group, the focus that is safest and most likely to be productive is the process consultant's own primary task or goals as a helper or manager. What are you and your client or subordinates trying to do? Where do you want to be by when? What next steps make most sense given what you are trying to accomplish?

In many consulting models this focus is often identified as "setting a contract with the client." That is usually *not* the right formulation. It is better to focus on our immediate goals in order to be able to intervene effectively from the outset, to be helpful to the client or subordinates from the moment of contact.

For the outside consultant, overt concern for what the client is trying to accomplish 1) signals interest in helping, 2) elicits data that are needed in order to decide how to help, and, most important, 3) is already a critical intervention, forcing clients to *articulate* what they are trying to accomplish. Often this turns out to be helpful in that it starts the client thinking about goals. The contract that may arise is a by-product, not the primary goal.

The same logic applies to managers whose subordinates come to them with problems. The manager who wants to be helpful should focus on what the subordinates are trying to accomplish, why they are having difficulty with it, why they are having difficulty right now, why they are coming to the boss for help, and so on, but always remain focused on the primary task. As the answers to these questions reveal other concerns, the focus can shift to them, but the initial focus should stay in cells 1 and 2 of Table 3–1.

Focus of Interventions: Task Content, Task Process, or Task Structure?

The client is usually pretty sensitive to the content issues but is likely to be *insensitive* to process and structure. The barriers to more effective task accomplishment often lie in the processes or structure, yet these are often the least visible aspects of how things are done. Hence bringing to light new data on process and structure, and helping clients to see such data on their own in the future, is most likely to be helpful. Generally the task content is something highly visible and chances are that the client is more expert in that area than the helper anyway. But the consultant or manager can really help by noting how the task process and structure helps or hinders decision making and problem solving.

The process of surfacing and changing *structure* may involve confrontive or even manipulative interventions where the consultant in the expert or doctor role directly manipulates portions of the structure in order to change other parts of a system that has become rigid. Such systemic interventions have become common in family therapy and are increasingly being applied in organizational settings, but they are rarely appropriate until enough process consultation has gone on to find out whether clients are genuinely "stuck," unable to diagnose or influence their own system (Madanes, 1981; Durkin, 1981; Borwick, 1983).

Another kind of structural intervention that may help to get the client unstuck is to define a new structure as an "experiment to be tried" rather than a final recommendation to be adopted. Such an intervention is likely to be powerful and confrontive in that it forces into consciousness routines that may be deliberately concealed.

Why Not Focus on Interpersonal Process and Structure?

Since interpersonal issues are generally very salient and easily observed, it is tempting to focus the interventions directly on such issues. The primary reason not to do so is basically cultural. In our culture task accomplishment, progress, goal attainment, and achievement are so central to relationships that most of the motivation for improvement comes from preoccupation with a task. Even if a personal relationship becomes a problem, we define relationship improvement as a "task" to be accomplished.

It is likely that in some other cultures where "effective relationships" and "harmony" are more important than task accomplishment, the focus for facilitative intervention would shift to interpersonal processes, but in the United States a focus on such matters at the outset is likely to be seen as a waste of time, irrelevant, soft, and motivated by false emphases on "humanism." Consultants or managers who try to promote harmony may fail unless they establish credibility by beginning with task process interventions.

A second reason for avoiding focusing on interpersonal process interventions is that management or consulting to organizations is itself task focused. Organizations are task oriented by definition. They are created to achieve certain goals, to accomplish tasks. Management is typically *defined* as the attainment of goals. Consultants who work with organizations are typically brought in by managers who are "hurting" because tasks are not being accomplished in desired ways.

Thus, interpersonal issues are seen as relevant by most client systems only insofar as they influence task accomplishment. If such relationship issues become primary we think not of consultation but of therapy, and we tend to place such therapeutic interventions into contexts outside of the work sphere. A family business may be engaged with a consultant working on business problems and be working with the same consultant or a different one on family issues (Beckhard and Dyer, 1983). It is important to differentiate these processes and to recognize that only in the therapeutic context is the relationship focus legitimately the primary one.

On the other hand, if interpersonal issues are clearly interfering with task accomplishment, and the consultant or manager believes that this is highly visible to the participants themselves, it may be entirely appropriate to shift explicitly to an interpersonal intervention. What kind of intervention to make and how to frame it will be discussed in later chapters.

Does it make a difference in the interpersonal arena whether one focuses on content, process, or structure? Is it important to distinguish content from process or structure in this area? The answer is yes because of the different consequences of interventions in the different cells of Table 3.1. You may readily observe interpersonal *content* in the sense of who actually feels how and is doing what to whom. Nonetheless, it is in this area where you should be most careful because people are most likely to be sensitive and defensive about the actual naming of names. When you "name names" instead of merely pointing out a general process, people feel they will lose face, and so naming names is taboo in most cultures.

For example, I may observe a pattern that Pete is always interrupting Jane and may conclude that this reflects a real enmity on Pete's part toward Jane (Cells 4–6). If I decide to intervene because I believe Pete's behavior is making the group less effective, I still have a choice around which cell to focus:

> Cell 4 (Content): "Pete, why are you always interrupting Jane?"
>
> Cell 5 (Process): "I notice that certain members tend to interrupt others, and wonder whether this is getting in the way of communication?"
>
> Cell 6 (Structure): "As our discussion has proceeded I have noticed that whenever we interrupt each other, the discussion is not as productive. Should we do something about this?"

Of course these illustrative interventions differ on dimensions other than content, process, and structure, but it should be clear that the highest risk is associated with the content intervention because it threatens to make both Pete and Jane lose face. The structural intervention is the safest but the least likely to be productive because it does not provide a specific reference for the group to organize around. The process intervention maximizes specificity without making people lose face.

In summary:

1. Process is always to be favored as an intervention focus over content.
2. Task process is always to be favored over interpersonal process.
3. Structural interventions are in principle the most powerful in that they deal with recurrent stable processes rather than the dynamic fluid ones, but they are also likely to be most resisted because there is comfort in structure, and also the most likely to be misunderstood because they are, of necessity, general.

Hence a focus on the dynamic task processes — how a client or group sets goals, gathers information, solves problems, makes decisions, and allocates work roles — is the focus most likely to be helpful. In the example given next the issue of where to focus interventions came up repeatedly. Because this case will also be used throughout the book, a certain amount of background is provided at this point.

Helping to Build a New Executive Committee: The Billings Manufacturing Company

Bill Stone, the president and founder of a small but rapidly growing manufacturing company, called me to seek some advice on hiring a new vice president for human resources. I had done a seminar on career development for the top fifteen managers of this company three years before, had known the corporate vice president for planning, and had worked with the recently departed vice president for human resources a year or so before when he had first joined this company. So I had various bits of knowledge about the company and they had various bits of knowledge about me.

Getting Acquainted with the Client. Stone mentioned in his first phone call that when the previous vice president of human resources was leaving, he had recommended that they might get someone from academia to take the job since Stone had a well-articulated philosophy of human resource management that had to continue to be well stated and well implemented. Stone asked whether this concept made any sense and whether I or some other professor would even consider taking an industrial job for a while. I said that I would not personally consider taking such a job but would be glad to examine the concept with him and see where we might come out. We agreed to meet for a long lunch at the Massachusetts Institute of Technology.

At the lunch Stone reviewed some of the decisions he had made recently. The fifteen-person executive committee was not working effectively, so he had begun to meet on a regular basis with two executive vice presidents, the chief financial officer, and the vice president in charge of new acquisitions. This group was a good nucleus for a more streamlined and effective executive committee, but they needed to add a vice president for human resources and had just launched a search for such a person.

Stone and I reviewed what he was really looking for in this role, and it became apparent that everyone in the new executive committee would have a big stake in deciding the kind of person to be hired. The idea arising from this discussion was that I should attend some of the meetings of this new executive committee, especially the meeting where the job description for the human resource VP would be hammered out. The other members agreed that my attendance would be helpful, though it was not at all clear to me whether I would be there as an expert telling them what they should be looking for, or as a process consultant helping them to figure out what they needed. I was tempted to try to clarify this point at the outset but decided that they probably were not sure themselves what kind of help I could offer, hence their answer might not be very meaningful until after we had had some contact.

Deciding the Intervention Focus. The first three-hour meeting I attended brought out many of the issues of what role to be in and what to focus on in the group's work. I attempted to make clear at the beginning of the meeting that I saw my role as that of helping the group to clarify its own thinking and that I would not be an expert on what their human resource VP should be — that is, I would not get into *task content*, but would focus on *task process*. I also said that Stone had asked me to work with this group over a period of several meetings to help it to become an effective group, which might involve me in clarifying and intervening not only on task process but also on *interpersonal process*. The group seemed to understand these distinctions and agreed that such a role could be helpful.

As the discussion began, I found myself intervening frequently on the line between task content and process. I kept raising content questions about the role that the new vice president was supposed to play in the new executive committee, especially vis-à-vis Stone, but I was careful to time the questions so that the group would have every chance to raise these issues on its own. I also framed the questions in the most general way so as to minimize my own content biases. In effect I was performing some problem-identifying functions that were missing in the group's discussion, but instead of simply saying that such functions were missing (which would have been a pure process intervention), I actually asked the content question to facilitate the group's forward movement.

I asked, for example, "Is the new VP expected to be only an implementer or is he expected to contribute to the architecture of human resource policies?" The group said unanimously that they wanted an architect. "Do you want a person who would argue with you and one strong enough to stand up to the kind of fighting that the group often engages in?" I asked this because it was obvious after fifteen minutes of observation that the group was used to intense debate and confrontation, and that Stone himself was often very strong in his own opinions. They said they wanted a strong confronter, and Stone agreed. Note again that I did not limit the intervention to simply noting that the group argued a lot and that Stone was a strong figure (interpersonal content and process), but embedded the data in a task content question that facilitated further problem solving.

"Do you want someone with a track record primarily as a human resource professional or someone with credibility as a line manager?" I wanted to force out into the open what the group really thought about the human resource function, because I began to suspect that they looked down on it. At this point my expertise and prior experience were seducing me into content opinions, but I did not have to voice those opinions. I could stay on the process level. To voice my suspicion would have raised issues about content structure (their stable perceptions of roles), which would have been dangerous because it might have precipitated a quick denial and some suspicion of me, so I chose a more neutral question. They said they wanted both things.

As consensus emerged on various of these criteria I wrote them down on the blackboard, since it was obvious that the group was having trouble remembering what it had said. (This was a task process intervention.)

Periodically I found myself having to deal directly with content and was forced to deal with perceptions that I had expert knowledge in this area. I was asked, for example, what kind of people were in comparable jobs in other companies that I was familiar with. I could not deny my expertise in this area, relative to the knowledge of the group, so I gave answers that I thought would aid their thinking without making specific recommendations as to what they might need. I emphasized the variety of such people that I knew in order to broaden the group's knowledge base of what was possible.

I was asked whether I had any knowledge of how this kind of function was organized in other companies such as theirs. Again I had to admit to some knowledge, but I was careful to offer a number of different options that I was aware of so as not to bias the discussion or get into a direct argument with any member of the group about the "right" way to do it. I found that I could give information but always tried to cast it in the form of an issue, the pros and cons of different approaches.

Interpersonal issues were obvious and ubiquitous. One of the executive vice presidents, Tom Riley, was obviously a central and aggressive figure in the group. He frequently argued with Stone and between them the two used up a large percentage of the group's discussion time. One of the members was somewhat hard of hearing and seemed to participate less, though it was not clear to me at the time whether or not his reluctance to participate was related to the hearing disability.

When real disagreements erupted, there seemed to be a norm to agree to disagree rather than to resolve the issue, a norm that often left me wondering what, if anything had been decided. It raised the possibility that the group knew that in such cases Stone would resolve the issue after the meeting, but I did not know enough of the history of the group to second-guess this aspect of their structure.

While all of these interpersonal issues potentially got in the way of clear resolution of the problem of developing the criteria for the selection of their human resource VP, at this first meeting I could not possibly intervene on such issues directly because I did not know enough about what was really going on. Later in the project, after I had interviewed all the members of the group and they had agreed to discuss "how the group functioned," it was possible to bring out these issues because they had been brought out in individual interviews.

The meeting ended with an agreement that Stone would take down all my notes from the board and circulate them. Considerable consensus had been achieved and a process agreed upon for interviewing candidates. Criteria were to be tested by applying them to each of the major candidates to be interviewed. At a later meeting that I would attend, the prime candidates would be reviewed by the entire group.

Lessons. As I reviewed my role in this meeting, it was clearly to force clarity of criterion setting by asking questions whenever I felt that the group was being vague or ambiguous and by testing consensus in areas of agreement. I also focused the group by recording their points on the board and helped to design the subsequent interview and selection process. All of these interventions were clearly *task process* oriented, but they involved the content of what the group was working on and thus did not divert the group into a pure process discussion, something that I thought they were not ready for.

Managing an Academic Group: Managerial Choices on Intervention Focus

Does a line manager have the same range of choices as the consultant in deciding on an intervention focus? I can answer this question best by reconstructing some of the decisions I had to make when I was chairman of a ten-person academic group within the Sloan School of Management at MIT. The managerial role obviously required the setting of goals and targets, but I found from the outset that if I did not get complete consensus on the mission of the group, any program of implementation was bound to fail. So my first task was how to design a process that would ensure consensus on what we were trying to do.

My first interventions were to create opportunities in individual conversations and in group meetings to discuss our priorities. These priorities were 1) to create an environment in which we could be productive researcher-scholars; 2) to develop a curriculum that met the needs of our students and drew on our own strengths; 3) to create a recruitment, hiring, and promotion system that would ensure that we get the best possible colleagues as positions opened up; 4) to ensure that we would attract the best possible Ph.D. students into our group by creating a program of education and training for them that would ensure their academic success.

I had been instrumental in bringing several new faculty into the group so one of my own main goals was to make sure that they be productive so that they would achieve tenure. In each of these areas, task process interventions were the key. We needed to develop a pattern of meetings that would be optimal for communication, we needed to marshal financial, space, and other resources that would make it possible for faculty to maximize their productivity, and we needed to minimize administrative duties and processes to conserve time for teaching and scholarly activities.

For example, in order to get optimal secretarial help and still have each secretary work for three faculty members, it was necessary to examine why secretaries were from time to time overloaded and demoralized. We involved our senior secretary in the process of figuring out what to do and discovered from discussing the process together that the main source of strain was being sent to the library and the photocopying machine all the time, thus interrupting desk work, phone answering, and other duties. We had incorrectly assumed that the secretaries felt overloaded with typing. Once we realized it was the constant errands that were the source of irritation we redesigned the secretarial process by hiring a student to be the all-purpose errand person to whom all the secretaries on the floor could give work that was away from the desk. We analyzed the work process, redesigned it, and cured the problem. We realized that the secretaries owned the problem and needed help and learned that our own diagnosis of the problem was, in fact, incorrect.

Another example of taking the process orientation concerned controlling phone costs. Each month I received a document that listed all phone calls made from each faculty member's phone. It was very tempting to delve into the "content" to see who was overusing the phone, but I feared that doing so would tempt me into confrontations with colleagues that would not only be embarrassing but would distract us from the more important mission of getting our scholarly and other work done.

Looking at this problem from a process consultant's point

of view led to the following procedure. I told my secretary not to show me the sheets at all but to cut them up so that each person could be given his own individual information. I wrote a memo saying that we needed to monitor our own phone calls because of rising costs and the report that some unauthorized calls were being made on our phones. Each person got a copy of the memo and his own data. At a subsequent faculty meeting we discussed whether anything further needed to be done about the phone situation. Everyone reported finding some useful things in their own data, an unauthorized person was located who had made over $200.00 worth of personal calls, and costs generally dropped dramatically.

Whenever general administrative issues came up, I reiterated our shared goals but then put the emphasis on how we could collectively design better processes for meeting those goals. I rarely had to "make a decision" because invariably we reached a consensus on how things should be done that everyone understood immediately. My job was to ensure that we identified the problem and took the time to design a process to fix it.

When individual colleagues or students came to me with problems, I found that the best stance was to keep asking questions that would clarify how the person was seeing the problem and, more important, to ask what the person had already tried to do about it. New ideas usually emerged that could be implemented. If I threw in my own ideas, however, they were often off target. I found myself to be most effective and helpful if I took a task process orientation unless I had specific information that needed to be shared, in which case I would, of course, share it.

Conclusion

Most of the illustrations given in this chapter refer to the consultant or manager working with a group. In reality the consultant will sometimes be working in a one-to-one relationship with a client, sometimes in a group setting, sometimes in a larger organizational setting, and sometimes will be recommending interventions that apply to organizational units not being directly worked with at all. For example, the consultant may recommend a special kind of meeting or the conducting of a survey. So a taxonomy of interventions must take into account not only the issues discussed here but also different client settings. (The variety of client settings is the subject of Chapters 7 and 10).

Which intervention is most appropriate depends also on the stage of the consultation project. The kinds of things the consultant can and should do when first establishing a relationship with a contact client may differ substantially from what can be done after the consultant has worked with various groups in the organization, understands something of the culture, and has multiple clients in the system. Becoming more familiar with what the various clients are ready for, the consultant can begin to shift to cells other than task process if interpersonal or content issues are interfering with effective problem solving.

Part II

Simplifying Models
of Human Processes

In order to be effective in helping others, a consultant or manager needs to know how things work — inside the individual, between people, in groups, in organizations, and between organizations in society. He or she needs to know a lot about the processes that occur in human systems. The consultant or manager need not have formal knowledge of psychology, sociology, and anthropology, although these fields contribute crucial insights into human processes. What the consultant or manager needs is practical models that simplify yet capture the essence of those insights.

One such simplifying model was presented in Chapter 3 to illustrate what is meant by the concept of "process." In the original version of *Process Consultation* (1969) I presented a number of such models dealing with communication, group growth, problem solving, leadership, and intergroup relations. Those earlier models have proved necessary but not sufficient in practice, so I have added in this book some additional models that I have found to be crucial to my own understanding of what goes on in human systems.

Insights into "what really goes on" are needed in order to diagnose a problem in an organization. To be effective in making helpful interventions the consultant or manager must supplement these insights with intervention skills, usually based on training and experience. Skill acquisition is not so much a matter of formal training as practicing observation and intervention and studying carefully the effects of one's own actions. But since one cannot practice observation effectively without some understanding of what to look for and how to analyze the observations, one must come back to the models that will be discussed in this part of the book.

The presentation of diagnostic models does not imply that in every helping project there must be a period of diagnosis followed by a period of intervention. Many consulting models present such stages as the correct way to proceed, but such sequential models distort reality. In fact, intervention begins with initial contact with the client. But one needs mental models of diagnosis in order to anticipate and decipher even the initial interactions with a client or subordinate. Diagnosis is both an instantaneous and a perpetual process, just as intervention is instantaneous and perpetual. Simplifying models help to put that instant process on target and provide the intervener with a way of thinking about interventions.

4

Intrapsychic Processes — ORJI

The most important thing for managers or consultants to understand is what goes on *inside their own heads*. If they cannot observe and assess their own feelings, biases, perceptual distortions, and impulses, they cannot tell whether their interventions are based on perceptions of reality, of what would really be helpful, or only on their own needs to express or defend themselves.

To understand what goes on inside the head and how this affects our overt behavior, we need a simplifying model of processes that are, in fact, extremely complex. The complexity arises primarily from the fact that our nervous system is *simultaneously* a data gathering system, a processing system, and a proactive managing system. That is, we observe (O), we react emotionally to what we have observed (R), we analyze, process, and make judgments based on observations and feelings (J), and we behave overtly in order to make something happen, we intervene (I).

In the simplest form we can lay this out as a sequential model as shown in Fig. 4–1. Although real intrapsychic processes do not occur in such a simple, logical sequence, the model permits us to analyze in more detail the complexity of what happens

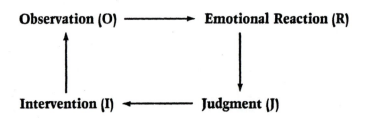

Figure 4–1
The Basic ORJI Cycle

inside the mind, what kinds of traps we fall into, and how this makes our interventions more or less effective.

Observation

Observation should be the accurate registering through all of our senses of what is actually occurring in the environment. In fact, the nervous system is pro-active, programmed through many prior experiences to filter data that come in. We see and hear more or less what we "expect" or "anticipate" based on prior experience, and we block out a great deal of information that is potentially available if it does not fit our expectations, preconceptions, and prejudgments. We do not passively register information; we select out from the available information what we want and need.

Psychoanalytic theory has shown us how extensive perceptual distortion can be. The defensive mechanisms of denial (refusing to see certain categories of information as they apply to ourselves) and projection (seeing in others what is actually operating in ourselves) are perhaps the clearest examples. To be objective we must reduce the initial distortions that the perceptual system is capable of.

One of the hardest tasks is to learn to suspend *prejudgment*, to become acquainted with one's own defense mechanisms, to correct for expectations and preconceptions so as to be able to "see" and "hear" more accurately what is going on. Some psychologists relate this to right brain versus left brain functions, arguing that it is the left "critical" brain that causes misperception. That theory is consistent with what many art teachers argue, that we cannot draw better because we do not actually see what we are drawing; we are drawing what we think things should look like (Frank, 1973; Edwards, 1979). To learn to observe, then, is to learn about traps that the rest of the ORJI cycle exposes us to.

Reaction

The most difficult aspect of emotional reaction is that we often do not notice it at all. We deny feelings or take them so for granted that we, in effect, short-circuit them and move straight into judgments and actions. We may be feeling anxious, angry, guilty, embarrassed, joyful, aggressive, or happy and yet not realize that we are feeling this way until someone asks us how we are feeling or we take the time to reflect on what is going on inside us.

Feelings are very much part of every moment of living, but we learn very early in life that there are many situations where feelings should be "controlled," "suppressed," "overcome," and in various other ways "deleted" or denied. As we learn sex roles and occupational roles, and as we become socialized into a particular culture, we learn which feelings are acceptable and which ones are not, when it is appropriate to express feelings and when it is not, when feelings are "good" and when they are "bad."

In our culture we also learn that feelings should not influence judgments, that feelings are a source of distortion, and we are told not to act impulsively on our feelings. But, paradoxically, we often end up acting most on our feelings when we are least aware of them, all the while deluding ourselves that we are carefully acting only on judgments. Forces we are not aware of cannot be controlled or managed.

If we can learn to identify our true feelings and what triggers our feelings, then we have a choice whether or not to give in to those feelings. If we do not know what they are or what causes them, we are de facto victims of them. It is not impulsiveness per se that causes difficulty, it is acting on impulses that are not consciously understood and hence are not evaluated prior to action.

Judgment

We are constantly processing data, analyzing information, evaluating, and making judgments. This ability to analyze prior to action is what makes humans capable of planning sophisticated behavior to achieve complex goals and sustain action chains that take us years into the future. The capacity to plan ahead and to organize our actions according to plan is one of the most critical aspects of human intelligence.

Jaques (1976, 1982) has noted that one of the ways that different levels of management can be distinguished is by the time horizon that they consider and by the length of the time units over which they are given discretion. Thus workers on the shop floor may have autonomy over minutes, hours, or days. Low-level managers may have autonomy for days or weeks. Senior managers plan for and have autonomy over months or years.

But all of the analysis and judgment we engage in is worth only as much as the data on which it is based. If we misperceive or if our feelings distort the data we operate on, then our analysis and judgments will be flawed. So it does little good to go through sophisticated planning and analysis exercises if we do not pay attention to the manner in which the information we use is acquired and what biases may exist in it. Nor does analysis help us if we unconsciously bias our reasoning toward our emotional reactions. It has been shown that even under the best of conditions we are only capable of limited rationality and make systematic cognitive errors (Simon, 1960; Tversky and Kahneman, 1981; Nisbett and Ross, 1980), so we should at least minimize the distortions in the initial information input.

Perhaps the commonest example of this dynamic has to do with our fear of being attacked and put at a disadvantage. Say I find myself at a meeting with fellow group members, one of whom has consistently undermined me or disagreed with me in past meetings. I make a particular point and it is followed by this person saying some words pertaining to my point. The cycle now may unfold as follows:

Observation. Steve is attacking me by disagreeing with my point. (What I may be unaware of is that I am perceiving what Steve said as disagreement because I expected it and am seeing disagreement as attack because I also expected to be attacked.)

Reaction. I am angry at always being disagreed with and attacked. I feel like really fighting back to make my position very clear. (What I may be unaware of is that my emotional reaction is now based not on what Steve's motives may actually have been, but on the motives I attributed to Steve.)

Judgment. Steve must be competing with me for status in this group and I can't let him get away with putting me down. I have to assert myself to protect my position. (What I am probably unaware of at this point is how this entire logical conclusion is premised on my initial interpretation and my emotional response.) If I now act on this judgment, I may or may not be acting appropriately because I do not in fact know whether my initial observation was correct.

The reconstruction of the cycle often reveals that one's judgment is "logical" but is based on "facts" that may not be accurate, hence the outcome may not be logical at all. And the most dangerous part of the cycle is the first step, where we make attributions and prejudgments rather than focusing as much as possible on what really happened.

Intervention

Once we have made some kind of judgment we act. The judgment may be no more than the "decision" to act on emotional impulse, but that is a judgment nevertheless and it is dangerous to be unaware of it. In other words, when we act impulsively, when we exhibit what are called "knee-jerk" reactions, it seems like we are short-circuiting the rational judgment process.

In fact, what we are doing is not short-circuiting but giving too much credence to an initial observation and emotional response.

Knee-jerk reactions that get us into trouble are interventions that are judgments based on incorrect data, not necessarily bad judgments. If someone is attacking me and I react with instant counterattack, that may be a very valid and appropriate intervention. But if I have misperceived and the person was not attacking me at all, then my counterattack makes *me* look like the aggressor and may lead to a serious communication breakdown.

When we say that someone acted "emotionally" instead of logically, we usually mean that he or she acted inappropriately to the situation, that we could not see the data that would warrant the kind of behavior we observed in the person. When we interview the "emotional" person we often find that the behavior was rational and logical from the person's point of view, that the person "observed" something that made him or her rationally react to that observation. If the behavior was inappropriate it was not because it was not rational but because it was based on incorrect initial observation.

A poignant example of this process was recently reported by an executive in one of our intensive executive development programs. Father (the executive) is deeply involved in studying for a finance examination to be taken next morning. He has isolated himself in the study and has asked his six-year-old not to disturb him. Half an hour later the child appears at the door and interrupts what the father was doing. Father gets angry because he asked not to be disturbed and "observes" the child's entry as doing something he had been forbidden to do. Father considers his anger to be entirely appropriate (judgment) and punishes the child by yelling at him that he was not to be disturbed (intervention).

Later on father notices that the child is very upset, aloof, and in other ways reacting more strongly than father thinks is warranted. This new observation triggers a new feeling of tension, concern, and worry about the child, leading to the judgment that he should find out what is going on, and causing him to intervene by asking either the child or mother some questions. These questions complete a second cycle.

What father now learns is that the child came down at the mother's request to ask him if he wanted to have a cup of coffee to help him work and to say goodnight. Listening to this explanation now makes father feel guilty and ashamed for blowing up. He makes the judgment that he was wrong to have acted so hastily before, so he now attempts to apologize and make up with his child.

More important, if father becomes aware of how he misperceived the situation and how this led to an inappropriate intervention, he can train himself to be more careful in future situations to check on what he is observing before he allows himself to respond emotionally. He discovers that emotions are not automatic, that they are based on what we perceive, and that if we can check our perceptions, we can, by this process, also control our emotions.

The More Realistic ORJI Cycle

If we were now to redraw what we have been talking about it would look more like Fig. 4–2. This figure permits us to summarize the traps involved in the ORJI cycle as follows:

Trap 1. Misperception. Due to prejudgments, expectations, defenses, or false attributions we do not perceive accurately *what* happened or *why* it happened.

Trap 2. Inappropriate Emotional Response. Because of misperception of what happened or why it happened, we "allow" ourselves to respond emotionally to our interpretation without being aware that it is based on incorrect data.

Trap 3. Rational Analysis and Judgment Based on Incorrect Data. Once we accept our observation and emotional response as correct, we can reason appropriately but still come out with the wrong conclusion if the input was incorrect.

Trap 4. Intervening on Seemingly Correct Judgment That Is in Fact Incorrect. If we allow ourselves to intervene without rechecking the whole cycle — that is, checking

GOAL: 1) Learn to distinquish *inside yourself* observations, reactions,
judgments, and impulses to act (intervene)
2) Identify *biases* in how you handle each of these processes

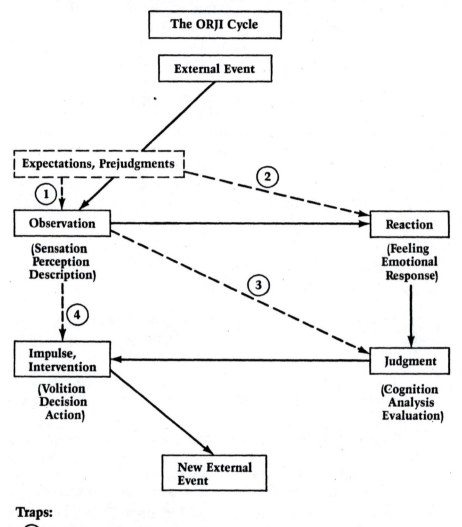

Traps:

(1) Misperception

(2) Inappropriate emotional response

(3) Rational analysis based on incorrect data

(4) Intervention based on incorrect data

Figure 4–2
A More Realistic Depiction of the ORJI Cycle

whether our observation and emotional reaction were correct and appropriate — we may act rationally but make the situation worse.

How to Avoid Traps

Communication breakdowns, hurt feelings, and destroyed relationships typically result more often from falling into various traps than from malice or intention. The manager dealing with subordinates, the consultant dealing with clients, and the group member dealing with colleagues all need to become highly aware of the pitfalls of intrapsychic processes, and need to learn some routines for avoiding or correcting these pitfalls.

Identify Possible Bases of Misperception

There are at least three distinguishable bases of misperception that need to be sorted out.

Cultural Assumptions. The same behavior in different cultural settings can mean different things. In one organization it may be culturally appropriate to argue all points; in another organization it may be culturally appropriate always to agree with a senior member of the group in public. If I, as the consultant, interpret either behavior in terms of my own cultural assumptions instead of theirs, I will misinterpret the meaning, react inappropriately, and make inappropriate interventions.

Personal Defensive Filters or Biases. Certain kinds of behavior in others may always be perceived by me as having a certain meaning because of my own defense mechanisms and biases. I may perceive all disagreement as attacks, or may perceive any silence as agreement (because I "need" to see it that way). As a consultant I have to observe myself in action over a period of time and get corrective feedback from others in order to identify the systematic biases in how I perceive things. Once I know what those biases are I can take greater care in checking things out before reacting to them.

Situational Expectations Based on Past Experience. If I have encountered a given situation or person many times before, I may come to believe that I know what to expect. In this case the potential source of misperception is my past learning, and this is perhaps the hardest to correct for because it requires one to "undo" one's own prior "knowledge." If I am trying to be a helpful consultant it is essential to be as objective as possible and to allow for the fact that situations and people do change. Hence I have to remain as observant as possible, even in situations in which I already "know" what to expect.

Identify Own Emotional Response Biases

If I have a systematic bias to respond to certain kinds of data with certain kinds of emotions, I need to know what that bias is in order to judge its appropriateness to any given situation. For example, if I tend to respond defensively and get angry whenever a client challenges me or tells me that I am wrong, I need to recognize this as a bias and learn to control or compensate for that feeling if my judgment tells me that it would not be helpful to the consultation process to get into an argument with the client.

Getting defensive and angry is not always wrong. Sometimes it is the appropriate response. But in order to make choices and decide what will be most facilitative in a given situation, one needs to know one's biases.

Identify Cultural Assumptions in Judgment and Reason

Reasoning and making judgments is not a culture-free process. Culture provides us with assumptions that tell us how to reason and what conclusions to draw from what data. If we do not know what our assumptions are, we may reason correctly from our point of view and still make errors from the point of view of others.

Errors occur often because of assumptions about time and space (Hall, 1959, 1966, 1983). For example, I might wish to have a "private" meeting with the client in order to provide some feedback. In my cultural setting privacy might be assured if we can find a quiet corner of a large office complex, but my client might define privacy as requiring being behind closed doors, out of sight of anyone. If I don't understand his definition of privacy I might not understand why he is so ill at ease when I try to talk to him in the open office setting.

Or, in my culture being on time might be a mark of efficiency and respect for the busy schedule of others, and I might be offended if my client keeps me waiting for fifteen minutes past the appointed time. In my client's culture, however, being fifteen minutes late might be appropriate and he might expect that both of us would keep others with subsequent appointments waiting for as long as we wished, and this is how he would show his respect for the importance of our meeting.

This kind of trap is so pervasive and difficult to identify that I question whether real process consultation can be done across major cultural boundaries. For example, I once did a seminar in Mexico for two groups in a bank. One of the managers was my client and he asked me to describe various kinds of organization development interventions. After I described an intergroup exercise in which each group meets to develop its own self-image as well as its image of the other group, both groups asked me to show them how to go through it. I reasoned that they wanted a clearer illustration by trying it out. I was not aware that they reasoned that this exercise would help them to resolve a major issue that had developed between them.

The exercise revealed that my client's group was quite dissatisfied with his leadership and when this was publicly revealed it led the other group to propose that many of the functions that the first group had performed now be taken over by the other. A big argument broke out and I lost control of the meeting because both groups suddenly broke into Spanish and refused to honor their original agreement to keep the conversation in English. My client ended up both losing face and losing political power as a result of the exercise, and I realized that I had completely misunderstood their motives when they proposed actually going through the exercise.

Institute Systematic Checking Procedures

The most important way to avoid traps is to test as best one can whether one's observations, reactions, and reasoning are correct or not. This can be done by more questioning, more observation before intervening, cross-referencing with the observations of others, and playing back to the client what has been observed.

   Silence as an Intervention. One of the most important interventions one can decide to make is to remain silent and continue to observe what is going on. Remaining silent and in an active listening mode may not seem like an intervention, but, in fact, it may be crucial in order to minimize the risks of misperception, inappropriate emotional reactions, and biased judgments. Often what we see and hear while we are struggling with ourselves to stay quiet reveals the further data we need to make a more facilitative response. The interrupted father in the earlier example need only have waited a few seconds in order to have found out that the child wanted to say goodnight and offer coffee.

   Spirit of Inquiry. The best overall protection to avoid the traps is a spirit of inquiry, a desire to decipher what is really going on, a commitment to listening and helping instead of actively displaying one's own impulses and feelings before one knows whether or not they are appropriate. One of the important differences between the three models of consultation is that in the expert and doctor–patient model less emphasis falls on being in an inquiring mode and more temptations exist to assume that one has the answer. The PC model argues that since only the client can solve the problem anyway, the consultant or manager practicing this model can and should comfortably stay in an inquiry role, knowing that, in the long run, this role will produce the best problem solution.

Applying the ORJI Model to the Allen Financial Service Company

   The ORJI model has to be considered at two levels. What possible distortions were operating within me as a consultant, and what possible distortions were operating in my client, Fred Ralston, in his efforts to manage his division? Looking first at my own behavior, I noticed throughout my early hours with Ralston that I tended to stereotype him, to assume that I knew what was probably going on in his department, and to seek confirmation of those assumptions in what personnel manager Ryan and others were telling me. The hardest thing to observe clearly was what Ralston's actual impact was, because he was having such a strong emotional impact on me.

In particular, I noticed that Ralston tended to overexplain, to tell me things repeatedly or in too much detail, and I had to fight off feelings of irritation and feelings of being belittled by being told too much. It was then very easy to project that his subordinates must be feeling the same way and to miss the possibility that they might react totally differently to this kind of behavior. I had to train myself to suspend judgment and evaluation until I had talked to the subordinates, and to keep an inquiring attitude. I had to consider seriously the possibility that everything my client was telling me about his subordinates was indeed true, especially the point that they needed education and strong parenting.

The emphasis on observation was easiest to maintain if I focused clearly on Ralston himself, his own feelings of overload, his frustrations, and his efforts to gain control of a difficult situation. If I could empathize with him and suspend judgment about his impact on others, I was more likely to be able to maintain an observant inquiring, minimally judgmental mode of intervening.

Hypotheses About the Client. To develop a mental picture of what might be going on in Ralston's division, I did have to formulate some hypotheses about the ORJI cycles that might be going on in his head, though, of course this remains speculative inasmuch as I cannot see inside anyone's head. Based on what he said about his own difficulties of implementing his programs, I hypothesize that some of his major difficulties could be attributed to his not observing accurately what was going on around him. He was so predisposed to prejudge the situation based on his past experience that he either did not see or did not interpret correctly the data available to him from his subordinates. For example, he did not see how much energy it took to follow through on some of his suggestions, and he did not see how much time it took to stay on top of all the indicators that he measured. When subordinates did not follow through on some of his suggestions he sometimes seemed to make incorrect attributions on what their motives might be.

I often felt that Ralston was angry with his subordinates for not following through on some of the things they had agreed to do, but when we analyzed this anger, it turned out to be based on questionable observations. It was almost as if Ralston perceived his subordinates to be children and that almost any explanation they gave for why they did not do something was treated as an excuse of the sort an unruly child would give. He attributed resistance to them instead of hearing accurately that they simply could not do everything that was asked of them.

In one of our many conversations I confronted Ralston with this interpretation, but his response made it difficult to know whether it made any sense to him. He did note that he felt very strongly about his subordinates and expected a great deal of them, so he measured them more against his ideals than against rational assessments of what was possible. We did not have enough time together to explore how Ralston could practice doing ORJI analyses on his own behavior to get a more accurate perception of his own feelings, but I believe they would have been helpful to him.

However, when Ralston was later pulled off onto another assignment that took him physically out of the division for long periods of time, he began to notice that if his group was left alone, they could act responsibly and competently in maintaining the cost reduction indexes while pushing other programs forward. Ralston gradually learned to be a better observer of what was happening in his own group, which helped him to avoid many of the traps of premature judgment and impulsive action.

Conclusion

If managers or consultants are to be helpful they must intervene in situations. But if those interventions are to be appropriate and helpful, they must be based on accurate observation, appropriate emotional responses, and a reasoning process that mirrors or at least takes into account to some degree how the client reasons. All of this requires some self-insight, and such self-insight is best acquired by maintaining a genuine spirit of inquiry toward oneself as well as toward others.

In the classroom I typically ask students to write a series of one-page papers describing simple incidents that occur in daily life in terms of each step in the ORJI sequence. At first this seems awkward and confusing because people are used to thinking of such cycles in holistic terms. But after some practice discriminating what is an observation, what is a feeling, what is a judgment, and what is overt behavioral intervention, people find that it is a helpful exercise in improving their observation ability and in avoiding premature judgments and inappropriate behavior.

5

Cultural Rules of Interaction

It is very difficult to manage effectively or to be an effective consultant across major cultural boundaries unless one is familiar with both cultures that are involved. Yet it is crucial to understand as much as possible the culture within which one is operating so that one can capitalize on that understanding in trying to be helpful. Being embedded in one's own culture can be a disadvantage cross-culturally but an advantage intraculturally if one understands the essence of one's culture. But deciphering one's own culture is also difficult precisely because one is so embedded within it.

One main source of regularity and predictability in human interaction is the rules that we learn in our culture for how to relate to each other (Goffman, 1967; Van Maanen, 1979). Every society develops rules to make life safe and predictable for its members, and the power of such rules derives from the fact that we need them to avoid the crippling anxiety of uncertainty and unpredictability (Schein, 1985a). As we examine these rules, we will see that they have primarily to do with protecting one another's social selves so that we can each feel secure at some very fundamental emotional level.

To introduce this topic we need to reflect on how our language gives us clues as to what is "really" going on. What do we mean by terms such as tact, poise, deference, demeanor, humiliation, embarrassment, and saving or losing face? Why do we describe social events or situations as "scenes," and talk of playing or not playing our "roles" properly? Why do we talk of feeling "cheated" in social relations or say that we need to "pay" attention when someone is talking to us or that we need to give people their "due"?

What our language tells us is that the simplifying models that best explain a great deal of what goes on between people has to do with a kind of *social economics* and a kind of *social theater* or *drama*. As we learn to perform on various life stages, we learn what is appropriate actor and audience behavior and we learn what kinds of exchanges are fair or unfair. Our emotional responses are very much determined by what we regard to be situationally appropriate and what we regard to be equitable social exchanges.

The relevance of all of this to the consultant or manager derives from the fact that help must be provided within the constraints imposed by the cultural rules. Even the definition of what is helpful is culturally determined, so the helper cannot function unless he knows a good deal about the culture in which he is working. Let us examine these models in somewhat greater detail.

Social Behavior as Fair Exchange

We all learn early in life that human interaction is reciprocal. If someone is talking to you, you are paying attention; if someone gives you something, you say thank you; if someone insults you, you defend yourself in some manner or another. We also learn when the reciprocating action is appropriate and when it is not, and we have a quantitative sense about this. If we are saying something important, we expect "more" attention and get annoyed when the listener seems to pay too little attention. If we give an important gift or throw a great party, we expect an appropriate level of thanks and feel upset if it seems the recipients or guests just took for granted what they were given. If someone insults us and we are unable to defend ourselves appropriately, we feel bad and vengeful. If we have "invested" a lot in a relationship and the other party casually breaks it off, we feel cheated, angry, and hurt.

Reactions like these tell us that we have a strong learned sense of what is an appropriate and fair exchange, and that this calculation happens automatically and silently. We only "feel" the results in the sense that when things have gone equitably we feel the situation is normal and we are satisfied, and when they have not been perceived as equitable we feel that something is wrong and we are dissatisfied.

If we add into the equation interaction across status or rank levels, we have additional rules. These rules tell us both what are the appropriate ways of showing the right amount of deference to someone superior to us, and how to display the right kind of demeanor to someone below us. The subordinate shows deference by standing up when the superior enters a room, asking questions rather than making assertions, taking the appropriate body posture, following orders, and making various gestures of deference such as not interrupting the superior, listening intently, not disagreeing openly, supporting the superior in public situations, and so on.

The superior, in exchange, must display himself as being in control of the situation, must communicate clearly so that orders can be followed, must show his own status by acting secure, by not getting inappropriately anxious or defensive, must maintain his bearing and not do things that would be embarrassing to the followers who are identifying with the superior. Subordinates can lose their cool; superiors must remain composed. Subordinates can give in to human foibles and be tactless; superiors must avoid tactlessness in public situations. The higher the rank of the superior the more his image must fit the stereotype in terms of bearing, dress, and other aspects of public behavior, so high-ranking leaders have to manage their public images very carefully, lest they "disappoint" their subordinates and leave them feeling cheated.

Equity in Helping Relationships

In our society self-reliance is very important, hence to need and ask for help is initially a disequilibrating social situation. The client puts himself "one down" in the social exchange vis-à-vis the helper, and the helper must be aware of the vulnerability this creates for both parties. To be specific, if the consultant/manager/helper who is sought out for help does not first equilibrate the relationship to make it feel equitable, he may be forcing the client to equilibrate it. One of the commonest ways that clients have of doing this is psychologically to reject the help and the helper by viewing the advice as off target, silly, uninformed, and in other ways a reflection of the helper's incompetence. The client in this scenario will not get help, but he will feel better about himself if he can tell himself that the helper doesn't know what to do either.

One of the main reasons why expert advice is often less successful than process consultation is that the client cannot stand the inequity of not only having given the helper status by asking him for help, but then having to give him further credit for providing a solution. If the solution does penetrate the perceptual defenses and the client realizes its validity, he still does not necessarily give the helper the credit. He reinvents the solution himself, attributes it to his own wisdom, and thereby makes himself feel "whole" again instead of one down. We should not be at all surprised, therefore, when others have to reinvent the ideas we gave them. Understanding of cultural rules of equity would make this a predictable response.

Process consultation often avoids this scenario because the interest the helper shows in helping the client to help himself serves at the outset to re-equilibrate the relationship. By showing interest and concern for the client, the process consultant helps the client to begin to feel better about himself. By taking the problem seriously, the consultant helps the client to feel less foolish for having a problem. By being willing to listen, the consultant shows deference to the client and allows the client to gain status by being allowed to control some aspects of the situation.

One of the most important things to do early in a client

relationship is to reassure the client that the presented problem is not foolish, dumb, or trivial. I take whatever the client says seriously and give it full attention, but do not fall into the trap of giving premature advice, and I do not take the problem onto my own shoulders. Rather, the goal is to help clients to gain status and a new equilibrium by gaining confidence in their own abilities to diagnose and solve their own problems.

Human Exchange as Drama

The rules of interaction and what we regard as fair and equitable do not apply in the same way across all situations and relationships. Rather, we learn early in life to play a variety of roles in a variety of scenes. The rules of appropriateness and equity are linked to those roles and scenes. One of the most amazing human capacities is our ability to keep in our heads the multiple sets of scripts that apply to the many human dramas we play out.

Helping as Drama

One of the complexities of consulting and helping derives from the fact that the idea of "helping" is not well defined or scripted in our society. There are many definitions and concepts of what it means to "help," and, to make matters more ambiguous, helping is one of those dramas that is defined more by audience response than by script writer. In other words, help is defined by whether or not the client feels helped, not by whether or not the helper asserts that he helped. Aspiring helpers must therefore vary their own behavior according to the stream of feedback signals they get from their audiences, the clients, and must be prepared to rewrite their scripts constantly.

Managers and consultants may have general principles in mind when they intend to be helpful, but they have to be innovative in the application of these principles in a particular situation. Helping is an art, not a science, but as in all arts the aesthetic elements introduced by the individual artist still have to be consistent with basic principles of design, color, and harmony. Or, to pursue the analogy, helping in the general sense is theater of improvisation, which requires not only the basic skills of acting and knowing something about audience response, but also improvisation skills and spontaneity.

If we go beyond these general social definitions and examine what goes on between client and helper over a period of time, we note that the helping process can be thought of as a complex reciprocal play in which the person seeking help is initially the actor and the potential helper is initially in an audience role. The client takes the stage and spells out his problem, often in painful detail, while the potential helper must listen like an attentive audience.

Once the client's lines have been delivered, there is an expectation that the helper will take the stage and deliver some dramatic lines of his own. This is the "role suction" previously identified that so often tempts us to become instant experts and doctors. The trap is that the client does not know what to expect when we play expert or doctor and often does not like the lines we deliver, so he rejects what we have to offer and no help is delivered.

If the helper stays in the process consultant mode a different scenario results. Staying in the PC mode is tantamount to refusing to take the stage, assuming instead a coaching role. The process consultant keeps the client on center stage and helps him to continue there by "forcing" him or benignly manipulating him into starting to work on his own problem. The helper stays in the audience role, watching with interest and support the efforts of the client as actor to solve his own problem. Therefore, one of the critical skills that effective managers and consultants must learn is to create the right scenes and to manage the dramatic process toward desirable outcomes. And they must do this without violating the rules of equity and the rules of saving face.

For example, when the client ends his dramatic tale of woe with "What would *you* do in my situation, Ed?" one of the most helpful things I can say is "Well, that sounds like quite a dilemma; tell me what you have done about it thus far, or what you think you might be able to do." If pressure mounts for me to give new suggestions, I can say, "If I were in your shoes I guess I would consider some of the following alternatives — x, y, z — would any of those work for you?"

The Sacredness of the Person: Saving Face and Face Work

One of the most centrally held cultural assumptions is that relationships depend upon mutual cooperation, giving all parties to the relationship as nearly as possible what they claim to need. Human dramas must come out equitably between actors and audiences, but both parties need some way of measuring "value" in the human interaction. Value is the amount of status that any given person claims within the boundaries of what externally ascribed social roles and statuses will allow. So the amount of value claimed in any given situation then depends upon the institutional conditions, the formal status system, and the motives of the person within a particular role. Audience response then validates or invalidates these claims.

"Face" can be thought of as the social value that an individual claims in a given situation and role. These claims are communicated early in any given situation through verbal cues, and the other persons in the situation generally feel obligated to sustain those claims if at all possible. Willingness and ability to sustain claims depend upon whether the amount of face claimed falls within the institutionalized limits accorded a given status or role.

To take a common example, if I say to you "Let me tell you a funny thing that happened to me the other day," you will gear yourself up to "pay attention," and you will be prepared to be amused as soon as I let you know through my tone of voice, inflection, and actual words when you are supposed to react. If the incident is interesting and funny this process will play itself out smoothly. If my claim to be able to amuse you is not sustained, if you are in fact bored or offended, then you will find yourself engaged in what Goffman called "face work."

"Face *work*" is what we *both* have to do if the claims made cannot be sustained in the short run, because cultural rules dictate that in the larger sense my social self and our relationship must somehow be sustained in spite of the disappointing interaction. *The cultural rules then dictate that you will pay attention anyway and you will smile and laugh appreciatively even though you don't really feel those feelings.* If you frown and say that it was neither interesting nor funny, you have not sustained my claim, and I have, therefore, lost face. You have told me that my social value at that moment in our relationship was less than I claimed it to be. Cultural rules dictate that you will not do that except under extreme circumstances. You will pretend to be amused and do your best to help me be what I claim to be. I, on the other hand, will make every effort to be amusing and interesting to help you sustain my face.

Every day we go through literally hundreds of situations like this in which we make claims on one another, and we sustain others' claims in our responses toward them even though we may feel that the desired response was not warranted. How often have we said *after* an encounter that we felt cheated and dishonest, that we did not like something that someone did, that they embarrassed themselves and therefore disappointed us, and yet have carefully concealed these reactions during the encounter.

In fact, cultural learning involves the routinization of emotional responses so that much of face work is automatic on the part of all the participants in the social drama, something we call poise, tact, appropriate demeanor, good manners, and the like. What we feel and how we feel is situationally scripted so that in many situations we do not even feel any conflict between what we are supposed to feel and what we "really" feel (Van Maanen and Kunda, 1986).

If people claim more than either their status or their ability to deliver warrants, as when we say that someone is "putting on airs" or "presuming too much," we do not tear them down, destroy their illusions, or in other ways make them lose face. But if someone consistently makes claims that clearly lie outside the boundaries of his status, as does the co-worker who tries to give us orders and "acts as if he is the boss," or the joke teller who is never very funny, we tend to avoid that person and not to interact with him. Nonetheless, we do not usually tell them to go to hell to their face, at least not in public where their loss of face would be visible to others.

The central point to understand in all of this is that we try always to grant others their claims and we go to great lengths not only to avoid losing face ourselves but also to keep others from losing face. We are careful not to claim too much in any given situation and to stay within the bounds of our status and roles, so that others will not have to do extreme face work.

The ultimate reason for face work is that unless we can reassure one another daily that our social selves will be acceptable, life becomes too dangerous and society falls apart. The very essence of society is the implicit contract we all have with each other to sustain each others' social selves as best we can. Persons are sacred objects, and the deliberate destruction of someone's face is equivalent to social murder. If I do that to you, I am licensing you and others to do the same thing to me, and that makes any form of society impossible.

The only condition under which deliberate destruction of face is culturally sanctioned is during the socialization process where selves have to be given up and reconstructed. Thus in moving from one organization to another or one status to another, one often suffers deliberate degradation in the process of learning a new role. But it is only during the transition that such face destruction occurs, and then usually only at the hands of teachers, coaches, drill sergeants, and other "agents of change."

Face Work in Helping Relationships

What does all of this have to do with consultation and management? Everything. There is nothing more dangerous to the person with a problem than to have a helper humiliate him by signaling in some way or another that the problem is trivial or reflects the person's incompetence or lack of toughness. The person with the problem is exposing his face in admitting a problem. He is saying that he is not as good as he thought he was, and is thereby making himself vulnerable. He will feel "one down."

Because of this vulnerability, potential clients will often not reveal their "real" problems, will deny that they really have a problem, will claim that everything is already under control, and in other ways "test" the willingness of the helper to really be sympathetic and trustworthy in the relationship. As any helper has learned over and over again, only after much listening and being supportive will the real problem surface. From this perspective the client's response is a normal and expected one, one that the helper must be prepared to accept.

If the listener shows impatience, laughs, implies that the client is silly or stupid for not having figured out what to do, or gets angry at the client for having the problem, he will be, in one way or another, humiliating the client, causing him to lose face. Given the cultural rules of face, he has then created in the client the license to express the anger caused by his humiliation and loss of face. The client then feels entitled to get back at the helper in any way he can. Solving the problem now becomes secondary to gaining revenge and, thereby, re-equilibrating the situation.

None of this is likely to be conscious. Cultural rules are so overlearned and automatically applied that most of the processes described happen outside of awareness. The humiliated client finds the consultant's suggestion silly or off target, or finds himself telling the consultant all the reasons why the solution won't work, without necessarily recognizing that he is doing this not because the solution is wrong but because he is angry at being humiliated and needs to get back at the consultant.

In the managerial relationship we have additionally to consider the rules of deference and demeanor. It is easy for a superior to humiliate a subordinate, and he should not later be surprised at the depth of anger that the subordinate may feel toward the boss. Similarly, subordinates who unwittingly cause their bosses to lose face should not be surprised at the extent of the repercussions in the form of poor assignments, lost promotion opportunities, and verbal abuse they may be subjected to.

Adopting the expert or the doctor role in a helping situation increases the risk that the client will feel humiliated and will lose face. This has happened most in my own experience with diagnoses or prescriptions that turn out to be things that the client has already thought of and rejected. The client feels foolish and put down by my suggestions because they imply that the client did not or could not have thought of them himself.

It is more helpful to start out with a PC orientation, because this orientation assumes that the client has the capacity to help himself and has probably already thought of some alternatives. One of the key questions always to ask before offering suggestions or advice is what the client has already tried or thought of himself.

If the helper can get across the message, "Your problem is real, but you can help yourself, and I will help you to help yourself," this is *granting face*, telling the client that he is worth *more* than he may have claimed. It also gets across the message that it is acceptable to have problems. One of the commonest early interventions I find myself using with a new client is to mention some other cases of similar problems that I have encountered, both as a way of testing whether or not I have understood the client, and as a way of telling him that his problem is neither unique nor something to be ashamed of.

Face Work in the Allen and Billings Companies

One of the dramatic differences between Ralston, the Allen Company's division manager, and Stone, the Billings Company's founder and president, is their totally different self-presentation. Ralston is a man of great pride. I have previously described him as a person who takes a very paternal role toward his subordinates. He is not easy to confront, because he makes high claims for himself in interpersonal situations and expects considerable amounts of deference. He presents himself as a teacher and communicates this by giving long speeches at department meetings.

If people disagree with him he will go to great pains to explain his position and to adhere to it. On the surface he espouses participation, but his manner, body language, and style of communication often send signals to his subordinates that his mind is already made up. To challenge him openly, therefore, runs the risk of making him lose face. Consequently his subordinates "work around him" rather than directly through him, and often are frustrated because they cannot figure out how to get a practical point across when it disagrees with Ralston's position.

The relationship between Ralston and his department heads was viewed by most of them as inequitable and they often felt unfairly treated. They felt that they accepted and met the challenge of Ralston's tough targets but that he did not give them enough credit. Instead of rewarding them and giving them a bit of rest, they felt he kept piling on more new programs. From their point of view there was no way to win. They felt that they were always disappointing their leader somehow or other. Such feelings of inequity and inadequacy are, in the long run, dangerous, so one of the primary goals of the consultation effort in the Allen Company was to resolve this issue, either by having Ralston demand less or by having him reward success more.

Stone, in contrast, presents himself as one of the boys, easy to confront, easy to argue with, ready to get into a scrap with anyone, but always powerful enough by virtue of his position to say, "Enough, I've made my decision." He is able to communicate clearly when he has had enough, though his subordinates sometimes complain that he does not sufficiently explain his decisions once they have been made.

Stone maintains less distance between himself and his subordinates and in meetings is willing to spend a lot of time listening to others. He views himself as a process-oriented manager and always asked me after the meetings whether I had any feedback that would help him to be more effective in that role. Deference rituals are much less visible in the Billings Company, therefore, though there is evidence that there are areas that Stone has declared as undiscussable, so the group will not challenge him in those areas.

In both organizations if one attends meetings one notices immediately how much attention is given by group members to the maintenance of others' face. The agreement to disagree rather than to resolve issues can be seen as an avoidance of running the risk of making someone lose face by backing down. When the Allen Company's department heads meet without Ralston they are more confrontive of one another and resolve issues, but they manage face by not going out on a limb. People present their ideas as trial balloons or ask for recommendations from task forces so that no one's own face is on the line with respect to a given decision. In this sense the group has learned how to manage task conflict without its becoming personally threatening to face, something that the Billings Company executive committee has not yet learned how to do.

The Billings group is a good example of a human drama. Stone and the key executive vice president are the main actors and, for the moment, at least, the rest of the group has been put into more of an audience role. They don't like it but don't know exactly how to handle the situation. One of the evolving goals of working with this group is to make the participation more even. The new vice president of human resources who was hired recently will play a major role to make this happen. He is a more dominant figure himself and he will use his process skills to help the group to achieve more of a feeling of being a team. My own role in this process so far will be described later.

Conclusion

Cultural rules of interaction are the most elusive but, at the same time, potentially the most powerful determinants of whether or not a viable helping relationship will be established. When clients seem to feel best is when they feel they have been helped without feeling they have been put down. Their dignity is intact, and, in fact, they feel stronger after the helping process than before.

When we consider managers as helpers, this point becomes even clearer. Subordinates consistently prefer a boss who makes them feel that they can solve their own problems, will coach them and help them, but not do it for them. A boss who is too smart and skillful and who always displays his superiority with his subordinates will get results but will be resented and, in the end, have a weaker and too dependent organization.

Maintaining one another's face is central to societal functioning. If someone loses face in a relationship, not only does that person feel embarrassed, humiliated, and ultimately vengeful, but the person who caused the loss of face shows himself to be unreliable in the human drama. And someone who cannot be relied on to play his proper role eventually gets ostracized and isolated. Consultants and managers must not only adhere to these rules but even play an active role in helping others to understand how important they are. They must be role models with regard to face work.

The ultimate dilemma of helping, then, is how to produce change in the client system without people losing face. The helper often finds himself for face reasons having to support assumptions that do not make sense. How can clients be gotten to see new perspectives, to consider new alternatives without being made to feel that their present mode is bad or valueless? To understand this process, we need to examine in more detail a simplifying model of the change process itself.

6

Initiating and Managing Change

Rarely is the goal of a helping process to maintain the status quo. Even if no great external changes will result, sometimes it is a significant change when a client accepts a situation and redefines it inside his own head. But one cannot conceive of human processes without conceiving of change, either evolutionary or managed.

Managers and consultants therefore need a simplifying model of what is, in fact, a very complex phenomenon. To produce "change" means to get the client to see and do things differently but without devaluing the client or his present concepts. The client must unlearn some old concepts and behavior without losing face. How can this be managed?

The model presented in this chapter was originally designed to understand the very complex process by which prisoners of war during the Korean War came to see some of their own behavior as espionage and as harmful to the Chinese and North Korean Communists. The model was adapted from Kurt Lewin's original model of social change, and has been elaborated at various times to fit the kinds of change processes in human systems that consultants and managers have to deal with (Schein, 1961, 1968, 1972, 1985a).

Change is a process that consists of a number of stages, as shown in Table 6–1. These stages overlap and may occur very rapidly, but they are conceptually distinct, and it is important for the helper to be aware what stage he is working in. To follow Lewin's original terminology, the stages are labeled

1. Unfreezing
2. Changing
3. Refreezing

and the key to understanding change is to understand the processes that occur within each stage.

The critical interpersonal processes that must be managed in each stage if change is to occur happen through the action of various "change agents," but the consultant is not always the change agent. Different people may play key roles at different stages. The consultant or manager must be clear what stage the

---

Table 6–1

A Three-Stage Model of the Change Process

Stage 1. *Unfreezing:* Creating motivation and readiness to change through
   a. Disconfirmation or lack of confirmation
   b. Creation of guilt or anxiety
   c. Provision of psychological safety

Stage 2. *Changing through Cognitive Restructuring:* Helping the client to see things, judge things, feel things, and react to things differently based on a new point of view obtained through
   a. Identifying with a new role model, mentor, etc.
   b. Scanning the environment for new relevant information

Stage 3. *Refreezing:* Helping the client to integrate the new point of view into
   a. The total personality and self-concept
   b. Significant relationships

---

change process is in and what his or her own role at each stage is.

Stage 1. Unfreezing

To unfreeze a system means to create a motivation and readiness to change. Potential clients must feel some pain or some disequilibrium somewhere motivating them to seek help, and they must be able to accept help. In human systems where we are talking of changing perceptions, attitudes, and behaviors, such pain or disequilibrium usually involves the *unlearning* of something, not only the learning of something new.

It is the unlearning that is often the most painful and causes so much resistance to change, because it involves the discomfort of giving up something that one is used to or letting go of something that one values. Unlearning may threaten face in implying that one has been doing something wrong or ineffective in the past and in forcing one to enter a period of uncertainty and instability while learning something new.

In order to become motivated and ready to unlearn something and to learn something new, three conditions must be met.

Disconfirmation or Lack of Confirmation

A person will not seek help unless something in his life space is not working properly. That usually means that some expected outcomes are not actually resulting — business results are not up to the expected level, deadlines are not being met, employee morale is lower than expected, inventories are too high, a subordinate is not improving his performance even after repeated appraisals and coaching, a plan is not working out as it is supposed to, a superior is not pleased with the subordinate's output, and so on.

What all of these situations have in common is that the person wanted and expected something to happen that did not happen. Usually the basic disconfirmation has occurred through information that comes from the outside or through information that higher level managers provide to subordinates, peers, or superiors. The situation is most problematic when a manager is disappointed in the performance of a subordinate or a unit of the organization and must communicate this disappointment to them. The initial disconfirmation is in the mind of the manager, but he then acts to disconfirm the expectations of the subordinates, who may have assumed that they had done a good job.

The reason this communication is problematic is that it is threatening to face, and if either the communicator or the recipient senses this threat, he or she will distort the message so that face can be saved. The boss may feel that the subordinate has really messed up and has acted stupidly, but the cultural rules say that he cannot say that directly to the subordinate's face without risking destroying the subordinate's self-esteem and labeling himself, in the process, as a socially dangerous character to have around. Even if the boss says it, the subordinate will find ways of pretending not to hear it, to deny it, and in other ways to preserve his self-image as a competent person.

The cultural dynamics around face operate to make us deny disconfirming information if we possibly can rather than lose face (self-esteem), so even if the information that something is not working as expected is available, this does not guarantee by itself that it will be perceived and assimilated. I have worked with product development teams in the food industry, for example, and have been told that the single most difficult part of the whole product development process is to *stop* the development of a "bad" product. Even though test marketing information comes in loud and clear that the product is not acceptable, the team continues to believe that the tests were not done right, or a slight modification in the product will change consumer opinions, or that the wrong promotional materials were used, etc., etc., etc. They continue to believe anything rather than admit that the product that they had committed themselves to is, in fact, no good.

Disconfirmation or lack of confirmation is not always a negative process. What ethnographers describe as "surprises" in the process of encountering another culture, or how we use information that does not "make sense" in the process of being socialized to new situations, would also precipitate change processes in the way I mean them here, but one assumes in those situations that there is already some motivation present to learn something new (Van Maanen, 1977; Louis, 1980). What this change model is designed to highlight is how change can be initiated despite initial complacency and lack of motivation.

In summary, disconfirming information of some kind is necessary for unfreezing to begin, but it is not sufficient. Two other processes have to work simultaneously: guilt or anxiety must be induced and psychological safety must be created.

The Induction of Guilt or Anxiety

The disconfirming information is more likely to be attended to if it reveals that some important goal is not being met or some important ideal is being violated. The former induces anxiety, the latter, guilt. Disconfirmations occur around us all the time, but most of this information is ignored or fails to induce motivation to change because it does not connect with issues that we care very much about. The ego is not involved with them, or we do not have any commitment to the goals and ideals that may be being disconfirmed.

When the weather does not turn out the way we wanted, or the traffic was heavier than we expected, or it took longer to do something around the house than we planned, or someone we were expecting did not arrive on time, we note it and maybe even grumble about it, but it does not ordinarily produce motivation to change our attitudes or behavior. Only if the disconfirmation involves an important goal or personal ideal is a change process initiated.

This can perhaps be seen most clearly in how a sales person attempts to structure the situation for a buyer. We assume that disconfirmation has occurred in that the old car is not functioning or is disappointing the person in some way. The car sales person will then try to make the potential buyer feel that by not owning a particular new car she is failing to meet her own ideals of providing herself the power, the status, and the convenience that owning the new car would provide. The sales person will work very hard to attempt to identify what the buyer "is looking for" in the sense of what ideals or goals are currently not being met, and will attempt to make the buyer feel anxious or guilty unless she buys the car. The sales person may point out that her present car may break down, or may not be suitable for the buyer's station in life, or if she waits prices may go up, etc. If the sales person can induce anxiety or guilt, he has a chance to get the person to buy.

The analogous situation occurs when a boss gives performance feedback to a subordinate. If he says that something the subordinate did took too long, or was too expensive, or wasn't of high enough quality, or whatever, this disconfirming information will matter to the subordinate only if it links with some personal goals or ideals of the subordinate. Otherwise it will be ignored or denied. Yet, if the boss and the subordinate have set some joint targets and if the subordinate has made a personal commitment to those targets, then failure to attain them has immediate personal meaning and will elicit guilt and anxiety.

So for performance feedback to produce change, there must be from the outset some personal commitment on the part of the person receiving feedback to some meaningful targets or goals. How often have we heard subordinates come out of meetings where they have been "chewed out" saying that what the boss wanted was unreasonable anyway, so they dismiss the incident as just an example of the boss's irrationality. However, if there is commitment that creates anxiety or guilt in the face of disconfirmation, the information will register and produce a motivation to change.

Will anxiety-producing information, feedback, or disconfirmation be enough to initiate a change process? These conditions are still not enough unless a third process, perhaps the most elusive, is well managed: the creation of psychological safety.

The Creation of Psychological Safety

The person receiving the disconfirming information can *accept* it only if it does not involve personal humiliation and loss of face or self-esteem. If there is personal commitment, targets or ideals that the person cares about, and if disconfirming information is received showing that the targets or ideals are not being met, then for the person to accept the information requires that he be able to continue to feel worthwhile even though a specific target or ideal has not been met. He must be able to feel the specific guilt or anxiety without feeling worthless as a whole person. If his basic sense of worth is threatened, he will find defense mechanisms that distort or in other ways undo the disconfirming information.

The biggest dilemma the consultant or manager who delivers disconfirming information faces is how to deliver it in a way that will not be a personal threat to the person with the problem. All of the "technology" of how to give feedback that has grown up around the performance appraisal process has to do with this central issue. Some theories advocate that one must ensure that the feedback emphasize positive reinforcement rather than punishment, that it occur soon after the behavior that is being discussed occurred, that it be specific rather than general, that it involve areas that the recipient is able to do something about, and that the motivation of the giver of feedback be perceived as constructive and helpful.

Other theories advocate that negative feedback — punishing information — be sandwiched between positive feedback: "You are a great salesman overall; you messed up the such and so account, but your basic performance is OK." The only trouble with the sandwich technique is that often the recipient only hears the two positive comments.

Making a client or subordinate feel psychologically safe so that fairly threatening things can be said is probably one of the most complex and artful of human endeavors, involving real caring on the part of the consultant or manager and a real commitment to helping the receiver of the disconfirming information to improve his situation.

There are no easy formulas for creating psychological safety. One key is to worry about "face" and to be very careful not to exacerbate the feeling of being at a disadvantage that the client already may have by virtue of admitting a problem. The process consultation model emphasizes building up the client's self-esteem and self-confidence. As a consultant I have to assume that the client knows deep down that there is a problem or I would not be in the picture, so he does not need me to remind him of his problems so much as he needs me to build up his confidence that his problems are solvable.

If the client or subordinate is very anxious about having to unlearn old attitudes and learn something new, the consultant or manager can play a temporary parentlike role and absorb some of the anxiety himself by reassuring the person that things will work out and that the transition period can itself be managed. Consultants often end up in the transition manager role because an outsider is needed to stabilize the situation while the insiders who are changing are experiencing disequilibrium and anxiety.

Sometimes psychological safety is created simply by the presence of the consultant reassuring people that the situation is under control, is not that unusual, has been faced by others successfully before, and can be managed. Clients often want reassurance that their problems are in the "normal" range before they will accept real responsibility for working on them; if the problem is not so unusual, they can feel that they are OK.

Summary and Conclusions About Unfreezing

The recipient of disconfirming information must feel psychologically safe enough to pay attention to it and to tolerate the anxiety or guilt that it causes. The potential client must also feel safe enough to expose himself to the discomfort of giving something up and learning something new. It is the client or the person needing to change who is in control of the situation. The change agent can escalate the disconfirmation, anxiety, and guilt, and can attempt to maximize psychological safety, but only when the client decides to let something go, to unlearn something and seek something new, can the next stage of the change process begin.

I have encountered clients and client systems at all stages of unfrozenness. Sometimes people see disconfirming information but do not connect it to their own important goals or ideals. Sometimes they openly display their defensiveness, guilt, and anxiety but hope that the consultant will help them to deny the disconfirming information. Sometimes they are ready to accept the information but do not feel psychologically safe enough to do so, looking to the consultant for the reassurance that he will get them through the painful unlearning and relearning without too much loss of self-esteem. And sometimes the contact client brings in the consultant to help him to unfreeze other parts of the organization because he does not know how to start the ball rolling himself.

In most of these situations the "change agents," the managers or consultants who want to induce change, are not sufficiently aware of the dynamics of unfreezing. They want to move directly into change, before the person or group to be changed is ready. Or they are aware of the need for disconfirmation, guilt, and anxiety, yet are oblivious to the need for psychological safety. How often have we heard a manager complain after a performance appraisal session that he presented bell clear information to the subordinate about areas needing improvement, yet somehow the message did not seem to get across?

One of the major functions of the early stages of the consultation process may then be to show the client both by example and by concept how important it is for people to feel psychologically safe before they can really change. The supportiveness of the process consultant in the earliest encounters, the initial acceptance of the client's formulations, and the gentle inquiring probing (rather than confrontation) all serve to create a feeling of safety in the situation.

If the client wants to talk about how to get others to change, the process consultant can point out the mechanisms of unfreezing and ask the client whether or not he has provided for each of the conditions in the model. The creation of psychological safety is typically the missing element. How complex the dynamics of orchestrating these conditions can become is illustrated in the following cases.

Creating Psychological Safety in the Chilton High Tech Company: Performance Appraisal at the Senior Executive Level

I had been working with a company president for years, primarily attending critical staff meetings and counseling him on various decisions. I had also become deeply involved with his immediate subordinates both as a counselor and as a clarifier of what is going on in the president's mind. Since I had spent a lot of time with Jim Dyson, the president, various of his subordinates would ask me what I thought Dyson meant by a particular remark he had made at a meeting. Most of the top group had used me as a communication vehicle as well, telling me things that they expected and hoped would be passed on to others when direct communication was not possible for any of a number of reasons. But it was clear that information on personal performance was often oblique and unclear.

Dyson was very comfortable thinking out loud in a group context, and, in fact, had a much harder time talking to his subordinates one-to-one. He would praise or criticize them from time to time in group meetings or even behind their backs, hoping that the right message would get to them. Everyone agreed that this mode of communication was less than ideal because it caused loss of face; worse, the messages often were denied and filtered in various ways so that Dyson ended up frustrated about his inability to get his appraisals across.

George Ross, the vice president of human resources, had felt for some time that the development of the executive team made it mandatory for Dyson to give more specific and detailed appraisals to each of his direct subordinates. He and I spent many hours discussing how Dyson could be gotten to do this, given his reluctance to talk face to face. Ross finally invented the following process, which he and I then refined and tested on Dyson and the subordinates.

Step 1. Ross sat down with Dyson and interviewed him about each of the direct subordinates, making detailed notes that were later typed and given back to Dyson for checking and elaboration. The notes would be used later to remind Dyson what he wanted to say to each of his subordinates.

Step 2. Each subordinate was scheduled for a two-hour meeting that would involve the subordinate, Dyson, Ross, and me. He was told that in this group his performance would be appraised and was asked if it was all right with him that Ross and I were present. Since most of the subordinates were anxious to have an appraisal and a chance to talk about it, they readily agreed to having the extra parties present. Dyson liked the idea of the extra people because he could then talk to us as a group about the subordinate being appraised, and there would be two additional people to help clarify the message and follow up on it. Dyson clearly felt more psychologically safe in the group situation because he did not always trust his own words, and needed the feeling that others were present to correct, fine-tune, and elaborate.

My role was follow-up with each subordinate, to discuss a development plan and to ensure that the message had gotten across.

Step 3. At each appraisal meeting Ross set the stage, having given Dyson a copy of the appraisal notes previously generated. Ross and I also had these notes so that we could prompt and lead Dyson as needed to ensure that he would get his full message out. The ground rules were that the subordinate could question, seek clarification, disagree, and engage in the action in any way that he saw fit, and it was my job to promote good two-way communication. In other words, I was there not only to help Dyson get his message across but also to help each subordinate respond as well.

The culture of this organization encouraged openness, confrontation, and debate, so it was essential to keep the climate as open as possible. I frequently found myself asking for clarification of points when I either did not understand the point or believed that the subordinate or Dyson had not understood a point. To force such clarification without threatening loss of face to others by implying that they did not understand, I always used myself as the foil, saying that *I* did not understand some point even if I did.

Toward the end of the meeting I also summarized and tested consensus on what I deemed the important areas of agreement and their implications for future performance and development needs.

Step 4. I made sure that as the meeting terminated I would leave the room with the subordinate in order to find a few minutes to discuss how he felt, what he had heard, and what inferences he had drawn from the discussion. Since I knew what message Dyson wanted to get across, it was important to check that the message had been received and how the subordinate felt about it. This often led to a half hour or so of additional talk with the subordinate as I clarified and counseled on next steps. If the subordinate was upset, this period provided a good opportunity to let him ventilate his feelings and put them into perspective.

Ross followed up later with further discussion and encouraged anyone who needed counseling or clarification to get in touch with me. I made appointments to see each person approximately three months hence to review development plans and to check on how things were going. These meetings confirmed that the feedback process had been effective in getting messages across clearly.

Although the feedback process seemed cumbersome and awkward at times, it was the unanimous feeling of Dyson, Ross, and all of the subordinates that it had produced the best appraisals they had ever had. The presence of the additional people not only clarified, but, more important, provided the subordinates some psychological safety in that there were witnesses to what was being said in both directions. We all agreed that the next round of appraisals should be conducted in more or less the same fashion.

Some Lessons. Several worthwhile lessons can be derived from this example. The process that worked was invented by Ross and developed jointly by both of us. Neither of us could have done it alone, and it was especially important for Ross to be involved since he knew better than I how Dyson and others would react to the seemingly cumbersome system.

Psychological safety does not mean privacy. Given the culture of Chilton, it was much more important for the subordinate to have "witnesses" so that allegations could be verified. We also learned that giving feedback is just as tough as receiving it, and Dyson needed all kinds of support to get his message out.

This process, once invented and tested, could easily be reproduced without my continued involvement. On future occasions Ross could play the role that I had played.

Unfreezing in the Allen Company

The situation with Ralston previously described further illustrates how unfreezing works. First of all, Ralston himself had to be unfrozen by me. He was very set in his ways and saw very little disconfirming information to what he was doing. The lack of support of his subordinates for his various programs was often dismissed as their ignorance, laziness, or failure to understand. Ralston seemed to believe that once he "educated" them, they would do all that was asked of them. What Ralston seemed to want from me was mostly reassurance, conceptual input, and guidance on how he could unfreeze his own departments.

I was getting plenty of disconfirming information from the personnel manager and the personal assistant, and I heard secondhand that various department heads had been quite blunt in telling Ralston that he was overloading them, so the disconfirming data were available, but not getting through. My tactic in this situation was to draw on Ralston's own frustration, pain, and overload. If I could get him to see that he was even asking too much of himself, then maybe he could realize that he was asking too much of others. I also used myself as a foil, saying that if I were in the shoes of a department head I would feel very overloaded.

When an opportunity presented itself I pointed out how Ralston's own goals were not getting met in the manner that seemed to suit him, thus inducing some anxiety and guilt. At the same time I was very reassuring that his goals were attainable if he could think differently about how to manage his division, thus making him feel psychologically safe. To reassure him further, I promised to help him in any way I could.

At the same time, as I got to know more department heads and started to attend some of their meetings, *I urged them to be very clear about their feelings* (escalate the level of disconfirmation), but to do so in a constructive way so that Ralston would not be forced into defensive denial. Over a period of months this combination of forces seemed to work in that Ralston gradually began to consider alternative ways of influencing his organization.

In summary, a client or client system is unfrozen if one or more relevant people in the system accept information that something they care about is not working properly, feel guilty or anxious about this situation, but accept the necessity to do something because they feel psychologically safe. If all of these conditions are not met, the client either will not perceive or will deny the information, and will terminate the relationship with the change agent rather than risk losing face by accepting the information.

The three consultant roles — expert, doctor, and process consultant — each have a key contribution to make. The expert and doctor are most likely to be useful sources of disconfirmation and to be able to induce guilt or anxiety, to see how a given client situation is failing to meet important targets and how this should cause the client to want to do things differently. The reason these two models are not more successful in causing change, however, is that they often do not create enough psychological safety to permit the client to accept the information. Hence no real unfreezing occurs until the more process-oriented consultant creates enough psychological safety.

Stage 2. Changing Through Cognitive Restructuring

For change to occur, there must be motivation and readiness to change, but that is generally not enough. We often know that something is wrong and accept it, but still do not know what to do. The effect of unfreezing is to open up the client to new sources of information and new concepts that permit him to look at his situation in new ways, to "cognitively restructure" it.

There are basically two distinct mechanisms by which information reaches us that permits us to restructure how we perceive things. We either have to find a role model with whom to identify, or we have to have the opportunity to scan our environment to locate new possibilities.

Identification

One way we learn new ways of looking at things is to identify ourselves with a role model, boss, mentor, friend, or consultant and begin to see things from that other person's point of view. If we see another point of view operating in a person whom we pay attention to and respect, we can begin to imagine that point of view as something to consider for ourselves.

Consultants as change agents often become the targets of

identification, and it is therefore very important that their own behavior and attitudes be totally congruent with the point of view they may be espousing.

If a client has been unfrozen and is very ready to change, he will seek out someone to identify with because this is the quickest way to locate a solution. However, identifying with another person can also be a very limiting way of learning in that it focuses the learner too much on a single source of information. And the point of view that fits the role model's situation may, in fact, be highly inappropriate for the client.

Given this dynamic, as process consultant one must 1) minimize putting oneself up as a role model, 2) help to locate relevant role models given the client's situation, and 3) emphasize that how others view a given situation is only one possible solution and that the client must search for what fits him. In other words, finding a role model is not necessarily the best basis for locating new ideas.

On the other hand, if there is a similarity between the client and the consultant, and they are working on a problem where the consultant has had personal and relevant experience, it may be efficient and effective to encourage identification with the consultant, especially if the consultant's own behavior is a good model for what will be needed in the client's situation. The danger is that the consultant lacks sufficient self-insight to determine whether or not he is, in fact, a good role model.

Scanning

If there is no readily available role model, the learner is likely to scan his environment for any information or concepts relevant to his problem. The consultant can be one source of information and ideas, but he can also stimulate the process of scanning by encouraging the client to read more widely, to talk to various others, to attend seminars, and in other ways to expose himself to new ideas, concepts, and methods.

Though this process may be slower and more difficult than identification, it is more likely to produce an outcome that fits the client's unique situation in that only information that is relevant will be taken in by the client. The key to both scanning and identification is that prior unfreezing has taken place so that the motivation to find a new point of view and new information is genuinely present in the client.

I have found over and over again that the acceptance of a new point of view by the client has much less to do with the validity of that point of view than with his readiness to consider any alternatives whatsoever. The building of that readiness is the unfreezing process, so much more of the change program typically has to be devoted to that phase. If there is real readiness, clients are very able to locate and evaluate new ideas by themselves or with the coaching help of the consultant. If they are not unfrozen, the best ideas in the world will not be heard no matter how hard the consultant works to make them visible.

Cognitive Restructuring in a Company's Culture Self-audit

To illustrate the dynamics of cognitive restructuring through a joint scanning process I will review the culture analysis session I conducted at the Delta Aerospace Company. Delta had been running a management development program for its most senior managers in an effort to get them to see their corporate as well as divisional roles more clearly. As part of this program they asked me to help the group to better understand the Delta culture, which seemed central to how they conducted their affairs but had not been recognized as such.

Delta was run by a top management team that had been in place for several decades. They had been put in place by a strong founder who was seriously committed both to technical excellence and to creating a human environment that would make employees at all levels feel like important contributors. The work of the organization was very technical so most of the managers were engineers, and they were expected to relate to one another in an atmosphere of informality, openness, communicativeness, and trust.

One of Delta's product lines, a weapons system, had been the original product of the company and was still contributing two thirds or more of sales. It was seen as dominating the rest of the company and preventing needed diversification. Almost all of the product was sold to the U.S. government, so the company felt quite vulnerable to swings in the Pentagon. The managers had always lived with this situation and were well adjusted to the Pentagon as the primary customer.

I was asked to spend half a day at the beginning of the three-week management development program to help Delta analyze its own culture. The managers attending the program were already unfrozen, since their bosses had planned the program and made it clear to attendees that it was a critical developmental step in their careers. They now needed a vehicle for analyzing something that they had not really thought about.

I had learned from other experiences not to try to tell people about their culture but, rather, to give them an analytical tool for developing their own insights. The tool used was a short lecture on organizational culture followed by the model that culture should be viewed at three levels (Schein, 1985a):

1. Visible artifacts such as any visitor to the company might observe
2. Espoused values such as those embodied in company literature or in the answers people might give when interviewed about why they did things as they did
3. Basic underlying assumptions that even insiders would not be consciously aware of until they really attempted to explain both their values and their artifacts in terms of the external survival and internal integration problems they had faced throughout their history

Following the lecture I asked the total group of twenty to give me some examples of Delta artifacts and listed those on the board. At this point an anomaly surfaced: the participants felt Delta was a very informal, egalitarian, open company, yet they noted that their headquarters building was extremely formal, had many levels of dining facilities, private parking spaces, an elaborate system for grading office size, furniture, and even decorations by company rank. We spent a half hour or so trying to figure out how the egalitarianism and informality could be reconciled with the obvious hierarchical and status-conscious headquarters.

As we explored this question historically the insight developed that the headquarters was modeled on the culture of the *customer* — the Pentagon. Inasmuch as most of their contact was with various Pentagon officials, the company gradually designed its most public areas to make the customer feel comfortable. They recognized immediately that in their laboratories and production facilities the egalitarian assumption was much more prevalent, so the analysis helped them to "make sense" out of something that previously had puzzled and even worried them. In this sense they were cognitively restructuring their perceptions of what the symbolic meaning of their headquarters building's appearance was and what function it served.

This process of identifying anomalies and then searching for the historical roots of the observed artifacts and values produced a number of different insights and illustrates well what I mean by cognitive restructuring once the client system is unfrozen. The participants in the program were ready and motivated, but they needed both to identify with one another and to scan all available information in order to understand what was really going on.

Cognitive restructuring is typically not as easy as this example implies. In changing the relationship between labor and management from an adversarial win/lose orientation to an integrative win/win orientation, companies often report that it first takes decades to unfreeze the system. This means convincing the union that the company's economic circumstances really do require a restructuring of the labor contract, linking this information to goals and values that the union is committed to, creating enough psychological safety in the work force to capture attention to the information, and then finally getting across a new integrative concept.

Cognitive Restructuring Through Charismatic Leaders

In one major American corporation that is known for its innovative design of plants, it was reported that under the new labor management system, which puts much more emphasis on worker autonomy, encourages multiple skill learning and job trading, and views management more as consultants rather than bosses, it was easy to train new workers in new plants to the system but virtually impossible to convert old unionized plants to this point of view.

Eventually economic circumstances forced the unions to come to terms with the need for some change, but it then took a group of charismatic plant managers each to call their entire plant population together into a mass meeting to sell the new concept. Such mass meetings served to restructure everyone's frame of reference at the same time, so that all of the workers knew that they were getting the same message. This combination of having unfrozen the unions and having the entire plant population be exposed at once to a new point of view worked and was viewed as a breakthrough by the company.

Inspirational leaders can produce change quickly if unfreezing has already taken place, but these same speeches would not have produced results had the unions not been ready to listen. And everyone agreed that what took the time was the unfreezing, not the cognitive restructuring.

Stage 3. Refreezing

Change can be very fleeting. We have all seen how clients can develop new concepts and points of view during training sessions and then revert immediately to their old point of view when they are back in the home environment if that environment does not support the new point of view. Refreezing is that portion of the change process, then, that embeds the new point of view both in the person's own psychic life space and in his various relationships with significant others.

Personal Refreezing

A new point of view will take root to the extent that it fits comfortably into the person's total self-concept and can be comfortably integrated with the rest of the personality. One of the reasons for arguing so strongly for the process consultation model over the expert or doctor model is that this model is more likely to guarantee that the client will accept only that which fits into his personality because he retains the choice of what new things to learn.

It is tempting to offer clients suggestions as a "doctor." Clients often accept the suggestions enthusiastically, then apply them in a stilted way that makes them seem incongruent, leading to disconfirmation and the erroneous conclusion on the part of the client that the suggestions were wrong. And, of course, the idea *was* wrong if one of the main criteria for a helpful facilitative suggestion is that it should fit into the client's total personality.

Relational Refreezing

Even if the idea fits into the client's own personality and self-concept, it is possible that it will violate the expectations of significant others around the client — his boss, peers, and subordinates — to a sufficient degree that they will either not reinforce it or actually disconfirm it. What the client must learn, painful as this process can become, is that he will have to retrain these others to his own new point of view, and that may involve a planned change program with them as the targets. The point is, there is nothing automatic about this process. It must be managed carefully if the client's new perceptions, attitudes, and behaviors are to survive.

The consultant or managerial change agent plays a critical role here in being for a time the only person who may be reinforcing the new point of view and behavior, helping the client to become comfortable enough with it to sustain himself in other encounters.

Refreezing in the Allen Company. As has been previously described, Ralston, the division director, was gradually learning to see how his own behavior as a strong "parent" was perceived by his adult department heads both as a source of inspiration and strength and sometimes as overbearing and demeaning. Ralston would cause the second perception particularly when he lectured and overkilled points, something that he sometimes did to me so I could see how it felt.

At one point in our relationship I found myself giving him direct feedback on what this behavior was doing to me; this further unfroze him and made him begin to consider alternatives. He decided that he should listen more, especially at meetings, instead of using up most of the time on his own sales pitch.

At first he had to practice this behavior on me and get comfortable with it himself. When he began to do it at meetings he received strong post-meeting confirmation from me, and, once his department heads overcame their surprise, they let him know as well how much is new approach was appreciated. At this point the new behavior was beginning to be refrozen.

Refreezing at Chilton. Dyson, the president of Chilton High Tech who used the unusual group meeting for his performance appraisals, was surprised that not only was he personally more comfortable giving appraisals in the larger group, but he got phone calls from various subordinates complimenting him on having given the best performance appraisal ever. Only when this feedback started to arrive did he begin to take seriously that he had now found a method that could be used on a regular basis because it fitted his own needs and those of his subordinates.

Refreezing at Delta. The cultural self-analysis that was done collectively in the general session described above was followed by two more steps that served to refreeze the new insights. We wanted to "stabilize" the insights in the participants' heads (personal refreezing), and we wanted to reach some consensus on how such insights would be used in their work following the management development seminar (relational refreezing).

Once we established some of the key underlying assumptions that characterized Delta, I broke the participants into three groups of about seven members and asked each group to take about one hour to 1) review the basic assumptions already identified and any others they could come up with, and 2) to identify and report back on those assumptions that they felt aided Delta's strategic posture as it looked into the future and those assumptions that they felt hindered their strategic posture and would, therefore, have to change.

By explicitly linking their cultural assumptions to their mission and future strategies it was possible for the managers to think through which assumptions really made a difference and which ones really did not matter so much. Doing this process in small working groups provided an opportunity for each manager's own new perceptions to be tested and reinforced by others so that following the meeting there would be a much more widely shared point of view.

For example, the groups all concluded that the headquarters

status system was necessary and harmless, so long as they all understood it and did not fall prey to status games in their important dealings with each other. But the assumption that their future economic welfare would continue to be tied to the weapons system that had been the source of their past success was strongly challenged as increasingly dysfunctional. One of the important outcomes of the seminar, then, even though this whole exercise had only taken three or four hours, was a consensus on a commitment to diversify and to develop future managers on a broader base than had been done so far.

From the Delta experience we learn that if a system is already unfrozen, if the client really wants and is ready for help, it does not take very long to make fairly significant interventions that produce cognitive redefinition and subsequent behavioral change.

Summary and Conclusions

This simplifying model of change theory emphasizes that change is a process that can be broken down into logical stages and that different mechanisms of change have to be managed at these different stages. At the unfreezing stage, the key is to provide disconfirming information, link it to important personal goals or ideals so that guilt or anxiety will be felt, and simultaneously provide enough psychological safety so that the disconfirming information will be attended to instead of denied.

If through these mechanisms the client has become motivated to unlearn something and to replace it with new learning, he will do so either by the mechanism of identifying with a new role model or by scanning the environment for information most relevant to his problem. The actual change can then be thought of as a cognitive restructuring or redefinition of his problem that leads to new perceptions, new feelings, new judgments, and ultimately new behaviors.

But the change process will not be complete until these new responses are tested for fit with the rest of the self-concept and personality, and, if they fit there, tested within the client's relationships. Only when the new responses begin to be confirmed by important others can one say that the change has really been stabilized.

The role of the manager or consultant as "change agent" varies widely across these stages. In most situations the client has already been partially unfrozen in having experienced disconfirmation, guilt, or anxiety, but most likely he has not felt enough psychological safety to become motivated to make a change. The most difficult situation occurs if the manager or consultant has to begin at stage 1 and somehow manage all of the unfreezing, changing, and refreezing processes. This is often time-consuming because the process simply cannot be short-circuited. Too many change programs or consultation projects fail because they attempt to restructure the change target's perceptions, thoughts, attitudes, and behavior before adequate unfreezing has taken place. And too many changes fail to survive because no attention is given to whether the new learning fits either into the personality or the significant relationships of the learner.

Change is a complex, drawn-out process. Crisis conditions can sometimes speed it up, but the early stages cannot be skipped. What the consultant or manager who is attempting to produce and manage change must realize is that whether or not he himself causes each stage to happen, the stages must be gone through by the client or change target.

Part III

The Consulting Process in Action

In this third section of the book the focus shifts to the strategy and tactics of consulting. How does one think about who is a client? How does one think about the actual things to say to a client in order to achieve the strategic and tactical goals of the helping process? Do these things differ as a function of the stage of the consulting process? Are managers as consultants in a different situation, or do the same principles apply to them?

Many more examples are used in the following chapters and concrete suggestions are made both to managers and consultants.

7

Who Is the Client?

Any helping or change process always has a target or a client. In the discussion so far I have referred to clients as if they were always clearly identifiable, but in reality, the question of who is actually the client can be ambiguous and problematical. One can find oneself not knowing whom one is working for, or working with several clients whose goals are in conflict with each other. And, as the consultation or managerial process evolves over time, the question of who is *really* the client becomes more and more complicated.

This point is obvious in the consulting relationship in that the contact client, the person who initially contacted the consultant, introduces the consultant to other people in the organization who, in turn, may work with the consultant to plan activities for still others in the organization. One must think, therefore, in terms of categories of clients:

- *Contact clients* approach the consultant or manager initially.
- *Intermediate clients* get involved in early meetings or planning next steps.
- *Primary clients* own a problem for which they want help.

- *Ultimate clients* may or may not be directly involved with the consultant or manager but their welfare and interest must be considered in planning further interventions.

Though it is not as obvious in the managerial situation, it is important to recognize that managers face, vis-à-vis superiors, peers, subordinates, and others outside their immediate organizations, the same set of "client" ambiguities when they are involved in helping. The manager can define any given subordinate as a contact client when working with that subordinate but is often planning activities that will involve others in the organization for the benefit of still others, who may be employees or people outside the organization, such as customers and suppliers.

One of the *ethical* dilemmas of management derives from the fact that the manager is always dealing with more than one client system, and some may not have the same needs or expectations as others (Schein, 1966). In the managerial context we think of these as different "stakeholders" and acknowledge that it is central to the managerial role to balance the interests of these groups. Managers and consultants, therefore, have something to learn from each other on how such multiple relationships can be conceptualized and managed.

It should also be noted that for managers to think of the members of their role network, their superiors, subordinates, and peers as "clients" may not initially seem appropriate because of the implication that there should be some professional distance between a helper and a client. Such distance is difficult to maintain when one thinks of the direct power that the manager has and the indirect power that the consultant has, but effective helping in both cases is possible if the relationship is structured according to the assumptions of PC. What the effective general manager does is to use his own power to create processes of problem solving and decision making that will empower the subordinates.

Contact Clients

The helping process always starts with a "contact" client who may be thought of as the first person with whom the consultant or manager meets concerning the problem, whether or not that person admits to owning the problem that is to be worked on. If I am to be helpful in terms of the assumptions of PC, I need to know as soon as possible what perceptions and stereotypes this contact client and others in his organization have of me and my consulting philosophy. I especially do not want to be cast into the expert or doctor role prematurely. Therefore, I must start with broad inquiries: Why has the person called or come? Why at this particular time?

The reasons contact clients give then provide a clue as to their perception which I can either reinforce or "correct":

- The contact has read a book or paper on my consulting style.
- He has been referred by a former or current client.
- He has been referred by a colleague who knows my style and areas of interest.
- He has become acquainted with me at a workshop in which I have done some teaching.
- He has heard a lecture or read a paper or book on some topic on which I have written, such as *Career Dynamics* or *Organizational Culture*, and perceives some connection between that topic and his problem area.

As I listen to the answers I calibrate as best I can whether the situation warrants continuing the relationship — that is, whether or not I can be ultimately helpful in the situation. I have to make an assessment of whether the contact client and others in his organization who may be involved have a willingness and readiness to engage in the process model I advocate. I have to discover whether the client's intent is constructive or not, so that I do not unwittingly become a pawn in someone's political game. As will be detailed in the subsequent chapters, I can only discover the answers to these questions through a process of careful questioning that is simultaneously exploratory and helpful.

I always have to operate by the overarching principle that whatever I say or do must be perceived as much as possible as *helpful* in the immediate situation. My goal is to have the caller feel that he not only received the information he sought but also got some help in thinking about the problem himself. In most cases this help would be in the form of suggestions of ways that the contact client can go back to his organization with his own helpful interventions and suggestions. One of these might well be to suggest that if other potential clients back in the organization want to explore the situation further, I would meet them for an hour or so to see whether it would make sense to get further involved, and would bill them for that time.

Billing for such an exploratory meeting is warranted because useful insights typically result from such initial meetings and there is often no need for further involvement. The contact client and whomever he involves in that meeting may learn from it what they need to do next, and those next steps often do not require any further help from the outside consultant. Billing for exploratory meetings has the further function of testing the contact client's motivation to get help, and, third, sends the message that help is available on an "hourly" basis and does not have to involve long projects or elaborate formal contracts.

Creating Clients from Inside

Managers and inside consultants are not typically in the position described above. They are more likely to find themselves being approached directly by a boss, subordinate, or peer for specific information or help and must decipher the role relationship immediately with the appropriate inquiries. The internal person often has the problem of "creating" a client in that he may see a problem in some part of his own organization, but no one has approached him for help. The manager or internal consultant must then play the difficult disconfirming role in the unfreezing process while, at the same time, trying to be helpful and supportive to create psychological safety.

To complicate matters further, the manager has access to the situation by virtue of his formal position, but the internal consultant often cannot figure out how to gain access to the potential client to start the unfreezing process. Is it valid for the helper to initiate the process even if the person needing help does not perceive his own need? In the managerial situation the answer is obviously yes since one of the manager's chief functions is to identify and work on situations that need to be improved. But even in the case of internal consultants, it can be valid to "create" clients because of commitment the consultant may feel to the ultimate client, the entire organization, the community, employees, or customers in general.

How then can "client creation" be managed? I have found that the key is to engage the potential contact client in an authentic manner with some problem or issue that the consultant or manager himself is experiencing. In order to establish the relationship, the helper must first seek help. The manager dealing with his subordinate would go to that subordinate and seek help in trying to understand why certain targets or standards are not being met by the subordinate. The manager makes it clear that he is concerned about the performance of the entire unit and would like to help the subordinate to succeed but needs help in understanding what is wrong. By making himself vulnerable the manager enhances the likelihood that the subordinate will reciprocate and seek his help.

When I functioned as a university department chairman and saw a problem in the way a younger faculty member was teaching a course, instead of taking a corrective attitude toward the person (the expert or doctor role), I found it more helpful to ask the young faculty member to brief me on what he was teaching, why he chose the topics and methods that he chose, and to be genuinely interested in understanding the course from his perspective. If he was getting low teaching ratings we could then puzzle out together why the low ratings were occurring. Most of the time I found that the person felt helped in solving what he already knew was a problem, though it would not have occurred to him to come to me for help. In other words, though the subordinate might never have defined himself as a client, it was within my power as a manager to think of him as either a subordinate or a client, and to structure the relationship accordingly.

The internal consultant does not have the same degree of access as the manager, but he can approximate the situation by going to managers in a department that seems to be in trouble and asking genuinely whether or not he could be of any help in working with that department. He could also focus on his own need to learn more about what that department was doing and suspend judgment on whether or not there was a real problem in the department that would require help. In any case he should avoid confronting them with his perception that they need help.

If, in the conversations with managers in the department, he is perceived as a helpful person to talk to, the likelihood is greater that he will then be asked to get more involved. The key is to be interested in learning what is going on and to come across in every contact as a helpful person.

The Power of an Honest Question

In all of these situations there is nothing more powerful than a genuine question along the lines of "I don't really understand what is going on here and why." When the manager or consultant comes into a new situation the only thing he actually observes is artifacts: poor outcomes, missed targets, waste, conflict, low quality, poor morale. He does not know *why* these things are happening. If the helper can avoid the psychological trap of thinking he is the expert or doctor who already knows why and what to do about it, he can genuinely inquire about the reasons for the poor outcomes, thereby helping the subordinates to think through and eventually to fix the problem.

We know that such genuine inquiry processes work because organizational researchers who have no intention of getting involved in consultation often find themselves pressed by members of the organization being studied to provide help. If the researcher is perceived to be a helpful person, even though he has not asked to get involved in problems, he will be asked to help. In other words, the manager or internal consultant who wants to create a client must first be genuinely inquiring as the researcher would be, and, through this inquiry, build up a level of trust. What typically does *not* work is the concept of trying to "sell" process consultation to someone unfamiliar and uninterested, or trying to explain how it works outside the context of an actual problem situation.

Intermediate Clients

The contact client is not necessarily the person who has a problem that must be worked on. He may even be just an agent for someone else in the organization who either does not want to take the time or is too embarrassed or troubled to seek the help directly. The contact client often just creates access to others who may or may not be the owners of problems. These "intermediate clients" in turn may create contact with the person who becomes the primary client or may themselves turn out to be the primary client. But initially one does not know.

For example, I often get calls from personnel or training departments of companies inquiring on behalf of line managers whether or not I do certain kinds of consulting. The caller admits to having a list of names and making the same inquiry of all the people on it.

If I were to treat this just as an information inquiry I could not answer the questions, because I would not know what kind of problem motivated the inquiry or how I got on the list. I would need to know what kind of organization and what kind of line manager would pass on such a task to a staff person and why. I would therefore define the caller as a contact client and try various exploratory interventions in order to determine whether or not to proceed further to identify the intermediate client:

> "Can you tell me a bit more about this manager and the situation?"

> "What is happening now that makes an outside consultant desirable?"

> "How does this manager relate to you in the organization?"

> "Can you tell me how you got my name, or why you are calling me in particular?"

My goal in asking these kinds of questions is twofold. First, I need to obtain information in order to proceed, and, second, I want to be helpful to the contact client to create the correct initial impression of the manner in which my consultation will proceed. Hence the questions also suggest some avenues for the contact client to explore on his own. They help him to structure his next steps with the intermediate client.

As the conversation develops, I may suggest alternative steps for the caller to offer the intermediate client: a meeting between me and the concerned line manager, a direct telephone conversation with the manager, or maybe just some further questions to put to the line manager regarding what he may have in mind.

The commonest version of this tactic is to ask the contact client to speculate on why this line manager is asking for help and why he has chosen the particular format of having someone else gather names of potential consultants. That gets the contact client thinking diagnostically and helps him to own his part of the problem.

If the contact client and I agree that the next step is for the intermediate client to call me directly or to set up a meeting, my focus shifts to the management of the intermediate client relationship. This involves setting a schedule, a time for a call or meeting, a decision on where to meet, who should be at the meeting, how long the meeting should be, and what the purpose of the meeting should be. Ideally, all of these decisions should be made directly with the intermediate client, the person who appears to own the problem.

In making these decisions, typically during a phone call, the goal is again twofold: first, to manage the process so that correct expectations are set up in the client as to how I will help, and, second, to be helpful during the phone conversation by asking inquiring types of questions and being generally supportive of moving forward without, however, offering to take the problem off the client's back. Part of the overall strategy is to get the contact client to own whatever next steps are taken. The jointly decided next steps then create a series of intermediate client relationships out of which a primary client evolves.

From the insider's perspective the choice is again the manager's. I have often been asked in my role as a colleague or formerly as a department chairman to attend a meeting in order to be helpful to "another group" who do not know they need help. It was then my choice whether during the meeting to come on strong as an expert or doctor, or whether to play the process consultant role by asking the right kinds of clarifying questions, summarizing, checking consensus, and so on. Managers and inside consultants are constantly in the situation where they can be helpful in the process consultant role in the normal work routine, and thus build up credibility as a person who is helpful to have around.

Primary Clients

A primary client is a person or group that has a particular problem on which we have agreed to focus and whose budget will ultimately cover my fees. Contact and intermediate clients may or may not become primary clients.

Ultimate Clients

Ultimate clients are the stakeholders whose interests should ultimately be protected even if they are not in direct contact with the consultant or manager. In other words, the helping process should not help a primary client if it will obviously harm some other group that the consultant or manager should be concerned about. If I am asked to help a manager to win a political battle over another manager, I must ask myself what will ultimately be best for the entire department or organization (the ultimate client). Only if I can justify in my own mind that the ultimate client will be better off can I justify helping this manager.

From a practical point of view I always think of the entire organization as my ultimate client if that organization is engaged in an enterprise that does not conflict with my own values. So whatever interventions are made, they must be guided by whatever estimates one can make of their impact on the total organization. By implication this makes the society and community another level of ultimate client. It is my presumption that I would not consult with an organization whose function or purpose in society was destructive or antithetical to my values.

Primary clients pay for the services directly. Ultimate clients are affected by the outcomes but may not even know that anything is going on. Ultimate clients, therefore, must be defined by the consultant or manager in terms of his own professional criteria. Should a second-level manager help a subordinate manager to exploit the workers under that subordinate, for example? Should a sales manager help his sales representatives to get better deals at the expense of the customers? Should an inside consultant (or outside consultant) help a company close a plant in a community that will clearly be harmed by such an action?

There are never easy answers to such questions, but it is important in all helping relationships to recognize the questions. That is, anytime we help someone we are, in effect, allying ourselves with the goals and values they represent. We cannot later abdicate responsibility for the help we may have provided if that help turns out to have bad effects on another part of the organization or other groups.

In my own managerial role as department chairman these issues came up frequently in regard to the interests of the faculty and the students. If faculty members asked me to help them to organize projects, teaching schedules, or consulting trips that would be, in my opinion, harmful to student interests I had to decide when the students as ultimate clients were more important than the faculty colleague who was the primary client. If questions about such issues arose in my mind, I found that the best intervention was always to share the question immediately so that the client had to own the issue as well. We could then work out together how to meet the needs of the ultimate client.

Client Complexity in the Multi Company

Client complexities in an evolving project can best be illustrated by reviewing some aspects of my work with the Multi Company (Schein, 1985a). I was initially called by a staff member, the director of management development, John Walker, and invited to consider giving a seminar to the top forty-five managers of Multi, a large multinational company, at their annual meeting six months hence. I tentatively agreed because I had met Walker at a previous seminar where he had heard me talk. He convinced me that a similar presentation would be very relevant to their company and I became interested because of the opportunity to make contact with a top management group of a large multinational organization.

Before the assignment was finalized, however, I had to meet the president, Richards, to see if we could agree on the purpose of the presentations and to test whether Richards would be satisfied with my approach to the meeting. A special trip was set up to meet Richards, who now became the intermediate client. Richards and I met, reached agreement on goals, established that we could be comfortable with each other, and, therefore, agreed to go ahead.

The next step was to meet a month later with the director of training, who designs and manages the annual meetings. He now became the *primary* client for purposes of developing a detailed plan of when and how I would give my presentations and how this would fit into the structure of the annual meeting. At the same time he became a consultant to me in helping me to design my sessions to be relevant to the issues that were salient in Multi at the time.

At the annual meeting itself I met many other managers. The members of the executive committee were clearly potential primary clients, as were some of the division heads and region heads. In each of these relationships the twin goals of inquiring and simultaneously being helpful were my criteria for how to interact with each new person I met.

During the annual meeting a planning group led by Walker which included the president and several other members of the executive committee monitored the meeting and replanned events as needed. They asked me to sit in with them and help them in this process, so they became a primary client for that purpose.

In terms of my actual presentation, the whole group of forty-five were my primary clients in the sense that they owned the problems that my seminar addressed. Individual members sought me out during the meeting and subsequently became primary clients concerning particular issues. After the meeting Richards asked me to continue to consult with the company to make it more innovative. He defined himself, the executive committee, and Walker as primary clients and asked Walker to manage my time during the visits, so Walker once again became the contact client.

As this scenario developed I ended up working with the senior group, various individuals in the executive committee, and with the participants at the next two annual meetings. The company as a whole was clearly one level of the ultimate client.

Walker and the training director continued in the dual roles of contact clients and primary clients in that management development and training issues became one of the prime foci for the later consultation efforts, but various other managers also became contact and primary clients in that they began to communicate with me directly about attending meetings or helping them with specific problems.

Consulting with Consultants:
The Jackson Strategy Consultants

An interesting example of the ultimate client issue came up in a project where I was part of a faculty group helping a strategy consulting firm to become more effective as consultants by participating in developmental seminars for the consultants. A number of faculty members worked with several senior consultants in the company on issues of marketing, finance, human resources, and consulting technique. The role of the faculty members was to provide research information and to help the consulting group to use this information to improve the tools they used in analyzing their clients' problems.

In my case the research focused more on method and process. In my individual sessions with members of this company and in group seminars we discussed issues such as how to decipher what the client really wants, what the client organization's culture is, and how the consultant can optimally manage the relationships. I provided conceptual maps and they provided case materials which we then used to discuss new analytical tools to be developed for their work with clients.

The ground rules were clear that faculty members would not get directly involved with clients unless there was some very specific reason to do so, so whatever help was provided to ultimate clients, the companies that Jackson works with, was provided through the intermediates, the Jackson consultants. On the surface this appeared to be a clear-cut case, but the unresolved dilemma was whether or not the faculty who was training the consultants had any say whatever over the kinds of clients who were ultimately taken on by Jackson, and whether or not we should have had such a say. I found myself monitoring this process by examining my own reactions to the cases presented by the Jackson consultants. Their cases and the approach they took generally fitted my own criteria of valid help, so the issue was resolved without conflict.

This case differed from the more common situation of functioning as a training consultant or a "shadow consultant" in that the faculty group contracted to help the entire consulting firm to become more effective. If the firm then hired people whose values we did not share or took on clients that we would not have approved of, such actions were entirely out of our control.

Conclusion and Managerial Implications

The most important point to be made about clients is that the consultant must always be clear who the client is at any given moment in time, and must distinguish clearly among contact, intermediate, primary, and ultimate client. Especially when the consultant has been working in an organization for some time with different units, it is easy to forget who the client is.

The managerial equivalent of this kind of situation arises in the process that has come to be labeled "management by walking around" (Mintzberg, 1973; Kotter, 1982; Peters and Waterman, 1982). The manager who tours his domain will find himself in several types of client situations. Someone will ask him for help directly; someone will identify a problem in another area that requires looking into; someone else will passively await questions from the manager. In each case the manager has to sort out mentally what role to play and, if he decides to play the process consultant role, will have to decide who is the primary client.

Managers who either cannot or do not want to play process consultant roles probably should not manage by touring or walking around because they will be tempted to become the policeman or spy instead of the helper, and this role may make matters worse instead of better. The manager trying to be helpful to his organization must be clear whom he is trying to help and in what manner.

8

Intervention Strategy

The helping/consultation process begins with the very first response you make to any inquiry. Imagine that you are a manager. One of your subordinates calls you or walks into your office and asks to talk to you about something. Or imagine that you are a consultant, your phone rings, and the party at the other end wants to know if you would be willing to help with a problem.

In both cases, the very first thing you say or do is your first intervention, and you need to think about the various choices that are available to you at that moment. What you say and do in effect begins to structure the situation, sets up certain expectations, and conveys a certain image you have of yourself and of the other person. Once the situation is structured, the other person will play by the rules he perceives to be appropriate to that situation. You have to be sure, therefore, that you are structuring the situation to be consistent with your own strategic objectives, values, and assumptions.

For example, if you feel yourself to be an expert at solving a certain class of problems and have advertised yourself previously as such an expert, you will want to find out very quickly whether the needs of the subordinate or potential client can be met by your expertise. If not, you will want to terminate the conversation or refer the person to someone else. If you see yourself as a doctor who can make a diagnosis and prescribe a remedy, you will invite the subordinate or client in and proceed to ask a series of diagnostic questions, conveying thereby your willingness and self-perceived ability to be helpful. You will also convey your willingness to tackle the problem, to take it off the other person's shoulders.

If you see yourself to be a process consultant who may be able to help the client to help himself, to be facilitative, or to be a catalyst, you will take a very different approach. In the initial interaction you do not really know whether or not you will be able to be helpful, what the client's intent or level of readiness for help is, how much the client will want to become dependent on you, and how willing you will be to accept this dependence. The same ambiguity applies to superiors vis-à-vis subordinates. By what criteria, then, will you decide how to respond to the initial inquiry?

Strategic Objectives of Initial Interventions

The dilemma of PC is that one is trying to accomplish several strategic objectives simultaneously. One must therefore invent interventions that permit each of these objectives to be met. The objectives can be classified into three basic categories as shown in Table 8–1.

In essence, what you have to do is to ask questions or make comments that

- Will be *helpful* in structuring the client's thinking further
- Will *reveal information* about what is really going on, thereby also teaching the client how to bring to the surface and analyze his own diagnostic information
- Will communicate clearly to the client that you will be willing to help but *will not take the problem onto your own shoulders*

The tricky aspect to this is how to structure the situation to leave your own options open since you do not know at the

Table 8-1

Strategic Objectives of Initial Interventions

1. *Provide Help:*   Whatever the manager or consultant does initially must be perceived as "helpful" by the subordinate or client.

2. *Diagnose:*   Initial interventions must create the conditions that permit the process consultant to find out "what is going on," in the sense of learning more about what the initial client wants from a consultant, why he is calling now, what the issues are in the client's organization, which individuals and groups are likely to become part of the client system, and what is expected of the consultant down the road. Furthermore, the diagnostic activity must be handled in such a way that the client himself develops diagnostic insight and skill.

3. *Build an Intervention Team:*   Because the process consultant will not take the problem off the client's shoulders, the initial interventions must make it clear that next steps will be a shared responsibility between the consultant and the contact client. As the consultation evolves and other people become clients, the interventions must be managed to continue to get shared ownership and responsibility for the total change process.

outset whether what is really going on and what the client really wants will fall into the range of things that you can be helpful about. You also do not know how you will feel about the implicit assumptions that the potential client may be communicating to you about what he expects. A subordinate bursting into your office or a client calling for advice can arouse a variety of feelings, ranging from annoyance at being interrupted or misperceived as an expert to joy and pride because someone is seeking help from you.

Given all of these considerations, it is very important to begin with a positive but fairly neutral attitude, not to let your feelings dictate your tone of voice or what you say. You have to develop instantly a "spirit of inquiry" and ask some questions or make some comments that will serve all three of the strategic objectives at once.

What often works best is to focus on the immediate "here and now" with questions that help clients to further explain what they want, why they have called me, and why they chose a particular time to seek help. I say very general things like

"Tell me a little bit more about what you have in mind."

"How do you think I can be helpful in this situation?"

"Can you tell me why you called me?"

"What is the timing on this? Is something particular going on that made you call me at this time?"

What I have to avoid is prejudgments of various sorts, stereotypes of the client or the problem, perceptual biases in listening, and emotional responses to the assumptions that the client may be making. It is the last category that is most dangerous in that the client often says things that imply things about me that are not true and may make me feel defensive.

For example, a person calls from a company and says: "Dr. Schein, I understand that you do seminars on communication. We are designing a middle management seminar next month and on the second day in the afternoon need a speaker for two hours on communication. Are you interested, and, if so, what is your fee?"

As I am listening to this, the following thoughts may be running through my head and the following feelings may be surfacing:

1. I am not a speaker on the management seminar circuit, and I have not done communication workshops, so how do I let him know this without turning him off.
2. I do not want to turn him off prematurely because maybe he is looking for something in the design of the seminar or in a topic area that I would be interested in.
3. The company or the department that he is in might be of potential interest to me.
4. I feel some resentment at being stereotyped, but I feel that I should always be helpful if that is possible so must try not to let the resentment show.

My response must somehow keep the door open even though I know already that I will not do literally what I am being asked to do. So I might say:

"I do occasionally do seminars for companies but would need to know a bit more about your program, what other topics are being covered, and how you got my name for this particular topic. Could you tell me a bit more about what you have in mind."

I will deliberately not answer the direct question or quote a fee, because that would validate the caller's stereotype of me and close off any options other than doing or not doing the seminar. As I get more information, if I decide that working with the organization might be productive for me and them, I would provide information on topics that I would be willing to deal with, say how much time I would need to cover a topic, and indicate what my hourly and daily fee might be, based on amount of preparation, travel time, size of audience, and so on.

The decision to work with a company would be based on several criteria. The first is my sense that the contact client was himself in a position where there was enough autonomy or power to be able to change things, or at least was linked to others who had sufficient autonomy or power. I do not want to get involved in situations where even if the client gets help, he is in no position to implement anything. Second, I want to have a sense that the client understands my general area of competence and experience as being in the realm of group and organizational psychology. I do not want to be involved in situations where I will be perceived from the outset as an expert in marketing, manufacturing, or some other functional area.

Third, I want to have a sense that when I bring up process kinds of issues even in the initial contact over the phone that there is some readiness to deal with such issues. If it becomes clear that the client wants a straight content input or an evaluation of a program, I am more reluctant to get involved. Fourth, I have to have a sense that the project is within my time limitations. Since I am not a full-time consultant I can only take on projects that will take no more than one day per week, on the average.

If my four criteria are more or less met, I will get involved even if the presenting problem is not one I would end up working on. For example, it might turn out that what the caller really wants or needs is some help in designing the whole management program, and this need would have surfaced from my questions about the other topics and their timing in the total seminar. We might agree to meet to discuss the seminar design, suspending the question of whether or not I do a segment of it, and I might end up being more helpful as a designer than a speaker. I might tell the client about some other seminars I have run or how some other companies have handled a similar problem by way of being helpful in enlarging the client's thinking. In this discussion I might switch back and forth between the expert role and the process consultant role.

If the client really wants just my two-hour presentation, this fact will surface fairly rapidly and we can then settle it based on topic, schedule, and fee, but it is essential from the process consultation point of view not to assume initially that what the client asked for is, in fact, what he most wants or needs. Several examples will make this clear and indicate how diagnostic and shared responsibility criteria can be worked in.

Suspended Team Building in Ellison Manufacturing

In this case an unwitting intervention produced help in a totally unexpected area. I had been working with the plant manager of a local plant for some months in a counseling relationship. He wanted to think out a strategy for developing more trust among his managers and between labor and management in the plant. He concluded that taking his senior management team (his immediate subordinates) to a two-day off-site meeting to build them into a team was a logical next step to take and scheduled a working lunch with me and the organization development advisor who was on his staff.

My role was to help design the two-day meeting and to plan what my own participation in that meeting would be. At the beginning of the lunch I decided I needed some general information about the setting and the people, so I asked: "Who will actually attend the meeting, as you see it, and what are their roles?" The plant manager started down his list of subordinates but when he got to the third name he hedged and said: "Joe is my financial person, but I am not sure he will make it; I have some reservations about his ability and have not yet decided whether or not to keep him or to transfer him." I asked if there were any others in the group about whom he had reservations, and he said that there was one other person who had not yet proved himself and might not end up on the team.

At this point, all three of us at the meeting had the same insight, but the plant manager himself articulated it. He said: "I wonder if I ought to be having this team-building session if I'm not sure about the membership of two of the people." I asked what he thought would happen if we went ahead but then later fired one or both of them. He concluded that this would undermine the team building, and that it was not really fair to the two people about whom he was unsure.

We discussed the pros and cons of having the team-building session at all until he had made up his mind about the marginal people, decided to postpone the meeting until he had decided, and all breathed a huge sigh of relief that this issue surfaced then rather than later.

Note that the crucial information came out in response to an innocent question, and that the process left the plant manager to reach the conclusion to cancel based on his own thinking through of the issues. He regarded the lunch as a most helpful intervention even though we ended up canceling the team-building effort for the time being. The strategic goals of the consultation process had been met.

The Unnecessary Management Meeting at Global Electric

A similar situation arose in a large multinational organization that wanted me to attend their annual management conference to help the president to develop something of a senior management committee. The divisions were operating in too isolated a fashion and, if we could use my educational input as an excuse to bring a small group together regularly, that group could gradually begin to tackle business problems.

The contact client was the director of management development and training, who briefed me during several meetings on the company's situation. They badly needed to find a vehicle to start the autonomous division managers meeting together but felt that such meetings would not work without an outsider to serve as both the excuse for the meeting (the planned seminar) and as the facilitator. So an educational intervention made sense even though the real goal was to build a more collaborative management team.

After our planning had proceeded and a date had been set,

we scheduled a meeting with the president at the headquarters in Europe to discuss the details of the project. The meeting with the president revealed a somewhat different issue. He was worried that two of his key division managers were fighting all the time and undercutting each other. One of these was too dominant and the other too subservient. What he hoped to do was to bring them together in a group situation where some feedback to both of them would "correct" their weaknesses. I was a bit skeptical about the potential of the group to do this, but he was prepared to go slowly. We decided that a seminar discussing career anchors and different management styles similar to what had worked well in Multi would serve their needs (Schein, 1985b).

Two months before the seminar I received a call from the contact client saying that they were terribly sorry but the seminar had been canceled and he would explain later. I was to bill them for any time lost, and they did not know whether or not they would do the seminar later. I only learned what had actually happened on a visit to another client who knew the Global people well, the adventures of Global having become something of a topic of discussion among others in the industry.

I heard that the president had become so upset at the "weaker" manager that he had replaced him, and with that replacement most of the difficulties that required group work seem to have disappeared. I learned from my contact client that the long interview with the president had partially precipitated this decision in that it got him to rethink carefully what he was doing and why. He had noted my skepticism about what the group could do and chose a different remedial course.

Here again, the consultation process was brief and seemingly terminated before it began, but in terms of the strategic goals of PC, the goals were met. The case has to be treated as successful in having provided the kind of help that the primary client, the president, needed.

Refusing to Play Doctor in Hansen Laboratories

This case illustrates a clear conflict in expectations. What I was willing to accept as strategic goals of the project clearly did not mesh with what the client expected from the consultant, hence the consultation was terminated at an early stage.

One of my former students was a senior manager in a small

company that conducted annual meetings of their key managers from all over the world. The company was run by his uncle and the uncle's brother the president, and he had proposed both to me and to his uncle that a consultant like me (hopefully I would have time to do it, he said) should attend their next annual meeting to be a facilitator during the discussion periods.

My job would be to "bring out" the silent members of the group by asking them confrontive questions about the presentations on future strategy that were to be made by top management. They felt that a "process expert" like me would be able to bring out these silent people in a way that they could not.

I asked a broad inquiry question — why they thought they needed an *outsider* for this, and was told that over the past several years the meetings had gone "badly" in the sense that the overseas managers usually failed to participate in the manner that they were expected to. I asked him to describe what went on at these meetings. This general inquiry pushed my contact to begin to think diagnostically and I learned that senior management gave lecture inputs on future strategy to which they wanted reactions but that the climate they created elicited only compliance. Furthermore, many of the managers who were supposed to respond to and critique the inputs had language difficulties and were in varying degrees of competition with each other. I suspected that it might not be safe to speak up at the annual meeting because one might create a bad impression both with one's peers and with senior management. Moreover, it was not clear whether senior management was serious about wanting to hear what others had to say.

At this point I felt that I could be most helpful by getting the contact client to see for himself that the conditions for participation might not be present and that bringing in an outsider would not fix this problem. I therefore asked a series of confrontive questions about how serious senior management was about wanting participation and about the nature of the climate they were setting up at the meeting. I was wondering whether they first needed to address their own commitment to participation before trying to figure out mechanisms for how to obtain it. I said that if they really wanted participation surely they could communicate that and set up their own mechanisms to draw out the silent managers. I offered to help them to design such mechanisms but did not agree that an outsider would help in this situation.

The contact client, my former student, felt that his uncle did not want the responsibility and that the president might not be very good at eliciting participation, hence they wanted to lean on an outsider. However, he believed that both were committed to participation.

As I thought about this I concluded that I did not want to get involved in the meeting because too little was clear about what would go on there. To be helpful in this situation I felt I needed to get the family to see their own problem more clearly. I asked my student to tell his uncle that I would be willing to meet with him to discuss the design of the meeting and whether or not it made sense to have any outsider present, but this would constitute a consultation visit for which they would pay my hourly rate. My purpose at this point was to test whether or not they were really motivated to work on this problem, and to learn more about the uncle.

The uncle did call and set up a two-hour meeting. At the meeting he reiterated all that his nephew had said and urged me to attend the annual retreat. We would all go up to a country hotel on a bus, spend three days, and then return on the bus. I could help to loosen up the group during the bus ride, question people at the meeting if they did not speak up, and further facilitate the process on the bus ride home. When I asked why they thought they could not set up a climate more conducive to participation themselves, the uncle hedged and argued that they did not have the skill, referring again specifically to his brother.

My emotional response was increasing tension and resistance. The situation felt wrong in that the motives did not match the proposed mechanisms. My judgment, based on talking to the uncle, was that they did not really know what they wanted, were probably sending mixed signals, or, possibly very accurate signals that they wanted only compliance, and that the consultant in this situation might only make matters worse by stimulating a level of participation that might not be welcome. I gently confronted the uncle with these thoughts and aroused a surprising amount of denial and defensiveness. He had his mind made up that an outside facilitator was the answer. I told him I felt I could not do it and hoped that he would try to solve the problem internally.

As far as I could tell, what was really going on would have made it unwise and possibly even harmful to agree to the next steps that the client was proposing. In effect they wanted a doctor to come in to fix a problem that they might have misdiagnosed, and they were not willing to share responsibility for the proposed intervention by doing more process management themselves. There was no way to tell whether getting junior managers to "open up" would be welcomed by their seniors or would be in the best interests of the lower level managers.

My help in this case was to try to surface all of this so that the nephew and his uncle could themselves gain some insight into these issues. I reinforced my verbal analysis with a long letter spelling out my analysis and concerns. I received my check for two hours of consultation but did not get any further communication so I do not know whether my interventions were, in the end, helpful or not.

Designing and Participating in the Annual Meeting at International Oil

In this example the three strategic objectives were met most clearly, but the process of getting there illustrates a number of the tactical complexities of staying in the process consultant role. The company is a large multinational oil and chemicals concern with headquarters in Europe. I knew a number of the people in the corporate management development group and had met one of their senior executives, Steve Sprague, years ago in an MIT executive program.

My involvement resulted from the interest that the company developed in looking at its own corporate culture and how that might or might not fit the strategic realities of the next decade. Several members of the corporate management development staff knew that I had just published some papers and a book on organizational culture.

I received a phone call from a man in the corporate staff group who was helping to design the annual three-day off-site meeting for the top forty executives of the company. The proposition was to come in for two days, listen to their internal discussions, and then lecture about culture, weaving in examples from their own discussion to provide feedback on their own culture. I was not to be involved at the very beginning and end of the meeting so this was defined initially as strictly an educational intervention during the second day of the meeting.

I was interested in this company and wanted to learn more about various company cultures, so this seemed like an ideal match. I agreed to the terms as originally stated and was then told that further briefing on the meeting would be provided by Sprague, who had become an executive vice president reporting directly to the chairman of the company. We arranged a meeting during his next trip to the United States.

At the meeting Sprague talked at length about the strategic situation of the company, saying that it was critical at the annual meeting to take a real look at whether the direction upon which the company had embarked still made sense, whether it should be slowed down or speeded up, and how to get the commitment of the top group to whatever was decided. I also learned at this point that Sprague was in charge of the overall design of the three-day meeting, and that he not only wanted to brief me, but wanted to review the entire design with me. The initial call had focused on my lecturing on culture, but Sprague was asking me to be an expert resource to help design the annual meeting and was making himself the primary client. I found myself switching roles from process consultant to expert because we were discussing the design of a meeting, a topic about which I obviously knew more than he, and we both understood this switch in role and made it explicit.

We reviewed the design of each component of the meeting in terms of Sprague's goals, and the idea emerged that a process consultant might be helpful at the meeting itself. Since my schedule permitted attending the whole meeting, it was decided by Sprague (with my agreement) to have me play several roles throughout. I would give a short input on *culture* and *strategy* early in the meeting and define my role as one of trying to see how these topics would relate to each other as the meeting unfolded. I would do my session on culture on day 2, and, most important, I would run the session on day 3 where the whole group would draw out what areas of consensus they had reached.

These areas of consensus would deal with the business strategy, but it would be easier for me to test for such consensus than it would be for any of the insiders, and it would free the chairman to play an advocacy role. It therefore made sense to both of us to have me play the consensus tester role, and I judged that Sprague knew the personality of the chairman well enough that an outsider's assuming such a role would also be acceptable to him. Sprague's insight throughout the discussion reassured me that he had a good grasp of the issues and knew the climate of the organization well. In any case there was not time to meet the chairman so I had to accept this role on faith.

My participation during the three days worked out as planned. The chairman was comfortable with having me present as an outside resource on process because he felt that this would permit him to focus more on the content, the strategic issues the group was wrestling with. It permitted him freedom that he ordinarily did not feel because he had played the role of consultant as well as chairman in prior meetings.

The interventions I made focused heavily on task process. I occasionally attempted to clarify an issue by restating what I thought I had heard, asked clarifying questions, restated goals, tested consensus when conclusions seemed to be reached, and kept a summary of areas of consensus for purposes of my formal input sessions.

When it was time to present my feedback on culture, I gave some formal definitions and descriptions of culture as a set of basic assumptions but then asked the group to provide the content. Several members of the group asked more pointedly how I perceived their culture, but I had found from past experience that it was best to remain very speculative about this because even if I provided an answer that was technically "correct," it might arouse defensiveness or denial. I kept emphasizing that only insiders really could understand the key cultural assumptions and invited members of the group to provide the answers.

On the final day I formally tested consensus by structuring the areas of discussion that had been covered and inviting the group to state conclusions, which I then wrote down on flip charts to make them explicit to everyone. By my playing this "up front" role, we made it possible for the chairman to be much more active in providing his own conclusions without using his formal power to override the conclusions of others. I sharpened many of the issues based on my listening during the three days and became somewhat more confrontive in areas where the group seemed to want to avoid being clear. In this role I was partly process consultant and partly management "expert" in giving occasional editorial comments on the conclusions being reached.

For example, the group talked of decentralizing into business units, but doing so would take power away from the units based in different regions. The business unit headquarters were all in the home city, so de facto they were really centralizing as much as decentralizing. I pointed out the implications of this for various other kinds of policies such as the movement of human resources across divisional or geographic lines.

The event terminated on a high note and the decision was made to revisit the results several months later. I met with Sprague to review results and learned that both he and the chairman had felt that things went as expected. They felt that bringing me in as an outside resource had helped very much, both at the level of process and content.

Conclusions: Complexities in Strategy and Client Management

What I hope these examples have brought out is the complexity of managing the multiple strategic goals of interventions as a process consultant. Not only does the client shift in unpredictable ways, but with each intervention new data are revealed that shift what it means to be helpful. Frequently one has to shift to being an expert, but then one must be able to shift back into the process consultant role smoothly.

Many descriptions of the consultation process describe it in terms of a contract that is clearly defined from the outset. The reality for me has been that the nature of the contract and who the client is with whom one should be doing the contracting shifts constantly, so that "contracting" is virtually a perpetual process rather than something one does up front prior to beginning the consultation.

One also should be clear, say many models, about precisely who the client is. As I indicated in the last chapter, clients have to be categorized, and their role shifts. I am always very clear about who the contact client is when I am first called or visited, but once I have begun to work with the contact client and we have defined a next step, the client base starts to expand in unpredictable ways.

The important principle is never to define a primary client unilaterally or without some level of understanding and consent on the part of that client. Such unilateral acceptance would violate the strategic goal of having the client continue to own his problem. Therefore, I am willing to be passed on to new primary clients only if the current one I am working with takes joint responsibility with me for the decision and if the mechanisms we jointly work out for involving the new client make sense to both of us.

9

Intervention Tactics and Style

Tactical Goals

How do managers or consultants actually frame their moment-to-moment behavior? What behavioral choices do they have? And what are the consequences of different forms of intervention? These are matters of *tactics* and *style*.

Structuring the relationship with the client or subordinate begins with the very first response that the consultant or manager makes. The biggest traps in the consultation process derive from a failure to recognize how one's initial responses send important signals to the client, especially if those signals are congruent with the client's preconceptions and stereotypes of what the consultant will do. The client's responses then subtly confirm an initial role that the consultant may not have intended but that becomes coercive in its effects. Before they both know it, they are off on an unanticipated and possibly undesirable trip.

The selection of the right response involves a choice among a number of tactical alternatives, as shown in Table 9-1. The consultant can attempt to maximize 1) exploration, 2) diagnosis, 3) action alternatives, or 4) confrontation.

Table 9–1

Types of Interventions in Terms of Their Tactical Goals

1. *Exploratory Interventions:* "Go on." "Can you tell me a bit more about why you are calling?" "Can you describe the situation?" "What do you have in mind?"

2. *Diagnostic Interventions:* "How do you see the problem?" "What goes on in these meetings?" "In what ways do you see me as being helpful in this situation?" "How can I help?" "Why is this more of a problem now?" "Why is an outside consultant needed?"

3. *Action Alternative Interventions:* "What have you tried to do about this yourself?" "Have you considered either of these alternatives?" "Maybe we need to sort out what you are really trying to do in this situation." "What would be the advantage and disadvantage of doing the following thing?"

4. *Confrontive Interventions:* "You should try the following course of action." "Why don't you do . . . ?" "You seem to be blocked and need to unblock." "You must define your goals more clearly if I am to be helpful to you." "It sounds to me like you feel angry at this person, is that right?" "Aren't your own feelings getting in the way of solving the problem?" "Shouldn't you be solving this problem yourself?" "Why did you come to me with this?" "What is keeping you from solving this problem?"

Exploratory interventions reflect my intention to make as few assumptions as possible about what may be going on so that the contact client can get out the story in whatever form it needs to come out. My tactical goal is to get information without sounding like an expert or doctor. It is much easier to do this in the consultant role than in the managerial role because the manager often has strong ideas immediately about what may be going on and what to do about it. As I reflect back on my own administrative days, if a student or faculty colleague came to me with a problem, the hardest kind of initial intervention was just to listen and encourage further exploration by saying "Go on, tell me a bit more."

As one moves from exploratory to *diagnostic* interventions, the focus shifts from just trying to find out what the client wants to *getting the client to begin to think about what might really be going on*, a step that is essential if the client is to learn diagnostic skills and is to take responsibility for next steps. Notice, however, that the examples shown in the table do not offer diagnostic insights. (Such interventions would be defined here as confrontive.) Instead they encourage the client to think diagnostically himself.

Here again the person in the managerial role wishing to operate more like a process consultant must suppress the impulse to give advice and instead encourage the subordinate or colleague to think the matter through for himself. The subject of the intervention should be the client's activity or thought process, not the helper's: "What do *you* think is going on," not, "Here is what *I* think may be going on."

If a junior faculty member was getting bad teaching ratings, it made all the difference in the world whether I said "What do *you* suppose *you* might be doing in the classroom that produced these ratings?" or said, "*I think* you are doing too much lecturing, or maybe you don't give enough concrete examples." Even if my suggestions were accurate, I always felt that the person learned less from being given the criticism and suggestions than being forced to think them out for himself.

As one shifts from diagnostic to *action alternative* as interventions, the focus shifts to *actual new behavior that the client might want to consider* on the assumption that if the client can begin to solve his own problem, he will have also learned something about the process of how to solve problems. In this kind of intervention the helper in the consultant or managerial role may begin to share his own perception of what may be going on, but it is by implication only and it is always couched in terms of multiple possibilities.

As the examples in the table suggest, one can simply ask the client to speculate about behavioral options, or one can suggest several options to consider. I could ask my faculty colleague to consider alternative ways to teach his class, or I could actually suggest several alternatives such as "Well you might try being more personal and giving examples from your own experience, or you might ask students to give examples of the general points you are trying to make."

The *confrontive* intervention shifts the focus to the client's *possible areas of resistance*, in that the consultant now combines some diagnostic insights that he might have with a *focus on the client's own behavior.* This becomes confrontive because the consultant is suggesting what might really be going on before the client might be ready to see it or accept it. The confrontive intervention would therefore typically be used only when the other three types did not produce insight or action alternatives from the client. Confrontation then becomes necessary as a way of both energizing the client and obtaining additional diagnostic information.

For example, if the client reacts with denial or defensiveness, the consultant knows that he should go back to an exploratory or diagnostic tactic to maintain the relationship as a helpful one. At the same time the consultant gains insight about what may really be going on by listening carefully to how the client's defensiveness or denial was put. Which aspects of what the consultant said triggered feelings, what precisely was the client denying and why, what feelings were elicited in the client and why?

When dealing with human systems, as Kurt Lewin noted long ago, it is only by trying to change them that we learn how they really work. This is what "action research" means, in the ultimate sense — that valid data often do not surface until the system has been perturbed or disturbed in some way. The problem, however, is how to intervene (perturb the system) without creating so much defensiveness that the consultant is no longer seen as helpful. In the PC model, remaining helpful is the first principle and major strategic goal so that the relationship continues to exist. Within that strategic goal, confrontive interventions can be tried, but they must be tried with care.

The consultant and the manager are in different situations here. If the consultant makes a serious error of confronting too soon or in an inappropriate way he will soon learn about it because he can be dismissed. If a manager is dealing with a subordinate and confronts inappropriately, the subordinate cannot dismiss his boss physically, but he can psychologically "not hear" what is being said. It is harder, therefore, for the boss to know when he has been psychologically dismissed; hence it is probably even more important for the manager to be careful in using confrontation as an intervention tactic prematurely.

I know that when I made inappropriate confrontive suggestions to junior faculty members they often smiled politely, dismissed what I was saying, and probably said to themselves that they would not seek my help any more. The problem, if this happens, is that the relationship itself suffers a setback, which makes it harder to recover and try some other tactic.

Another way to put this issue is to relate it to change theory. Which intervention tactic to use in consultation depends upon the degree to which the client is already unfrozen. If he has had prior disconfirmatory experiences and is already feeling anxious or guilty, then the consultant need only worry about creating psychological safety. If the client only feels vague pain but has not connected it in any specific ways to his own goals and ideals, the consultant must move much more carefully to help to bring disconfirming information into focus. Such disconfirmation must often be confrontive, but it has the constructive effect of unfreezing only if there is simultaneously the psychological safety to accept the information.

In practice I find that the degree to which I am confrontive is based on my immediate perception of how helpful I am perceived to be, and how much the client trusts me not to be hurtful or to threaten his face. I therefore need to gather some data by exploratory, diagnostic, and action alternative interventions about the readiness of the client to be confronted and the ability of the client to hear and accept certain kinds of confrontive remarks or questions from me. I have to be ready to back off fast if I discover that I have misjudged the situation.

Tactics will also shift as the consultant becomes more familiar with the culture of the client organization and can assess what clients are or are not ready for. A confrontive intervention that would be unthinkable in an early stage might become routine at a later stage. But the consultant must be careful not to go beyond his own level of understanding of the culture and the idiosyncracies of the client, because moving too fast and offending or arousing too much defensiveness is often impossible to reverse.

If the client is unfrozen, motivated to change, and feels psychologically safe, the diagnostic and action alternative interventions seem to be most helpful in that they are the most likely to help restructure the client's thinking, to provide new cognitive insights and new behavioral alternatives. Confrontive interventions should not be necessary because the client is motivated to explore on his own and should be able to hear the consultant's point of view as simply more alternatives to be considered. If sudden resistance is encountered, the consultant must ask himself whether he had misjudged the degree to which the client was unfrozen and be prepared to go back to stage 1 in the change process.

The examples explored below mostly focus on the dilemmas and problems that arise around confrontive tactics. The exploration, diagnosis, and action alternatives usually present no difficulty, but inevitably there comes the temptation to confront, and often it is at that time that the process consultant realizes some of the deeper dynamics of the helper–client relationship.

Confronting Management with a Culture Analysis — The Multi Case Revisited and Reviewed

As previously reviewed in Chapter 7, I was asked by Multi to attend their annual four-day meeting of the top forty-five managers to give a seminar on leadership, innovation, and management development. The seminar involved the participants in various kinds of exercises on career anchors and job role planning (Schein, 1978, 1985b) and was perceived as stimulating and helpful. As a result I was asked to consult with the company on the whole process of change and innovation, and was invited back by the president to the next year's annual meeting in a more complex role involving some presentations and some immediate process consultation to help the annual meeting itself to be more effective. The process role was difficult for them to grasp because their culture was strongly oriented toward the use of outside resources as experts, but it was agreed that if I also gave some lectures, such inputs would validate my expert role sufficiently to justify my attendance throughout the rest of the meeting.

I worked closely with the director of training in the design of the annual meeting, which turned out to be complicated because the company had to launch a major redirection project that would involve the shrinking of the headquarters and some divisions and, in general, a few years of restructuring to make the company more profitable. A member of the company's board of directors who was also a professor of business policy was also invited to the meeting to help get the financial message across.

The annual meeting turned into a giant unfreezing event.

After an unsuccessful effort by the vice president of finance to convince the division and country managers that a crisis was at hand, the professor/board member led the group through a very confrontive exercise that "forced" them to face the disconfirming evidence that their financial picture would be bleak indeed if they did not launch a major redirection project. At this point the group became extremely anxious and depressed, so the professor and I took a long walk to consider what to do next. We came up with the formulation that the group needed to be able to see some positive next steps and to be reassured that the situation was not hopeless. That is, we had to introduce some psychological safety.

We decided that my role should be to attempt to create such psychological safety by giving a lecture on change theory that would legitimize the feelings the group was having and would provide some further change tools, such as force-field analysis, to show them how to move toward solving their problem. Following this lecture the participants were sent off in small groups to examine various forces that would aid or hinder the redirection project. They were to report back with their main conclusions.

Among the major forces listed as both an aid and a hindrance to change was the "company culture," so an effort was to be made by me to get a better understanding of the culture and to report back on this at the third annual meeting. In the meantime the group organized a large number of task forces and projects to launch the redirection project. They asked me to be available during my three quarterly visits in the subsequent year to work with various of these task forces as needed. In the meantime I was to gather information on the company culture and be prepared to make a presentation at the next annual meeting on how it aided or hindered the change program.

Complexities in Defining the Client. The work with the annual meeting was relatively well defined, but as I got into regular visits between annual meetings it became less clear who was a primary client. In part this complexity was the result of how the company was structured. Multi was run by an executive committee of nine, with the president acting as chairman, but this committee was legally liable for all decisions and, therefore, functioned by consensus. I had met all members of the committee but could sense from the meetings that their reactions to my presence varied from enthusiasm on the part of a few to downright skepticism on the part of others. During my several visits to the company the president encouraged all members of the committee to hold individual sessions with me, but only three or four took advantage of this opportunity.

In terms of "who is the client," therefore, the picture was very mixed. My contact clients, the director of management development and director of training, continued to be the primary organizers of my visits and the ones to whom I was directly accountable for billing, travel arrangements, and so on. They were also primary clients in that they were responsible for the design of the annual meetings, and they needed my help and counsel in the overall management development program.

The president was also my primary client in that he really wanted to create some change in the organization and saw me as a catalyst to such change. However, he was extremely busy and became ill during the second year of my consultation, so I saw less and less of him. Three members of the executive committee and various divisional managers became primary clients because they wanted counsel on various aspects of the redirection project, and various lower level managers in the training and organization development function sought me out as an expert resource.

The Culture Presentation. In preparation for my presentation at the third annual meeting, I had checked out all my perceptions of the culture with various members of the organization and knew that what I would say was accurate. However, during the actual presentation I referred to some aspects of the culture as resembling the military (a term I used neutrally, not pejoratively). I immediately got an argument and a defensive reaction from two key members of the executive committee. They, in effect, dismissed what I had said as incorrect and irrelevant, saying that I "did not understand *either* the military or the company." More important, in spite of subsequent reassurance by others that I had been on target, these two executive committee members and an unknown number of other managers subsequently indicated in various ways that my use as a consultant should henceforth be curtailed since I clearly did not "understand" the company.

This confrontive intervention (telling them about their culture) polarized the situation in an undesirable fashion, with some managers rallying to my defense while others wanted to disassociate themselves from me completely. The president had been the prime force in maintaining my role, but, because of his illness, he was forced to withdraw more and more from active management. With his departure the division of opinion within the executive committee on whether or not I could be useful in the change program became more salient and led to my being asked to limit my future consultation to working with the management development group. The main intention of the president had been to get me positioned well with the executive committee so that I could play a continuing role in helping the company to become more innovative, so the decision to limit my participation to helping management development was costly in terms of the original strategic goals of the main primary client.

Lessons. Several lessons can be derived from these events. First, I learned from the culture presentation that premature confrontation can have very serious negative consequences, especially with that part of the client system that has not developed a strong and trusting relationship with the consultant. Most of my prior interventions were more congruent with their culture. I had delivered lectures and introduced new concepts; I had played an expert role in helping to design the meetings by becoming part of the planning group, in which I played a combined expert and process role; I had been facilitative by clarifying concepts during the meeting itself; and had counseled various individuals on how to handle critical parts of the meeting and the subsequent redirection projects. When I talked about the culture I not only sounded wrong about some of the content to some of the people, but the very act of talking about it turned out to be a violation of the culture itself, demonstrating in my behavior that I did not really understand it.

I could easily have managed my culture presentation differently by having members of the company articulate their own content in categories of analysis that I would have suggested to them, but I fell into the trap of believing that I really did have some important diagnostic insights with which to confront the group. The irony of this situation is that by speaking publicly about portions of the Multi culture, I was in effect violating that culture because there is a deep sense of privacy in the organization and the assumption that cultural matters should be left implicit. This aspect of the culture only became visible when violated. Insiders were not aware of their own assumptions about it until those assumptions were confronted.

If I had had a better relationship with some of these individuals we might have been able to work through my error, but, given that some of them were skeptical about the need for an outside consultant once the redirection project was well under way, and given their assumption that the use of a consultant is a sign of weakness, there was no way to salvage the situation.

A second lesson has to do with the confrontation that occurred in the annual meeting concerning the financial problems in Multi. The two-stage presentation by the head of finance and the professor/board member was a clear illustration of a disconfirming intervention designed to unfreeze in a potent manner. After gentle efforts to get the management to accept the financial crisis had failed repeatedly, the planning group decided with the help of the outside board member to confront more directly and forcefully. The negative psychological reaction was predicted, was considered necessary, and had to be dealt with therapeutically within the meeting itself by offering some psychological safety through a new set of concepts for dealing with change.

Confronting a Group with Process Data About Itself: The Kolson Manufacturing Division

Some years back I was asked by a manager of a manufacturing group to sit in on his staff meetings to help diagnose why the group was having difficulty. They said they were always overloaded and felt that decisions were not based on all the best input. The manager and the group were willing to have me come in, so I started to attend meetings. We agreed that at the end of each meeting we would take some time to analyze the process of the meeting, at which time I would make whatever observations I considered appropriate.

One of the first things I observed was that one older member of the group was consistently being interrupted or ignored when he attempted to make a point. After watching this for a couple of meetings I decided to confront the group with what I considered to be potentially destructive behavior. Immediately after I made the observation that the group seemed to consistently ignore this member, I noticed a sharp rise in tension, some embarrassed side remarks and attempts at humor, and an immediate effort to get onto another topic.

I realized that I had "touched a nerve," and therefore did not pursue this line of intervention, but I found out later from the manager of the group what had happened. The older member had been an important contributor when the company was first founded but had gradually become obsolete. The company did not want to release him because of his important earlier contributions so they put him into an area where he might have been able to continue to contribute. The group had learned over time that his ideas were obsolete and they considered it merely a matter of politeness to let him come to the meetings. He seemed to realize his marginal role and accepted the interruptions and being ignored. My bringing up the issue caused him to lose face and embarrassed the group.

Lessons. There are two critical lessons in this example. First, I realized after the fact that I had made an intervention on the *interpersonal* instead of the *task* side of group events (contrary to the advice I offer in Chapter 3), without really finding out whether the seemingly destructive interpersonal behavior was or was not in fact interfering with the task. Second, I had confronted the group prematurely with data about itself that I did not fully understand myself.

I could have accomplished my helping goals better by staying at the inquiry level and asking whether the group was satisfied with its own pattern of participation and its own use of member resources. I should have limited my inquiry to task content and task process issues. There was no need to pinpoint what I thought might have been misuse of member resources. I fell into the trap of imposing my preconceptions of how a group should operate on this particular group without sufficient information about its own history (see the section on traps in Chapter 4).

Confronting a Manager with a Diagnosis: Lorton Research Division

One of my earliest and most problematic consulting experiences involved the interviewing of a group of engineers in a laboratory in order to report back to the laboratory director and the vice president of research the state of morale of the group. This assignment fell to me and a colleague because the VP had approached a senior member of our faculty who had worked for years with this company. The senior faculty member was too busy to do the assignment so he obtained the VP's permission to pass it on to us. We were told that the VP and the laboratory director wanted the survey and that we should proceed with the interviews.

My colleague and I found out many things that were working well and not so well in the laboratory, but one consistent theme was some dissatisfaction with the autocratic manner in which the laboratory director set goals and instituted administrative controls. Our findings were to be embodied in a final written report that would be reviewed with the laboratory director. In this final report we noted the point about the director's management style but carefully embedded it among a dozen or so other themes in an effort to minimize his potential defensiveness.

We had an appointment to give feedback to the laboratory director and to explain and elaborate on what was in the report. Shortly after we handed him his copy, we noticed him leafing through it rapidly and zeroing in on the section dealing with his management style. He became visibly angry, thanked us very much, and dismissed us!!! We could not subsequently find out either from him or the VP what happened and why.

Lessons. As I review this experience two lessons emerge. First, we should never have undertaken the survey without personally speaking to both the VP and the laboratory director.

We did not really have a clear enough idea about who wanted what, and what degree of readiness there was to hear various kinds of survey results. In other words, our contact client had been our fellow faculty member and we had never developed a real primary client within the organization.

Had we spoken to the laboratory director we would have had a chance to ask him how he would react if the engineers discussed his management style. If we sensed that he might be defensive we could have left that section out of the written report, or we might have realized that we should not undertake the project at all because of his sensitivity. We went to a confrontive level of intervention without any inquiry or diagnosis of what might have been going on in what we assumed to be our primary client.

Second, I learned from this experience not to agree to written feedback without knowing much more precisely what the client is looking for and may be anticipating. Once things are on paper they become public and therefore much more threatening. In many instances the client will accept the feedback and deal with it provided he can keep it private. We might have been able, even given these errors, to salvage the situation had we not put the critique of the director's management style into the written document.

It is, of course, possible that the VP was looking for precisely what we found, in which case we had unwittingly become a pawn in the VP's game and had precipitated an unknown degree of trouble both for the laboratory director and his engineers because it was possible that he would now behave very punitively toward them for criticizing his managerial style.

In summary, the tactics of intervention should focus initially on exploration, inquiry and diagnosis. Only when the consultant feels that the client is ready to think about alternative next steps is it appropriate to move to action alternatives and confrontive interventions. As the above cases illustrate, it is easy to misjudge this readiness and to confront prematurely. Since the overarching strategic goals are to remain helpful, to find out what is really going on, and to build a relationship in which the client will own his own problem, it pays to be conservative when considering a confrontive intervention.

Tactical Alternatives in the Stylistic Form of Intervention

Question or Assertion?

I have found that the major stylistic choice I have when I intervene is whether to couch my point in the form of an assertion, a declaration of some sort, or whether to put the same content material in the form of a question. In my experience the question is generally the more helpful intervention because it encourages, even forces, the client to maintain the initiative. If I want to move out of the process consultant role and to take the initiative, then assertion of one kind or another is better. But if the goal of process consultation is to help the client to solve his own problem, to own the responsibility, then the question is the best way to communicate that expectation.

Questions need not imply passivity on the part of the consultant. They can be highly confrontive, even aggressive, such as when you ask "Why didn't you do anything about that yourself?" or "Why don't you try the following?" or "Don't you think you should have solved that problem by now yourself?" But note that the question leaves room for further diagnostic information to surface, whereas the assertion leaves no room for inquiry, only action or defense. Therefore, most of the concrete examples of interventions shown in Table 9–1 are framed as questions, even in the area of confrontive interventions.

Single or Multiple Diagnostic or Action Alternatives?

Whether or not the intervention is couched as a question or an assertion, what are the pros and cons of making a single suggestion or recommendation about a diagnostic possibility or an action alternative versus offering two or more alternatives? Much of the consulting literature implies that consultants *must* come up with a single specific recommendation or they are not doing their job. My view would be that there are at least two reasons why this logic is fallacious.

First, if we are dealing with dynamic, open human systems, the consultant rarely knows enough to come up with a single diagnostic insight or action recommendation. Only the client has enough information to know for sure whether the recommended alternative would work in his situation. Second, even if the consultant was sure of a single action alternative, as he might be if it concerns the management of some processes, the philosophy of process consultation would argue that it is better to help the client to choose the right answer from two or more alternatives than to give him a single one. Here again the logic is that the client should be helped to stay in control, to retain initiative, to learn how to think out his own solutions.

The consultant can be quite forceful in arguing for one of several alternatives, but I believe that it is always helpful to have those alternatives available as contrasts and as reminders that there are other choices. If the client forces the issue and asks point blank, "What would *you* do?" the consultant can say what *he* would do but still remind the client that he is not in the client's shoes and, therefore, what the consultant would do is not necessarily valid for the client.

Conclusion

The strategy and tactics of intervention have to be guided by the ultimate assumptions underlying the helping process. If the assumptions of process consultation are the most applicable to the situation, then the consultant must act consistently with those assumptions, which means to help the client to own his own problems, to maintain his own initiative, and to help him to make his own diagnosis and select his own ultimate interventions.

Within those broad strategic objectives the consultant must choose between very open-ended *inquiry, diagnostic* questions that begin to stimulate the client's own diagnostic thinking, *action alternative* interventions that begin to suggest what the client might do, and *confrontive* interventions that test the client's level of insight, motivation, and readiness to act.

If the client is unfrozen and some level of trust has been established, the consultant can work comfortably across the whole range of intervention choices. If the client is not unfrozen, then the consultant must be much more careful in not moving too fast. Staying at the inquiry and diagnostic levels until the client's state of readiness and motivation is really known would seem to be essential at that stage.

10

Toward a Typology of Interventions

The previous two chapters have focused on the general questions of the strategy and tactics in process consultation. These general categories are designed to highlight that PC is a way of thinking, a philosophy of how to give help. If the manager or consultant clearly has this philosophy in mind, it is possible to go beyond these general categories and attempt to build a typology of interventions that apply to the many kinds of situations that managers and consultants find themselves in.

The reader will have noted that in the case examples I displayed all kinds of behavior from lecturing to interviewing to counseling to making suggestions. But all of these were predicated on knowing what role I was in and maintaining a PC perspective whenever I felt that to be appropriate. In other words, if we have the underlying assumptions clearly in mind, it is possible now to build a more concrete typology of interventions.

The consultant and manager both find themselves on any given day or project in a multiplicity of situations and relationships. They are sometimes alone thinking about things, often on the phone talking to someone on their own initiative or in response to a call, talking to an individual face to face either in a formal setting or during an informal run-in with the person, managing or participating in a meeting of some sort, planning and organizing activities that involve wider groups both within and outside the department.

Some of these relationships involve the creation of new settings, new expectations, and a heavier emphasis on diagnostic types of interventions. Other relationships have been operational over long periods of time and may involve much more intimate confrontations, where the consultant or manager knows the essence of the diagnosis, but the implementation of change runs into various kinds of difficulties that need to be managed.

In most consultation models these matters are treated chronologically, implying that the best basis for classifying interventions is to think of them as hooked to some "stages" in the consultation process, such as scouting, entry, diagnosis, intervention, disengagement. Many of the typologies that have been proposed also are biased strongly toward interventions in face-to-face and small group situations, paralleling some of the taxonomies of managerial behavior.

In fact, one of the misunderstandings about process consultation is that it is viewed as an activity that goes on *exclusively* in small group meetings as part of team-building or meetings-improvement activities (see, for example, Dyer, 1977). As I hope I have shown with my examples, group settings are only one category of the many in which the consultant and manager operate.

Process consultation is a way of conceptualizing the helping process and the role of the helper that applies equally to

- A single manager or consultant working with a single client or subordinate
- A manager or consultant working with a small group or as part of a meeting
- A group of managers or consultants such as a strategy consulting team working with an entire top management client system
- An individual consultant or team working with an organizational department or the entire organization planning major structural revisions, administration of surveys, or other systemwide interventions

Table 10–1

Types of Interventions

1. Active, Interested Listening (Exploratory)
2. Forcing Historical Reconstruction (Diagnostic)
3. Forcing Concretization (Diagnostic)
4. Forcing Process Emphasis (Diagnostic)
5. Diagnostic Questions and Probes (Diagnostic, action oriented)
6. Process Management and Agenda Setting (Confrontive)
7. Feedback (Confrontive)
8. Content Suggestions and Recommendations (Confrontive)
9. Structure Management (Confrontive)
10. Conceptual Inputs (Potentially confrontive)

The categories of interventions presented in this chapter are therefore geared more to the structure of the intervention itself than to its strategic goals, its tactical goals, or the setting in which it occurs. Ten categories of intervention are discussed; they are listed in Table 10–1.

The first five types of interventions can be thought of as being primarily client centered, the next two as being interactive between client and helper, and the last three as being more helper centered. The types move from being primarily inquiry oriented toward diagnostic and ultimately confrontive (the categories of Table 9–1).

The Intervention Types in the One-on-One Setting

The key tenet of process consultation philosophy is that clients own and must continue to own their own problem. The goal of consultants or managers must be to provide help without taking the problem onto their own shoulders. No matter how tempting it may be to perceive similarities between what the client is talking about and what the consultant has already experienced a hundred times, and to deduce from those perceived similarities what the client should probably do, the temptation to give advice prematurely must be firmly resisted. What kinds of interventions can be most helpful, given this imposed limitation and given the strategic and tactical goals outlined in the previous chapters?

1. *Active, Interested Listening.* The consultant or manager must develop the ability and requisite attitude to see the uniqueness of what the client is talking about, try to develop empathy, and try to understand the problem or issue from the client's perspective. Whatever else the consultant or manager does by way of intervening, he will soon learn that without constant active and interested listening throughout, the process of helping will deteriorate.

2. *Forcing Historical Reconstruction.* Clients often dump their problem out in abbreviated form and then wait stonily for some advice. How can the consultant "open up" the situation in order to have something to listen to? What works best for me is to ask the client to reconstruct some of the events that led up to the problem.

Such historical reconstruction can deal with the client's own job or career situation, with the events surrounding the problem, with the organization in which the client works, or whatever else is handy. The goal is to find something that the client can get comfortable about so that he talks freely and naturally.

3. *Forcing Concretization.* Problems are usually stated in very general form. The subordinate, John, goes to his boss and says: "What am I going to do about Joe who keeps messing up? He is always late for work, and generally doesn't seem to be motivated no matter what incentives I give him." This sounds concrete in that it deals with Joe, but the problem is actually stated in very vague terms and in very general form.

In this kind of situation I find myself wanting to know in concrete terms what is actually going on, so I ask questions such as the following: "When is the last time an incident took place that made you feel this way about Joe?" "Tell me the details, what happened, what led up to it, how did you handle it?" "Can you give me some examples of what you mean when you say that Joe is not motivated. How does that manifest itself?"

The goal of concretization is to accumulate enough concrete instances to begin to see the *pattern* of how the problem manifests itself, how the client perceives it, what role he takes in it, what his own diagnostic insights are, and so on.

4. Forcing Process Emphasis. Problems are often stated in content terms and the consultant/manager must find a way to get the client to restate the problem in process terms in order to locate where the problem might have developed. Using the example above, note that one of the effects of forced historical reconstruction and concretization is that the client must translate his vague difficulties with Joe into stories that will reveal both what he did and what Joe did.

If the process does not come out clearly enough, the helper can focus the issue more by asking questions such as: "Tell me exactly step by step what led up to this or what happened. . . . What did you do next? . . . What did Joe do in response to what you did?" By forcing a reconstruction of the process, the consultant not only learns the details of what went on but teaches the client the value of thinking about process and how to diagnose it himself.

5. Diagnostic Questions and Probes. If the consultant begins to feel that he understands partially and wants to test that understanding he can put his tentative insight into the form of questions. "Could it be that this is happening because . . . ?" "Have you thought of the following possibility . . . ?" "I don't really understand why you feel this way about the situation." "How much more can you tell me about what happened?" "What is your own theory about why this problem exists?"

Such questions and probes fall tactically into the confrontive intervention category and should, therefore, only be used when confrontation is called for. They are, in effect, "leading questions" that are intended to get some ideas and content across, to stimulate the client's diagnostic thinking, and to check out possibilities that the consultant has thought of. They should not be stronger than questions, however, to give the client room to reject the idea and, thereby, make more information available to the consultant and to correct whatever diagnostic hunches he may have.

6. *Process Management and Agenda Setting.* As the consultant or manager feels that the relationship can tolerate or requires more active management, he can suggest, propose, or actually order that certain agendas be covered. All such interventions are by definition confrontive, inasmuch as they contain diagnostic assumptions within themselves. Such agendas might focus on either content or process. For example, the consultant might request information on content: "John, I want you to tell me a lot more about Joe's personality." Or the consultant might suggest a process exercise: "John, let's role play this situation. You be Joe and I'll role play you."

The consultant might suggest that at some future meeting Joe be brought to the meeting, or that certain topics be discussed, or in other ways take charge of the relationship and what will be worked on. Note that this taking over of the process can be quite autocratic without in any way taking over the problem. What the consultant is doing is taking charge of the helping process if and when he feels that is appropriate.

7. *Feedback.* Once the consultant or manager has some idea of where the client is trying to get, it is possible to provide feedback on how he is doing relative to those goals. It is important to note that feedback is "information on how someone is doing relative to *their own goals*," not any reactions that the consultant may have to the client.

For example, if John reports that he is trying to be generally more assertive in his relationships and thereby gain better control of the situation with Joe, and if the consultant notes that John's behavior is indeed becoming more or less assertive as he directly observes it, then it may be appropriate for the consultant to share his own direct observation. But feedback will have beneficial effect only if it is solicited, timely, concrete, and relevant to the client's own stated goals.

8. *Content Suggestions and Recommendations.* If the consultant feels confident in his understanding of the problem and has accurately assessed the client's readiness to hear a suggestion or recommendation, he can provide specific content help. He can say to John: "Why don't you try sitting down with Joe once a week and lay out specific performance targets and review these with him at the end of the week?" or "Why don't you and Joe get together and you share with Joe your various frustrations with his behavior and invite him to provide you with some information on how he sees it?" or "Leave Joe alone for a few weeks and see what happens."

In my own experience, such interventions are rarely appropriate until a great deal of joint inquiry has taken place. Usually such joint inquiry leads the client to the content or process solution without the consultant having to provide specific suggestions or recommendations. The consultant can still be very helpful by throwing out lots of possibilities from which the client can select ones that make sense to him.

9. Structure Management. The consultant/manager may feel that the most helpful intervention is one that would change the structure of the situation. Depending upon his own ability to control that structure, he might either manage it directly or make a suggestion or recommendation to the client that the structure be changed.

For example, he might decide that Joe should not work for John; if he is their boss, he might simply reassign Joe. Or, if the boss is not part of the system, he might suggest that John consider assigning Joe to another unit. Or he might ask that John and Joe both come to the next meeting so that their problem can be worked on directly.

Obviously such interventions imply that the consultant has reached a definite conclusion about the nature of the problem and is ready to intervene in a very potent manner. One would expect such interventions to be very rare, therefore.

10. Conceptual Inputs. The final category of interventions involves the set of activities often called "educational interventions." The consultant/manager listens enough to formulate ideas as to what kind of concepts and information might be relevant to the problems that the client is experiencing and then shares general ideas, information, and concepts without necessarily relating them directly to the client. The connection between the problem and the concepts is left to the client unless, of course, the client asks the consultant to make a more direct connection.

John's boss in the example might ask John to read a book on supervision that contains ideas that the boss thinks might be relevant, or he might ask if John would like to attend a seminar that deals with topics of similar content, or might deliver a brief lecture on the general problems of handling difficult subordinates, or might use his own experience as a basis for telling stories of how he handled problems such as this.

The dilemma in using this intervention is that it may be off target and, therefore, time wasting. It may also make the client feel put down if the ideas come across as too elementary or if they are things he had already thought of.

Summary. This preliminary classification of types of interventions is not intended to be exhaustive and, in practice, the interventions overlap. The important point to note is that the interventions lean strongly toward keeping the problem on the client's shoulders and putting the consultant as much as possible into the position of trying to help the client to help himself. If the consultant is the expert on helping and on process, he must, of course, use that expertise. But he can usually do that without becoming an expert on the content of how the client should actually solve his problem.

In the remainder of this chapter I want to illustrate how some of these intervention types apply to groups and larger systems. As will be seen, the basic intent of the intervention remains the same regardless of the setting in which it is employed, but the tactics of how to make the intervention can vary dramatically with the setting.

The Interventions in the Group and Intergroup Setting

Each of the ten intervention types has its counterpart use in various kinds of group and intergroup settings. There is, however, an important difference between the one-on-one and the group settings that has to do with cultural rules of interaction. If

I am dealing with a person face to face and am trying to concretize things, it is difficult to do that without being somewhat confrontive; the person has to speak for himself and put himself on the line.

In group settings, on the other hand, it is possible to raise issues in a general way without forcing any given person to deal with the issue, thus permitting those persons who are least defensive to deal with the intervention. For example, if I ask the subordinate in the example in the preceding section to reconstruct some process, he has little choice but to deal with his own part in that process. But if I ask a group to reconstruct some prior decision, any of the members can take up the challenge without any given member feeling under pressure to respond.

In making interventions of a diagnostic or content sort, the consultant can refer to "some members" or "the group" without naming any given individual, thus permitting the shoe to fit where it will. The consultant can ask whether "anyone feels a certain way" or whether "anyone" is willing to provide some data or feedback that the group may need. In the group and intergroup setting, therefore, an additional choice is provided for each of the intervention types — whether to make it personal or to keep it deliberately abstract.

1. Active, Interested Listening. Much of the time of the consultant or manager will be spent in group meetings, in negotiation sessions, and in presentations of various sorts where different departments are holding forth on various issues. If the goal is to become helpful, the active, interested listening orientation must be maintained, and the consultant must remain alert to the many process forces that can be observed.

The key is to learn to listen for *process*. As the group is working or the meeting is progressing, the consultant can observe who talks, who talks to whom, what communication style is being used, who interrupts whom, how people react to interruption, what kind of group problem-solving process and decision mechanisms are being used, and so on (Schein, 1969).

Powerful interventions that result from such listening are clarification, summarizing, and consensus testing. If the consultant notes that people do not understand each other, he can clarify by asking what was meant, by asking whether everyone understood, and by asking for restatement. If he feels the group is confused about its goals or direction, he can summarize what he has heard so far and check how much consensus there is on the points he brings out. Each of these interventions clearly will aid in the task process, and that is where the emphasis should be.

In the *intergroup* setting it is especially important to learn to listen sympathetically to both sides of a conflict so that at an appropriate time an agenda managing intervention can be made to bring the different points of view into better alignment. The PC must be especially careful to listen for his own biases and to maintain a neutral stance if this is possible.

2. Forcing Historical Reconstruction. This type of intervention is most relevant when a group or organizational unit is puzzled about unexpected and undesired outcomes. Several hours may have been spent in a meeting and no decision has been reached, or a decision has been made but members feel uncomfortable about it, or conflicts have arisen between members and no one quite knows why, or participation levels have become very uneven and the group cannot figure out whether that is a product of some personalities being more dominant than others, and so on.

In all of these instances the most helpful initial intervention (provided there is some time to do it) is to say "Well, let's look back over the meeting and see if we can reconstruct what we did the last couple of hours. . . . How did we set our goals, how did we decide how to work on the issue, what can you remember happening early in the meeting? . . ." The goal is to get historical, to get concrete, and to get a process focus so that the group can discover for itself when and how it may have produced outcomes that it later considers desirable or undesirable.

3. Forcing Concretization. Forcing the group to be specific and concrete flows almost automatically from asking it to be historical, but the consultant or manager should be alert not to let generalizations go by unchallenged. Someone says, "The meeting began in a very autocratic way," or "At the beginning everyone was speaking all at once." The consultant should step in and ask, "What do you mean by 'autocratic'? What exactly happened that made you use that label — who actually did what?" Or, in the second example, the consultant could say "Everyone? Can we be more specific about who actually spoke up?"

In the intergroup or organizational setting the same logic applies. If parts of the client system are attempting to figure something out the consultant or manager can force reconstruction and can keep emphasizing the need to be specific and concrete in the reconstruction.

4. Forcing Process Emphasis. As reconstruction takes place the consultant or manager can keep raising process questions if the group is too focused on content. Someone says, "Well, the first thing we decided was to launch that new advertising campaign and then we moved on to what we would ask the sales force to do." The consultant can then say, "How did we make that first decision, and how do we feel about the decision process used?"

5. Diagnostic Questions and Probes. These kinds of questions can be brought up confrontively as in the one-on-one situation. But the group and intergroup context also makes it possible to test diagnostic insights less confrontively by embedding them in general remarks that may be made to various groupings as part of a feedback session or educational input.

For example, I may be working with a company as a consultant and be asked to give a general lecture to top management on some topic such as organizational culture. I may have observed that the group's process problems have something to do with its cultural assumptions about how to make decisions, yet may feel that I cannot share this observation without risking being too confrontive. I can, however, insert in my lecture several general examples of decision processes that include the ones I have observed and raise the question of whether any such processes apply to the group I am addressing.

6. Process Management and Agenda Setting. This area is the most complex to describe and analyze because much of the technology of organization development that has grown up over the last thirty years fits into this broad category of interventions. Such techniques as confrontation meetings, intergroup exercises, conflict reduction exercises, community role plays, survey-feedback processes based on interviews and questionnaires, educational interventions of various sorts designed to bring groups together that must work together, responsibility-charting meetings, open systems planning, and various other kinds of planned change processes all have in common that the consultant designs the process with some key members of the primary client group and then "stage manages," administers, and monitors the process as needed (Beckhard, 1969, Beckhard and Harris, 1987, Burke, 1978; French and Bell, 1978).

In order to be consistent with the philosophy of process consultation, the design of such activities must highlight that the consultant is managing only the process, not the solution. The client is being helped to locate a solution that his own problem-solving processes have not been able to genera' ?. The following example is an excellent "pure" case.

The Use of a Delphi Process to Make a Strategy Decision in the Wilson Foods Company. Wilson Foods is a large multinational that had experienced some years of slowed gr˥wth and declining profits. The president and his four-person ⌐xecutive committee undertook to rev˩alize themse˩ves by exam˥ning their major strategic options, selecting one of them, and put˩ng major effort into actualizing the option they had decided on.

There were four options: 1) major emphasis on research and new product development, 2) aggressive expansion of domestic markets to capture more market share, 3) expansion of the overseas business, and 4) aggressive programs of productivity by simultaneously improving marketing and cutting manufacturing and other costs. Each of these options was associated with one of the members of the executive committee who was its "champion" and, as might be predicted, this group after months of debate could not reach consensus on which option to pursue.

The president called in a process-oriented strategy consultant to see what could be done. He interviewed all of the members of the group and concluded that the basic problem was that each member understood the nuances of his own preferred option very well but did not really understand the other options well enough to make an intelligent choice among them. A process needed to be invented to make everyone equally familiar with each of the options so that the group could collectively examine all of the pros and cons.

I became involved as part of a team that was put together by the strategy consultant. He proposed putting the executive group through a delphi exercise. Each option was presented in the form of a set of questionnaires asking the group's members each to predict the consequences of pursuing that option. These predictions were fed back and a second round of predictions asked for, now based on what each member knew the others had said. Following the feedback of the second round of predictions a summary was prepared of the consequences as perceived by them, and the next option was subjected to the same process.

This process was jointly designed by the consultants and key members of the Wilson Company's planning staff. They were frustrated that so little of the data they had on potential consequences was being attended to. Given their insights into the options it was fairly easy to design a set of questionnaires to give to the committee members, and to get acceptance of the entire process because the executive committee felt some need to use their own planning staff resources. So even though this whole process would last two months, it was decided that the time and energy investment was worth it since a major strategic direction for the company was involved.

Following the two months of work on the delphi process, the executive committee again met in a two-day off-site meeting to see whether they could now reach consensus with the strategy consultant and me in attendance to help with further process issues as those might arise. The climate was completely different. The members of the group acknowledged how little they had understood the options that they had not championed but were now able to discuss each one with full understanding. The delphi process had educated them in a way that the mutual give and take in the meetings had not been able to do. In effect they had been seduced by the process into listening to one another. Once they had reached this stage, it was fairly easy for them to agree on which of the options to adopt, and to have full consensus on the decision.

Reducing Conflict Between Sales and Product Lines in the Chilton Company. Process consultants are constantly designing organizational and intergroup processes to help members work out solutions without getting involved in those solutions directly. For example, in Chilton High Tech there was a time when a major conflict developed between product line managers, who were measured on the particular sales of their product, and regional sales managers, who were measured on total sales. The regional managers would push whatever seemed to sell well, often ignoring products that given product line managers were pushing and to which they had committed marketing and sales dollars from their own budgets.

The company did not want to organize differently; they wanted these groups to work it out. The personnel manager who had a strong PC orientation decided to call a two-day off-site meeting of the five product line managers and six regional managers and designed an intergroup exercise for the two days. Each of the two groups was to examine its image of itself and the other group; they were to share these impressions by listening to each other. Each group then had to examine the other group's views of itself and to develop hypotheses to explain those views. At this point the groups were encouraged to share data about each other directly so that the hypotheses the groups had about themselves could be checked out.

The effect of this process was "to get the garbage out of the system," to reconstruct and undo stereotypes and the historical enmities to which they had led, and start afresh on developing a system for how to work together. Once the entire group had gone through this historical reconstruction they were able on the second day to design a series of processes for managing the sales effort in such a way that no product line would feel unfairly treated. They created a set of specialty salesmen, decided on quarterly meetings of the group to review how things were going, and basically committed themselves to being "one group" instead of two warring factions.

The personnel manager had "solved" the problem without in any way affecting the actual new working relationships. He had created a process that made it possible for them to work things out among themselves.

7. Feedback. Feedback is information relevant to the attainment of goals that have been set by the client. Unfortunately the term has acquired a much broader and looser meaning in the context of organization development work in the frequent use of "survey-feedback" methods. The consultant decides with the primary client to gather data from other parts of the organization through some survey method, and then "feeds back" the information to various groups (Nadler, 1977). Feeding back data to the client system involves the client in the diagnostic process and such joint inquiry is then labeled "action research."

From my point of view the issue is what kinds of questions are asked initially, how involved are the people who are being asked questions in the design of the process, and to whom is the information fed back initially. In most survey-feedback models several levels of employees are interviewed or given questionnaires to determine their morale, the problems they perceive in the organization, and their reactions to programs that the organization may have instituted. The data are typically aggregated and given to top management first, and then are "cascaded" down the organization level by level, department by department, with each supervisor being required to share his group's data and elicit a problem-solving discussion about the points that the employees may have raised. The notion is that the employees are giving feedback to management, following which management responds to the issues that the employees have raised.

This top-down, cascading model violates the basic tenet that the problem will be fixed better if the person owning the problem is responsible for fixing it. By encouraging employees to "tell" management what is wrong, we are encouraging them to abdicate their responsibility. Now management has to "fix" what the employees don't like.

If, instead, we think of the employees as primary clients in a survey (because they are being encouraged to air their problems), the feedback process should encourage them to own their own problems. The process consultation model would argue, therefore, that the data only be gathered around issues that employees themselves are involved in (or else the feedback will be meaningless), and that any data gathered on a given group of employees be fed back *to that group before anyone else has seen them.* Top management does not have to see the data first, because many of the problems identified will not even involve them.

Giving employees back their own data in a group meeting before anyone else has seen them has several advantages.

1. The data can be checked for accuracy: "Here is what you said on the survey. Is this what you meant to say? Is there anything that needs correcting? Can you elaborate or give some examples? Is there anything that needs highlighting?"
2. The group can be asked to sort the problems identified into those that *they* can do something about and those that need to be passed up to higher levels of the organization, a process that locates each problem at that place where it can best be worked on.
3. The process of working on the data and sorting the problems involves the employees as a group in owning their problems and becomes an important step in building teamwork for fixing the problems. Following such meetings employees typically respond that they feel genuinely involved and real participants in the organization's effort to improve itself. In contrast, the top-down model makes the employee feel dependent and uninvolved because clearly the initiative is in the hands of higher levels of management.

As problems are identified that need to be passed upward the next layer of management gets involved in the same way, looking at their own data and what was passed up from below. After they have sorted the problems they pass up what needs to be passed up until eventually top management sees those problems that only they can do something about. In the meantime all the lower levels have been energized to get to work on fixing that which can be fixed, instead of sitting around waiting for senior management to "respond" to their "gripes" and "suggestions."

This process requires much more patience on the part of senior management, and it requires them to suppress their curiosity to see everything. The more senior management gets involved in seeing all of the data, the more they will be tempted into doctor and expert roles that may undermine their own goal of getting the employees involved in the organization development program.

8. Structure Management. These kinds of interventions would be relatively rare in the process consultant role, except where the consultant is an expert on structural issues that directly impact organizational performance. Thus the consultant would get involved in the design of meetings, survey-feedback processes, educational interventions, training events, and other issues where process was crucial, as in the case of International Oil, above.

The consultant or manager operating in the process consultant role would rarely involve himself in deciding who should report to whom and how some given project or department should be organized. Instead he might be very active in raising questions that would make different structural options very clear, that would force thinking through of the consequences of different structures, and in general educate the client or subordinate to the implications of structural decisions.

9. Content Suggestions and Recommendations. As in the case of structure management, the process consultant would only suggest options and help think through consequences.

10. Conceptual Inputs. Conceptual inputs and various kinds of educational interventions can become a powerful tool in the process consultant's intervention kit, especially when done with groups where threat to individual self-esteem can be minimized by speaking to the group in general. Thus corporate seminars, lectures to executive development programs, and special training events on specific processes such as performance appraisal all can be designed in such a way that they not only maximize the learning of content, but also facilitate the solution of the fundamental problems the consultant was hired to address.

For example, I have used the device of an educational intervention to reduce intergroup conflict or tension by having the two concerned groups attend a joint seminar during which problem solving or case discussions are planned for small groups, and the groups are designed to be half from each of the conflicting groups. The process goal is to get people acquainted on a more personal and informal level as a prerequisite to building trust for more formal problem solving.

What makes such interventions work is the fact that cultural rules of interaction make it difficult for people to admit and confront conflict directly because of the risk of losing face. But both groups will willingly lend themselves to a neutral event like a seminar and begin to work out their intergroup issues informally (all the while denying publicly that there is a problem).

Another example was the previously cited use of a lecture on organizational culture to have the senior managers of the Delta Aerospace Company analyze the relationship between their own culture and some of the strategic necessities that were confronting them. What the consultant must do in these instances is to be ready to shift gears from continuing the educational input to helping the group to work on its on-line problem.

Finally, educational interventions can be powerful unfreezing forces by allowing the client organization in a nonconfrontive and psychologically safe educational environment to recognize some of its problems. The consultant can speculate on various diagnostic possibilities and let the shoe fit if it will, without anyone feeling personally threatened.

Summary

I have tried to illustrate how each of the types of interventions can be utilized in the group and organizational context. To give a full listing of all of the possible uses would be beyond the scope of this book, but it should be clear to the reader that process consultation as a philosophy can be applied across all types of interventions and settings. It is not the particular intervention or setting that defines PC but the assumptions underlying the intervention and its structure and timing.

Conclusion: The Concept of Facilitative Intervention

The effectiveness of a given intervention is primarily related to the degree to which it facilitates forward movement in the client or client system, as defined by the client. The consultant or manager who wishes to be helpful must therefore figure out where the client is trying to get, and must decide what form of intervention will most facilitate movement in that direction.

The worst thing the consultant can do is to intervene in a manner that disrupts, delays, or otherwise interferes with the client's agenda and sense of direction, unless the consultant is deliberately attempting to disrupt, something that would rarely be appropriate in the PC model.

To be properly facilitative is difficult because the consultant's own needs to display knowledge, skill, and insight often override his judgment on what will be appropriately facilitative in any given situation. The commonest example I have witnessed as well as perpetrated is to introduce process observations and feedback at a point in time where the group has neither the time nor the energy to deal with those observations.

For example, I might be observing (with only ten minutes to go in a meeting) that the group is wrestling with three different decision alternatives and that each is being advocated by a strong member. At this point I could make a diagnostic observation by saying, "Perhaps we are having trouble making this decision because there is a power struggle among members A, B, and C." This might be accurate and worth testing, but totally disrupt the group process.

If I am trying to be facilitative and sense that the group is really trying to make a decision in the remaining ten minutes, I could make instead of a diagnostic intervention a process suggestion: "Why don't we take the three decision alternatives we have identified and take a quick poll of the group to see whether the group leans toward one of them." I might even sense that there is some consensus around one of the decisions and say by way of a content intervention: "It seems to me we are leaning toward decision X. Am I reading the group correctly?"

Consultants are often overtrained to make diagnostic observations and to avoid process or content suggestions, but if the observation is disruptive or delaying, it may be better to be more action oriented and help the group to move along. The observation is still relevant in that it tells the consultant what he should be doing, but he does not have to reveal his observation to the client system at that moment.

The "bottom line" for the consultant or manager as consultant is whether the intervention really helped accomplish the shared goals, not whether it fitted some theory of what would have been appropriate at any given moment. The skill of intervening is to be so tuned in to what is going on that one's sense of timing and appropriateness is based on the external events, not one's internal assumptions or theories.

11

Emerging Issues in Process Consultation

Much of this book has focused on how process consultation begins, though the illustrative cases have shown that some of the most interesting and difficult issues arise after the consultant has been working with a client organization for some time. The reason for the intense focus on the beginning is that I have learned over and over again if I have problems down the line it is because I have sent incorrect signals up front.

In this chapter I want to discuss what some of the "down-the-line" issues are and how they can best be managed. I also want to touch on some specific issues having to do with billing, contracting, and the ethical problems that can arise in the consultation process. Most of this chapter will work around case materials, using primarily ones that have already been partially expounded.

The change process, as argued in Chapter 6, can be thought of as a series of stages, but consultation as a process should not be thought of in this manner primarily because it allows the consultant/manager the illusion that there is a period of diagnosis during which nothing much happens to the client system. The central point of process consultation as a philosophy and model is to note that *diagnosis is intervention* and that how one intervenes determines both what kinds of diagnostic information become available and how the relationship with the client evolves.

Contracting and Fees

In most of the cases I have been involved in the question of how I will charge for the consulting is raised either by the contact client or me in the very first conversation. I typically quote a daily rate and indicate that this can be broken down into an hourly rate if only an hour or two is sought. My goal is to make it as easy and comfortable for the client to proceed as possible. I bill for all preparation and working time but typically will not add any fee for travel time unless a long trip is involved. I generally charge a slightly higher rate if I have to make a presentation for an entire day, as contrasted with attending a meeting for a day, based on my experience that this requires more energy and preparation, as well as a longer time to "recover" after the event.

Whether or not I bill for an exploratory meeting depends upon the circumstances. I am usually willing to explore an issue over the phone or during a short visit without automatically charging for this, but, as I have pointed out before, it has been my experience that the most important help is often provided in those first meetings. Therefore, if someone really wants to spend an hour or two "exploring" an issue, I typically charge for this time.

I avoid attempting to define "contracts," in the sense of clearly articulated project goals, budgets, total numbers of days of consulting, retainer fees, and other devices that would bind either me or the client to a situation that might no longer feel useful or helpful. The object is to create a relationship that can be terminated by either party if it ceases to fulfill its function. However, such an open-ended arrangement can lead to problems of its own. On a number of occasions I have had a very clear initial understanding with the contact and intermediate clients only to discover that there was a serious mismatch between my assumptions and the assumptions of the primary client. The next case illustrates most clearly how such assumptions can lead to stress, potentially poor consulting, and awkward terminations.

Misunderstanding at Mason

The Mason Company is a division of a large U.S. corporation doing primarily defense-related high-technology projects. There are two departments within one of its major divisions, one more research oriented, the other more development oriented. The division management has an organization development and training unit but each department has its own organization development and training people.

I received a call from the *division* training manager, Bill Macy, asking me if I would be willing to visit their division to do the following: 1) give one major talk on organizational socialization and career development to a large group of technical people and managers in one large development department, followed by lunch with a working group to draw out implications for their department, and 2) conduct an afternoon work session with a smaller management group from the research department to work on specific applications of how to better utilize their technical people.

This would amount to a very full day but would be feasible because the afternoon group was highly self-motivated and I would function primarily as a process consultant in that meeting. In other words I would not have to give two major lectures in one day. We both agreed that two lectures in one day would not make sense, but it was also clear that budgets were tight and they wanted to limit the total program to one day's consultation for budget reasons.

Macy explained to me in the initial telephone inquiry that the division had had an unsuccessful formal mentoring program, had abandoned it, and wanted some perspective on why it might not have worked. This was to be discussed with senior management at the lunch. The afternoon departmental discussion of how one could best use technical resources in a research and development organization would be a small and highly interactive group.

As it was initially described it sounded like a feasible and interesting combination of an educational intervention and some on-the-spot problem solving. The day fitted my travel schedule since it was in a part of the country where my wife and I could do some sightseeing after the day of work, so I agreed and set my fee for one day plus a couple of hours of preparation. Given the description of what they wanted, not much more preparation time would be involved since I had a prepared lecture on socialization, and the rest of the work would be on-line process consultation.

Troubles Start. Roughly one month before the seminar I received a letter from one of the *department* training managers, Lucy Brown (I had not talked to her previously), confirming my morning talk and luncheon meeting. But her understanding of what I would talk about was very different from what Macy had described on the phone. She wanted a specific analysis of their mentoring program, a review of research on mentoring, and other research findings on career development, pointing out that the audience would be very skeptical if I did not base the talk on a lot of empirical findings. This created an immediate dilemma inasmuch as I had not budgeted for additional preparation time, nor would I have agreed to give this type of talk if it had been proposed originally.

I telephoned Macy to share the dilemma and was reassured by him that I should not worry about this issue, that the kind of conceptual talk about organizational socialization that he had heard me give would work out fine for this audience, and I need only make general references to mentoring, based on skimming the material they had sent me. We reconfirmed the original arrangement and agreed to meet on the Sunday night before the meeting to get acquainted. We also discussed my sightseeing on the subsequent days and he gave me advice and help on where to go.

New Dates. In the following week Macy called again and told me that the second department meeting scheduled for the afternoon of our consulting day could not be scheduled then, but that perhaps I could work them in on a morning following the sightseeing excursion inasmuch as I would be there for several days. Since the excursion involved a 200-mile drive each way, I had to examine in my mind how this would be feasible, and decided that we could get to the site on the afternoon of the first seminar day, and get back after a day and a half to do the second seminar on the morning of our departure. This was not ideal, but we agreed that it was workable. I was concerned, however, about my fatigue level on the first seminar day, and was definitely not looking forward to driving 200 miles after a lecture and a working lunch.

What I had not given enough attention to at this point was that I was beginning to feel like I was being taken advantage of. The original plan for a one-day meeting followed by two days of vacation fitted my plans much better than what was now being proposed because two long half-days would be more tiring and inconvenient than what had originally been described. I also had not figured on how much extra time would be involved in studying their mentoring program materials. But I wanted to be helpful and the contact client clearly had a schedule problem to resolve.

The Sunday Night Surprise. When we arrived at the hotel on the Sunday before the first seminar I called Macy and we agreed to meet at 7:30 after dinner to get acquainted and for final briefing. His agreement to the 7:30 time implied a short get-acquainted meeting and arrangements for pick-up the following morning at 7:45 A.M.

At this point the roof caved in. Macy arrived with Lucy Brown and Linda Pierce, the two training managers from the two departments involved, and said that each of them wanted to give me additional information on their departments and to share their expectations of what the session with their department should involve. Lucy Brown then revealed a substantially different set of expectations about what we would be doing from what I thought I had agreed to.

Monday morning, I was told, was to be a three-stage process: 1) a lecture on socialization to a large audience of 100 or more; 2) a follow-on lecture that would get into the mentoring issues for all of the key managers, an audience of about 50 to 60; and 3) a working lunch of the 25 senior managers where *I would present* my conclusions and recommendations.

I was in a panic and angry because I knew that I could not handle three such successive lecture situations, and the design did not make any sense anyway in that it cast me completely into the role of an expert lecturing to them about their program. Brown indicated that her boss, the department head, had wanted this kind of design for maximum exposure of his people to my point of view, but she had not forewarned me of any of this.

Given the total situation, I concluded that I could not back out or insist on the original agreement since machinery was in motion for my talks. My only realistic alternative at the eleventh hour was to raise some questions about the validity of the design in terms of *their own goals*. It would not allow for enough involvement and interchange and hence would not really start the kind of problem solving that they claimed they wanted. We spent about two hours considering various alternatives and finally worked out a three-stage process with smaller groups in the second two stages, so that some immediate work on their own program could be done in the groups instead of my lecturing the whole time.

This meant that Brown had to renegotiate things with her boss, but she thought this would be possible even at this late hour and early in the morning so we fixed on the new design. She clearly agreed that what the department manager had wanted did not make sense and that the new design was much better geared to their own needs. What, in effect, we had done is spend two hours on redesign on the night before the event to ensure that the event would be maximally helpful.

At 9:45 Linda Pierce, the other department training manager, then brought out a large batch of materials on her department and indicated that there was so much interest in the session that many more people would be attending, apparently not realizing that I had contracted to do a working session, not another lecture. I had been led to believe that the department issues would come out in the discussion instead of my having to be briefed for an additional hour or so on Sunday night and having a batch of background reading to do on my own time in preparation for what would now be another lecture. I was frustrated and angry, but there was little to be done at this point except to go along with it.

I went to bed at midnight quite angry at the way the situation had developed and knowing that I would be much more tired both for the talks themselves and for the subsequent drive than I had bargained for. This bothered me because I am never at my best in an interactive situation when I am tired. It was also clear to me that the prior preparation, the Sunday night intensive working session, and the additional time that I would have to spend prior to the second department meeting now amounted to a full day's worth of preparation that had not been budgeted for by me, nor by the client. I decided that since this extra time had been spent on genuinely improving their program I should charge the client for the additional time.

I mentioned this to Macy on the way to the first lecture at 8 A.M. on Monday morning. He seemed surprised and shocked and said he would look into it.

The Event and Thereafter. The talk was well received and the two working sessions did produce genuine problem solving of the sort the client system wanted, leaving all of us with a great feeling of satisfaction that the goals had been accomplished. We agreed that the planning session on Sunday night had been essential to working out a feasible design.

I took time out from sightseeing to redesign the second department meeting, which also went very well and, following the talk, led to some real problem solving of the sort that the client wanted. The larger numbers were a problem, but not an insurmountable one. The managers of the departments and the training managers voiced satisfaction that all had gone extremely well.

However, on the matter of the additional day's work, Macy told me *in a very brief letter* a week later that he would hold me to the original contract of paying me for one day of work, *without offering any explanation*. This curt way of dealing with my request made me very angry. I could have understood if he had given some explanation about budgets, or being caught in the middle, or even acknowledging that the extra work had been "rung in on me" and that I had helpfully changed my schedule to accommodate his problem. So I wrote a long memorandum indicating that I had spent all of Sunday night on planning, an activity he himself had acknowledged as essential to the success of the program, and had spent several additional hours preparing for the second meeting at their request. His next reply was another curt note saying that he had reviewed my various points but that the original arrangement that I had agreed to would have to stand.

I then wrote back saying that the money now was not as much of an issue for me as to understand what had happened so that I could learn something from this for future reference. This led eventually to a phone call from him that permitted me to clarify some of my feelings and led to my asking him to clarify what had happened at his end. He then revealed that it was his assumption that any "professional" consultant would expect to do the kind of "fine-tuning" that we had done on Sunday night, that this was not additional work, but simply a "normal" process that he expected me or any consultant to do as a matter of course. He again reiterated how helpful the whole exercise had been, that the department managers had really liked the interactive nature of our design, that they felt they were working on their own problems and had moved forward. But my request for additional fees was viewed as unreasonable and unprofessional.

Some Lessons. The matter ended there, but in retrospect, I realized that in this case I had not been consistent at all in my own inquiry process, that I had assumed that the contact client had control of a situation that he clearly did not entirely control, that he got caught in the middle (he probably could not go back to *his* clients and ask for more money), that what would be helpful to the two departments required input from them that I did not have until Sunday night, and that there was much confusion in the training managers' minds about the difference between lecturing and working on-line with the groups. This confusion required me on Sunday night to shift to an expert role redesigning the morning to better meet the goals they had articulated for that morning.

I also concluded that up-front "closed" contracts are probably inappropriate for situations where the consultant does not know exactly what is ahead. If I contract for a day's seminar, I need to have a way of separately billing for whatever planning time may be involved in preparing for the seminar, and it is often very hard to predict how much time that will take. I recall other occasions where I agreed to do a half-day presentation to a company and was subsequently expected to spend two full days visiting the company to get acquainted with them.

The Mason case made me realize that since *time* is the scarcest resource, it must be managed most carefully. It is essential, therefore, to have a separate understanding about the *preparation time* that may be involved for an educational intervention. My current policy is to bill separately for preparation time, which permits me and the client to decide together how much time will be needed to do an adequate job of preparing for a meeting. If more time is required, it is then understood that this time will be billed for.

A Concluding Note on Contracting. Many consultation models put a heavy emphasis on clearly defined contracts, both legal and psychological, up front before the consultation even begins. Such a process sounds ideal in that it should avoid the kind of confusion that arose with Mason, but it is totally unrealistic in my experience. None of us could anticipate where the problems would arise.

For me a better model is to focus on the sharing of mutual expectations throughout the project and with each client as I encounter them, so that the "contract" becomes a perpetually evolving thing. Budgets in time and money can be estimated, but I believe it is a real mistake to make up-front commitment to given amounts of time and money before the consultant has any idea of what may really be going on.

The Consultant as Organizational Catalyst

As projects with a given organization evolve, I have often found myself playing catalytic roles where I was deliberately and knowingly being used by various primary clients to make things happen that otherwise would not happen. For example, in one organization I was asked to provide some career counseling to two senior executives who, I was told, had been asked to leave the company. I made appointments to see them and discovered in both cases early in the discussion that they had not yet been told clearly that they were expected to leave. My "counseling" was, in fact, a primary communication vehicle to let them know that a serious mismatch was involved and that they might as well leave for their own sake.

I was tempted to avoid getting involved in such organizational games, but realized in each case that if I could get them to review their own history in the company they would find out for themselves that there was indeed a mismatch, and that it would indeed be in their best interests to leave the company. Getting the message across and getting them to initiate their own departure would cause them less loss of face than their being fired. The situation also provided an opportunity for each of them to express their anger at the company and to experience catharsis.

In the catalyst role, one can serve as a communication channel between parts of the organization that for one reason or another cannot talk directly with each other. The goal in these situations from a PC point of view is to play that role only as long as is necessary while helping the organization to develop its own processes of communication and feedback for future use.

Opening Up Communication in Billings

In the previous descriptions of my relationship with the Billings Company and Fred Stone, its president, I emphasized helping the executive committee with its selection of a vice president of human resources, and with helping it to become an effective group. After a number of meetings with that group, Stone and I decided that it would be helpful to interview each of the members individually and to explore two particular agendas: 1) How could the group be more effective?, and 2) What feedback would they give to Stone to help him to become more effective not only as the chairman of the group but, in general, as their boss?

Stone felt that he had a pretty good, open channel of communication with each of his subordinates, but he was anxious to check that perception and to improve his own managerial effectiveness. He asked whether I could recommend a process that would allow him to get feedback and to make the group more effective. The process I suggested, functioning now as both doctor and expert, was to interview each member about the two issues, to collate the data so that if at least two people mentioned a given issue I would report it back to the group as an issue, and, after the group had approved this process, give Stone individual feedback based on any comments that at least two or more members of the group had made. Following this, the group would meet with

Stone and discuss openly the issues that had been raised in the private interviews. My role as catalyst would protect face for the participants and allow both the group and Stone to calibrate how serious their communication difficulties were prior to their committing themselves to open discussion of such issues. Stone agreed to this process and also agreed to be the first to be interviewed.

Over the next several months I interviewed each member of the group, describing at the outset what the process of collecting and reporting the data would be. I stressed that their individual comments would remain completely confidential but that I would collate what any two or more people said into a report that would be checked with them and eventually become the basis for feedback to Stone and a discussion in the total group with Stone present. Every person so briefed thought this was a good idea and was ready to talk.

I spent the next two months setting up and conducting the individual interviews and found that the managers were more than ready to talk about the group and their feelings toward Stone. These feelings were mostly positive but there were some aspects of Stone's style that his colleagues really did not care for so they were glad to learn of his interest in examining his style.

A meeting to verify my conclusions with this group was difficult to schedule, so I put most of them into a written report designed to be given to Stone, and asked the committee members to correct or elaborate if there was anything in the report that I had misunderstood or misinterpreted. Two people responded, mostly with comments to the effect that they agreed with what was in the report. The ones who did not respond told me later that they assumed that I would take their silence as consent.

The next step was a private meeting with Stone at which I reviewed the group report and added an individual report that pulled together all of the comments about his style, provided that at least two or more people made the same comment. Mostly these were descriptive, analytical comments. They could easily be taken as critical, however, and they implicitly suggested some real changes in Stone's behavior. We went over the comments in detail and decided that it would be useful now to open up the discussion in the executive committee.

This process was greatly facilitated by Stone's own suggestion to use the individual feedback report in the group. We would give everyone copies and encourage people to elaborate in person some of the points in the report. At the meeting I led the discussion through the two reports, clarifying wherever I could and inviting members to elaborate in their own words on what they meant. Stone was very encouraging, so a really good session on how the group could improve and how Stone could improve as the group's boss ensued.

What the interview and feedback process had facilitated was a careful face-preserving entry into the dangerous waters of mutual feedback between Stone and his group. Everyone was aware of the dangers and handled each step sensitively to ensure that the door would be open in future meetings. The meeting turned into an equitable exchange in that it also allowed Stone to give some feedback to group members that he had been anxious to get off his chest.

Lessons. This process made it clear to me that the outside consultant can serve the critical function of preserving the social order and everyone's face while the group tries to change the social drama from one in which everyone is guarded and polite to one where people confront each other on a more personal level. Everyone seemed to want to do this, but they could not safely rewrite the script themselves. I served as a kind of director of the new process, and, once this process was attempted and worked, the group could take it over.

Multiple Agendas of Different Primary Clients in One Company: Ethical Dilemmas in the Consultant Role

One of the most difficult aspects of consultation is how to balance the different agendas of different primary clients within the same company, especially if the agendas of two primary clients conflict. In the Billings Company everyone was headed in the same direction, but I have been in the situation where the interviews revealed information that would harm either the person being discussed or the person giving the information, depending upon how that information was ultimately used. The consultant then finds himself having to make an ethical choice of which is the least harmful alternative.

A common example is the situation where the primary client, as part of a team-building process, asks the consultant to interview all of the subordinates, and one or more of the subordinates reveal, in confidence, that they are planning to leave the organization to start a company of their own that will be in competition with the present one. The process consultant cannot vi olate the confidence, yet he has some obligation to protect the interests of the primary client. From the point of view of the assumptions of PC, the only valid intervention would be to urge the subordinates to reveal their information to their boss themselves so as not to compromise themselves, the consultant, and anyone else to whom they revealed their plans.

If they choose not to reveal their plans, the consultant must remain silent, because the value of his role hinges on the degree to which people feel they can trust him. If there is any evidence of violating anyone's trust, regardless of where they fit into the client structure, the basic process consultant role is permanently damaged, and others will cease to provide valid information to the consultant.

A variety of such client issues emerged in the Allen Company as I worked further on the project, so I will turn to that analysis as a way of illustrating the complexity of these issues.

Further Developments and Multiple Agendas in the Allen Financial Services Company

In the previous discussions of this case I brought out the fact that Ralston, the division general manager, had involved me in helping him to rationalize and sort out his agenda for the division. He had launched many programs, all of them individually worthwhile, but their cumulative effect was to overload the department heads. Ralston suspected them of procrastinating and claiming to be working on things harder than in fact they were. Ralston was not always sure he was getting good information on how his programs were going. We decided that it would be useful for me to get to know the department heads in order to see whether or not I could help. I made it clear and Ralston understood that if I started to work with the department heads I would treat them as clients in their own right, not merely push Ralston's agenda. But this dual client focus made sense because Ralston realized that he could not achieve his goals without the support of the department heads.

Focus on the Job Redesign and Reorganization Survey. We decided that the best vehicle for my conversation with department heads would be the implementation of the job restructuring and reorganization program. The basic survey had already been done by an outside consulting firm and there was evidence that many of the service clerks would welcome having their jobs broadened. It was also recognized that with job redesign there would be an opportunity to cut out an entire level of supervision, thereby making the whole division much more cost effective. It would also ensure that the service clerks would be able to become more market oriented and could be trained to bring in more business. The implementation of this project logically had the highest priority among the various projects.

For all of these reasons it was imperative that the survey results be fed back and that the departments begin the process of reorganization and job redesign. One possibility to speed things up was to use the survey firm to set up more meetings for the implementation of the feedback process, but their standard feedback methodology was to cascade the data down from the top, a method that I strongly disagreed with, given Ralston's goal of stimulating more participation at all levels. So Ralston and I decided that I should start talking not only to the department heads but also to the senior consultant in the survey firm to convince him to feed the data back from the bottom up, giving each work group a chance to look at their own data prior to sharing it with the supervisor, then having an entire supervisory level look at their data prior to sharing it with department subheads, and so on up the line.[1]

The Survey Task Force and Its Chairman. The survey consultants agreed to design the process in this manner and to

---

[1]This process is described in detail in Chapter 10.

take the new recommendation to the task force that was in charge of the project. One of the key department heads, Paul Miller, had been made the chairman of this task force so he was logically the first of the department heads that I spoke with. I asked both Ralston and Ryan to brief Miller on my role so there would be no confusion.

Establishing a relationship with Miller was not easy because it remained very unclear whether or not I was acting merely as Ralston's agent to put even more pressure on, or whether I was really willing to help Miller with his own problems as a department head and task force chairman. I had a half hour with him and made every effort to provide facilitative interventions that would get across the message that I was really interested in helping him *at his level,* not merely there to implement Ralston's agenda. I mostly asked questions about what was projected and told him about my conversation with the survey consultant and my suggested bottom-up feedback plan. Miller liked this idea and agreed that the task force should proceed with it.

I also told Miller about the plan to talk to other department heads and asked for his help in briefing them. Primarily I wanted him to reassure them that I would view the department head group as a primary client in its own right and help them in their dealings with Ralston. I made it clear that I believed that Ralston might have been asking too much of them and that my role was to be helpful to them as well as to him. I also assured Miller that any individual dealings with any department head were strictly confidential.

Getting to Know the Department Heads. In the subsequent monthly meeting I met roughly two thirds of the department heads. Ralston and his assistant set up a schedule of meetings in a conference room next to Ralston's office, an arrangement that was not ideal inasmuch as it symbolically put me too much into the role of Ralston's agent, but there seemed to be no good alternative since their offices were widely scattered and it was really easier for them to come to the conference room.

The focus of each meeting was the job redesign project. I reviewed what had happened, what the plans were for feedback, and asked how they felt about that project and others that the department was involved in. I expressed my own concern about their overload and encouraged them to talk out whatever feelings they had. My criterion for what to focus on was based on the principle that the primary task (the job redesign project) and the processes for accomplishing it should be the guide to my inquiry Feelings and related matters would come out on their own.

What this inquiry revealed was a wide variety of reactions, with some department heads expressing strongly the sentiment that Ralston had overloaded them, was not giving them enough credit for what they had accomplished, and was causing them real stress and strain. At the other extreme, some felt that things were finally going at a pace that they needed to be going and that "weak" department heads should just work harder or be replaced. Most people were for the job redesign project, but the problems of implementation were going to be difficult and would vary widely by department.

Everyone agreed that it was a good thing for me to be involved with the task force and to continue to work with Ralston to help him to get some perspective. Even though I had not yet met all of the department heads, Miller and I decided that I should attend the next off-site meeting of department heads one month hence because the survey consultants would be presenting the detailed implementation plan for the job redesign project at that meeting.

The Department Heads' Meeting. The meeting on implementing the job redesign program was organized and designed by Miller and the senior consultant from the survey consulting firm. My role was to attend as a process consultant and to be helpful in whatever way I could. I described this role at the outset of the meeting so that those department heads whom I had not yet met would have accurate expectations of what I was there for. This meeting would also provide me an opportunity to meet all the department heads and to work with them directly since Ralston was not attending the meeting.

I formed several impressions as I listened to the discussion. The department heads were well motivated, bright, energetic, and committed to the division goals. They were articulate and strong, willing to argue with each other but in a constructive manner. Even though they were not really officially a team, it was not difficult to see how they could become a real collaborative team with a little practice. To create such a team was one of Ralston's goals; hence most of my interventions were geared to helping them to understand one another and to reach consensus on critical items where they disagreed. Both the survey consultant and I threw in alternatives for resolving conflicts to ensure that the meeting would end up with some clear decisions to move forward. We assumed that the goal of becoming a team would also be shared by the department heads, but this was not tested explicitly.

Two critical decisions were made: 1) to produce an inventory of the manpower of the division to see which clerks and managers could do what in the future, and 2) to think through the roles, career paths, and reward systems for the people who would end up in the enlarged jobs. Not only would their roles be different but the supervisors of such professional service workers would have to be less of a boss and more of a team leader and consultant. This would require setting up a training program for both the new clerical and the new supervisory jobs.

A communication program had to be planned to assure people that with the reduction of one level of supervision, people would not be laid off but redistributed in an equitable way since some departments were overstaffed while others were shorthanded. What complicated the effort is that different departments were at different stages of readiness to make all of these changes, with some claiming they were practically there already while others claimed that they could not get going for months because of other problems they had.

I played an active role in repeatedly pointing out how the more "advanced" department managers could, by sharing their experience, help the ones not yet started. This notion of sharing problems and using the meeting to "help each other" was a new thrust for the group, inasmuch as it had been used to seeing itself as a collection of autonomous and even competing actors. If someone brought up a problem I intervened by asking whether there were others in the group who had encountered similar situations, and whenever help was offered, I strongly reinforced such behavior by noting it and pointing out how this would ease tensions for everyone.

It was agreed that the group should devote one meeting per month to the reorganization project and my consulting visits were to be timed so that I could attend these meetings and continue the group team-building effort.

Miller and the Department Heads as Clients. During the time I was getting acquainted with the group Ralston acquired some additional responsibilities, which kept him away from the division for long periods of time. He appointed Miller as the acting division head. My own meetings with Ralston became less frequent because he was busy with his other assignment, but I kept him informed by sending him short feedback reports following my meetings with Miller and the department heads.

Miller used me more and more as a counselor in planning and designing the department head meetings. The survey consulting group was phased out and the project feedback, setting up of training programs, developing the inventory, and redefining the new roles was taken on by various subgroups or individuals in the department head group. Miller, the group as a total unit, and various individual department heads each became primary clients at this point, and Ralston virtually disappeared from the scene but obviously approved of what was going on because he could see forward movement.

If individuals or the group brought up the problem of how to deal with Ralston, I played a mediator role, trying to point out to them what Ralston might have wanted from them, and asking them how they might more effectively deal with Ralston to get their own point of view across. Some were obviously very frustrated with Ralston's managerial style and needed real help in figuring out how to deal with him.

At the same time I was increasingly able to reassure Ralston when I did see him that the group was working effectively and he should trust them more to get done what he wanted of them. He could and should continue to monitor those indicators that he felt were critical to the division, but he should relax a bit on the pace of introducing the new programs. Ralston did admit that since he had spent less time in the division he had noticed that the group had kept up its performance pretty well without his daily input. Confidence was growing on both sides.

In relation to Ralston I was increasingly functioning as a tension reducer, anxiety absorber, and catalyst, reassuring him when necessary and counseling him on how to handle his own concerns. But all of these interventions were made from a process consultation perspective, trying to get Ralston to develop his own solutions.

The Zero Defects Program. One of Ralston's strengths was his keeping up with new approaches to management. He was an avid reader and attender of seminars. Since errors in the division were a costly problem, Ralston had been worrying about some form of quality control program and discovered that he liked the approach used by Crosby (1979). He went to an executive briefing, liked the concepts, ordered many copies of the book, and decided to introduce the program into the division by asking all of his department heads to attend the Crosby seminar as a first step toward a full-scale introduction of the program into the division.

The only problem was Ralston made all of these decisions unilaterally and introduced the program just as the group was developing a comfortable working pace with the reorganization project. I did not know anything about it until all the orders had been given for department heads to attend the seminars and prepare to institute the program.

It was obvious to me that the department heads would be angry and frustrated, and most likely would drag their feet even though the program made sense. So my role evolved into one of seeing how the job redesign, reorganization, and zero defects programs could be conceptually and practically combined. I had to find a way to be helpful both to Ralston and the department heads, though on the surface the two clients wanted opposite things.

One obvious point was structural: Don't have a *separate* task force on quality. Such a group had already been created so Miller and I spent a lot of time figuring out how to integrate that group with the reorganization task force. At the same time I tried to convince Ralston to think integratively about the two programs, at least to the extent of allowing the department heads to figure out themselves how best to introduce both things to their subordinates in an integrated fashion. Ralston was willing to allow this, a real change in his managerial style, and a clear signal to the department heads that they had earned some clout. He was still the strong initiator, but he would listen to their ideas of how to manage the implementation.

This new power balance was tested some months later when Ralston introduced another very difficult budget reduction exercise and was going to show each department head exactly how to do it. I found myself confronting him quite strongly on the desirability of giving them the targets but letting them figure out how to meet them. He agreed. At the subsequent meeting of department heads it was clear that his agreement was critical. They had not minded the targets but had been ready to revolt if he had imposed his methods of meeting them. Both sides were learning to change their style and how to influence each other.

The Hiring and Firing of a Chief of Staff. Amidst these activities another set of issues arose that raised some ethical questions on top of the multiple-client agenda issues. Ralston decided that his administrative assistant of a year or so needed to broaden her experience in the line operations of the company, and that he needed a different kind of assistant, more familiar with operations, who could really serve as his "chief of staff," operating with power in his absence, handling all the mail and administrative routines, and generally easing the work load for Ralston.

The personnel manager, Ryan, suggested a candidate, Martins, as being ideal. Ralston interviewed him and considered him as a serious possibility, but he wanted me to get involved as well in discussing the role, talking to Martins about Ralston and his style, giving Ralston an opinion of Martins, and testing whether Martins could work directly with me. Martins visited me at MIT and we spent three hours discussing very frankly all the possible benefits and pitfalls of this role.

Martins was very open about his reservations but felt that if he could work his way into the job and if he had my counsel during this time it would be a good move for him and might really help Ralston with his overload. I shared these impressions with Ralston, again emphasizing the possible pitfalls, especially the fact that Ralston liked to supervise very closely and might not really delegate enough to get good mileage out of a chief of staff, but on balance it looked like a risk worth taking.

The role that both Ralston and Martins wanted me to play added some unusual dimensions to what I was doing in the Allen Company. In interviewing Martins to give Ralston an opinion on the likelihood that this role would work, he was clearly putting me into an expert role and counting on me to give him advice. He also wanted me to be very honest with Martins about his own style and for me to test how ready Martins was to work with someone like Ralston.

Martins, for his part, wanted me to communicate clearly to Ralston what some of his requirements were for the job, and to use me as an expert resource on what Ralston was really like. As we will see, when the relationship began to run into difficulty, I not only learned how "inexpert" I had been, but also began to have to play a mediating role to keep some semblance of productive effort going between the two men.

Within a matter of weeks Ralston was dissatisfied with Martins, mostly concerning his interpersonal style. Martins was "not neat enough," "did not follow through enough on simple projects," "made some decisions without consulting Ralston" (as his job description asked him to do, but Ralston did not like Martins's "judgment" on which decisions to make and which ones to refer upward for consultation).

What made matters worse was that Ralston did not share his clear dissatisfaction or Martins did not hear the feedback. When I had my first meeting with Martins one month into the job, Martins told me that things were going well and that the two of them were successfully accommodating to each other. I found myself with the very delicate task of trying to get Martins to think about his own style without point-blank telling him that Ralston was dissatisfied. At the same time I strongly urged Ralston to be more open and direct in expressing his dissatisfaction. I clearly had become a kind of mediator between the two and found myself very confused about whom to tell what since we were dealing with feedback that threatened loss of face.

When I visited a month later the situation from Ralston's point of view had deteriorated even further, to the point where he was more critical than ever of Martins's messiness, his poor judgment, his failing to take action on items that Ralston perceived to be critical, and continuing to make decisions where he should have referred the matter up. Ralston claimed that he had given Martins clear feedback, but, when I talked to Martins, I again heard him say that there were only minor problems and that basically things were working out very well.

Again I had the delicate task of getting Martins to see that he was failing without causing him too much loss of self-esteem or becoming, in effect, a direct agent of Ralston's to fix a deteriorating organizational situation. Had I told Martins more directly how Ralston felt, he would have denied it or been furious at being told this by a third party. I had to go back to Ralston and urge him even more strongly to deal with the situation firmly and clearly.

After two more months of talking to both people, Martins finally began to recognize that he was not succeeding in the job and began to consider his own options. He felt that Ralston owed him some help in relocating, and Ralston provided this help, so that after several more months a suitable new job was found for Martins. During these months I had several more meetings with Martins that were devoted primarily to helping him save face and maintain self-esteem. I emphasized the stylistic incompatibility between the two men and deemphasized the success/failure metaphor that Ralston was using; Ralston could only see Martins as incompetent, whereas Martins appeared to have some real talents that were, however, not needed in this particular job.

In due course Martins was relocated and Ralston found another personal assistant who was experienced in the company and was more compatible as a personality with Ralston. I talked with her from time to time, primarily to make it clear to her what I had learned about Ralston's style so that she would not be too taken by surprise or upset at the level of detail that Ralston was willing to pay attention to and the amount he demanded of people.

Lessons and Implications. The ethical issues as I review this situation had to do with how much to share. How much did I "owe" Martins an earlier account that he was failing instead of trying to help him save face? How much did I "owe" Ralston an earlier account that Martins did not recognize any of his failings as Ralston saw them? Should I have brought the two men together to precipitate an earlier confrontation or was it better to let the drama play itself out? Looking back on the outcome, it seemed better to take the low-key approach and to continue to urge each person to work more actively on what he saw to be the problem, the process consultation approach, but it is not clear whether it might have been better to move into a doctor role, using all of the information that I had.

The Allen Financial Service Company illustrated many of the complexities of the consulting helping role, for both the consultant and the manager. My primary client, Ralston, is in many ways a highly successful and effective manager, but he feels overworked, is under constant stress, and is frequently very frustrating to the people under him. He could be far more successful if he were more of a process consultant and less of a doctor, expert, or even parent. So one of the main goals I have set for myself in this project is to help him to see the consequences of his managerial style and to test whether or not he can learn some different concepts and behaviors of how to manage. His goals seem very sound, but his methods of implementation cause him and others problems.

There is evidence that some changes have already occurred in that he has been more willing to let the department heads run things, has given a lot of authority to Miller as the acting division head while Ralston is away, has been more willing to listen to arguments from department heads, and has changed his mind about how to do things after listening to those arguments.

With respect to the job redesign and reorganization survey, I had defined two different primary clients. I worked systematically with Miller, counseling him on the design of the department head meetings and the planning for the overall project. We also discussed how he could best help Ralston accomplish his goals and, at the same time, help the department managers succeed in theirs. Though Miller was the acting division head, he had not yet been given formal authority because Ralston wished to retain the division manager's job himself while doing the additional projects that the company has asked him to do. In the last year I spent more time with Miller than with Ralston, and I continued to be active in explaining each person to the other. It is likely that Ralston will have more time to devote to the reorganization project in the near future, which will escalate the pace and possibly the tension between him and the department heads.

The department heads collectively became another primary client. I attended a number of their meetings, especially those devoted to the reorganization project, but also found myself intervening in a task process role on other department business and around the agenda of helping them to become more of a team. Individuals sought my counsel on problems within their department or on how best to relate to Ralston. From these contacts the client base was building and broadening so that gradually I was beginning to see the division as more of a total organization. Recently I interviewed members of the layer below the department heads and found still other feelings and opinions about the job redesign and organization project that will need to get factored into the plans.

At the request of two department heads I interviewed supervisors and clerks to get more of a feel for what their departments do and how the clerical staff members, who are the ultimate target of the job redesign program, are feeling about what is going on. This has provided useful information but also further opportunities for direct process consultation with those individuals on the problems they were experiencing. In other words, in each of those interviews my strategic and tactical goals were *to be helpful,* and not to let pure diagnostic activities override those goals.

In summary, this project evolved in a fairly typical manner toward multiple primary clients, a variety of process consultation activities mixed with occasional periods of providing expert recommendations or confrontively pushing certain agendas, playing other roles such as being a go-between and conflict reducer, and, throughout, gradually finding out more about what was really going on, what the culture of the place was, and how best to be helpful in it.

Conclusions

Consultants and managers find themselves in all kinds of helping situations with all kinds of client issues. I have tried to illustrate some of the complexity of the helping process and to provide some simplifying models to help the helper think his way through the complexity. The most important conclusions can be stated as follows:

1. It is critical for the helper to know what role he is in at all times (expert, doctor, process consultant), and to assess the pros and cons of being in that role.
2. It is important for the helper to know whether or not he can play the process consultant role from a temperamental and skill point of view, because if he can, that is often the most appropriate role to take in a complex human helping situation.
3. The process consultant role is the least vulnerable to mismanaging the helper–client relationship because it keeps the initiative in the hands of the client, where it belongs.
4. The helper must at all times be clear about who is a contact, intermediate, primary, and ultimate client, and must pay special attention to the needs of the primary and ultimate clients.
5. In dealing with human systems the best focus for interventions is task process because that is most congruent with the larger cultural assumptions and with the stated goals of organizations.
6. Ultimately process consultation is a philosophy or a perspective on how to provide help to human systems, not a technology or a given intervention style. The roles that a consultant will find himself playing in different kinds of organizational settings and at different stages in a consulting process will vary widely, but the philosophy of maintaining a process consultation orientation toward all those roles and settings is a feasible and, in my view, desirable way to maximize help.

References

Beckhard, R. 1969. *Organization Development: Strategies and Models.* Reading, Mass.: Addison-Wesley.

Beckhard, R., and Dyer, W. G. 1983. "Managing Change in the Family Firm: Issues and Strategies." *Sloan Management Review* 24:59–65.

Beckhard, R., and Harris, R. T. 1987. *Organizational Transitions: Managing Complex Change,* 2nd Ed. Reading, Mass.: Addison-Wesley.

Borwick, I. 1983. "Footnotes to Change." Unpublished paper.

Burke, W. W. 1978. *The Cutting Edge: Current Theory and Practice in Organization Development.* San Diego: University Associates.

———. 1987. *Organization Development: A Normative View.* Reading, Mass.: Addison-Wesley.

Crosby, P. B. 1979. *Quality Is Free.* New York: McGraw-Hill.

Durkin, J. E. (Ed.) 1981. *Living Groups: Group Psychotherapy and General Systems Theory.* New York: Brunner/Mazel.

Dyer, W. G. 1987. *Team Building: Issues and Alternatives,* 2nd Ed. Reading, Mass.: Addison-Wesley.

Edwards, B. 1979. *Drawing on the Right Side of the Brain*. Los Angeles: J. P. Torcher.

Frank, F. 1973. *The Zen of Seeing*. New York: Vintage.

French, W. L., and Bell, C. H., Jr. 1978. *Organization Development*. Englewood Cliffs, N.J.: Prentice-Hall.

Goffman, E. 1967. *Interaction Ritual*. Hawthorne, N.Y.: Aldine.

Haley, J. 1984. *Ordeal Therapy*. San Francisco: Jossey-Bass.

Hall, E. T. 1959. *The Silent Language*. Garden City, N.Y.: Doubleday.

——— . 1966. *The Hidden Dimension*. Garden City, N.Y.: Doubleday.

——— . 1983. *The Dance of Life*. Garden City, N.Y.: Doubleday.

Jaques, E. 1976. *A General Theory of Bureaucracy*. London: Heinemann.

——— . 1982. *The Forms of Time*. London: Heinemann.

Kotter, J. P. 1982. *The General Managers*. New York: Free Press.

Louis, M. R. 1980. "Surprise and Sense Making." *Administrative Science Quarterly* 25:226–51.

Madanes, C. 1981. *Strategic Family Therapy*. San Francisco: Jossey-Bass.

Mintzberg, H. 1973. *The Nature of Managerial Work*. New York: Harper & Row.

Nadler, D. A. 1977. *Feedback and Organization Development*. Reading, Mass.: Addison-Wesley.

Nisbett, R. E., and Ross, L. 1980. *Human Inference: Strategies and Shortcomings of Social Judgments*. Englewood Cliffs, N.J.: Prentice-Hall.

Peters, T. J., and Waterman, R. H., Jr. 1982. *In Search of Excellence*. New York: Harper & Row.

Schein, E. H. 1961. *Coercive Persuasion*. New York: Norton.

——— . 1966. "The Problem of Moral Education for the Business Manager." *Industrial Management Review* 8:3–14.

——— . 1969. *Process Consultation: Its Role in Organization Development*. Reading, Mass.: Addison-Wesley.

—— . 1972. *Professional Education: Some New Directions.* New York: McGraw-Hill.

—— . 1978. *Career Dynamics: Matching Individual and Organizational Needs.* Reading, Mass.: Addison-Wesley.

—— . 1985a. *Organizational Culture and Leadership.* San Francisco: Jossey-Bass.

—— . 1985b. *Career Anchors: Discovering Your Real Values.* San Diego: University Associates.

Simon, H. 1960. *The New Science of Management Decision.* New York: Harper & Row.

Tversky, A., and Kahneman, D. 1981. "The Framing of Decisions and the Psychology of Choice." *Science 211:*453–58.

Van Maanen, J. 1977. "Experiencing Organizations." In J. Van Maanen (ed.), *Organizational Careers: Some New Perspectives.* New York: Wiley.

—— . 1979. "The Self, the Situation, and the Rules of Interpersonal Relations." In W. Bennis and others, *Essays in Interpersonal Dynamics.* Homewood, Ill.: Dorsey.

Van Maanen, J., and Kunda, G. 1986. "Real Feelings: Emotional Expression and Organizational Culture." In B. Staw and L. L. Cummings (eds.), *Research in Organizational Behavior.* Greenwich, Conn.: JAI Press.